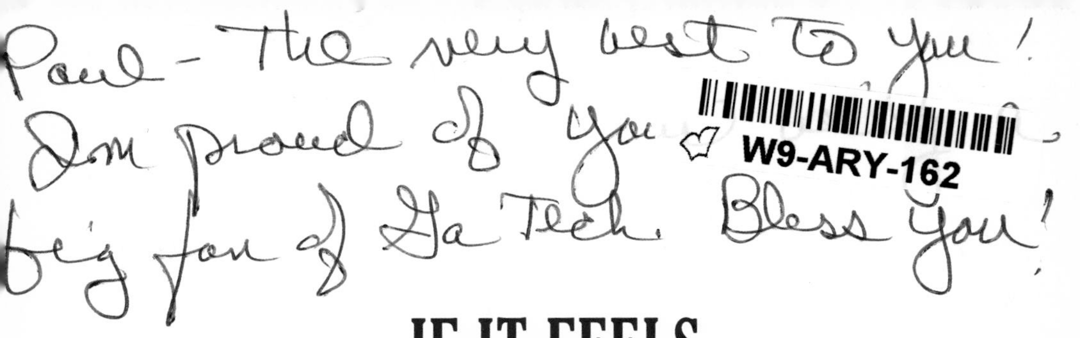

IF IT FEELS LIKE LEATHER, SHOOT IT

The All-American Life of Roger Kaiser

By Richard Hyatt

Cover Art by Don Coker
www.doncokerart.com

978-1-329-08249-6

Contents

Introduction

by Jim Minter

The problem with a book about Roger Kaiser, I fear, is that in this current climate of college athletics and society in general, it will be mistaken for fiction. Even while it was dominating sports pages, the Roger Kaiser story was hard to believe. It still is.

In the late 1950s and before, basketball at Georgia Tech, as throughout the football-dominated Southeastern Conference (Kentucky excepted), was an orphan sport. Then a young man came South from the basketball hotbed of Indiana. With a supporting cast of names like Blemker, Randall, and Denton gathered by an unassuming coach called Whack Hyder, Roger Kaiser put Georgia Tech basketball into the local and national limelight.

Kentucky and Adolph Rupp were no longer invincible. Grant Field wasn't the only "in place" to be seen at a college sporting event in Atlanta. Alexander Memorial Coliseum became a hot ticket. Georgia Tech basketball headlined the *Atlanta Journal* and *Atlanta Constitution* sports pages. Tech basketball and Roger Kaiser were national news.

Not long ago, a young reporter asked me to recall the most unforgettable happenings from my more than half-century of writing and observing sporting events. This one immediately popped into mind:

January 31, 1961, Alexander Memorial Coliseum. Roger Kaiser's fifteen-foot shot with five seconds left to cap a heroic game-long performance to upset a Kentucky team favored to win a national championship.

There were others. High on the list being the long basket as time expired in Athens, sending frustrated Bulldog fans into the streets to join rioters protesting enrollment of the University of Georgia's first two black students.

Kaiser's record, games won as player and coach, basketball and baseball; individual honors; national championships, West Georgia and Life University, are much too lengthy to list in this introduction. Richard Hyatt will detail that part of the story in the pages that follow.

This long in the tooth journalist/observer/fan will only say that in his studied opinion in the fabled roster of Georgia Tech heroes, the White and Gold has never listed a greater athlete than Roger Kaiser, or a finer person.

After being invited to write this introduction, I called two of my old *Atlanta Journal* colleagues from the 1960s to solicit their memories of Roger Kaiser and his time at Georgia Tech.

Gregory Favre, who went on to become the editor of several big-city newspapers and president of the prestigious Society of American Newspaper Editors, had this to say: "I remember his humility on and off the court. Georgia Tech was a football school, and basketball was sort of like the bastard cousin at the family picnic. Nice to see him, but do we really have to embrace him?

"Roger made it okay to get excited about basketball at Tech. He put people in the seats, and with his skills, electrified what was a small arena by most standards. He led Tech to its first NCAA appearance in 1960 and set the table for guys like Mark Price, who followed. And he made Tech basketball a sport that demanded more space and attention in the paper."

Favre added: "I found it interesting that at Furman Bisher's funeral in 2012, he walked up to me after all these years and immediately said, 'Hi, Gregory. Remember me?' That was reflective of the young Roger that we knew, a man who was confident in his own abilities and with his own identity, and who let his talent speak for itself. He didn't have to remind folks that he was good. So unlike the basketball stars of today."

John Logue played basketball for Joel Eaves at Auburn. After his years of writing sports in Atlanta, he became the managing editor of *Southern Living* magazine, founding editor of book publisher Oxmoor House, and a prolific author of his own books. John is famous for his memory. Here is his 2014 memory of the young Roger Kaiser, more than a half century ago:

"The jump shot had come into basketball. But Kaiser took it to another higher level. I can see him at the top of the circle, bending his

knees, launching himself directly up, hanging there, and then releasing the ball above his face, with a high arc and deliberate backspin, giving it a soft landing. About 50 percent of the time it went in the net. That percentage from that far out was a rare and winning shot.

"He was the go-to guy. Especially in close, tough games and especially on the road. He had to make shots for Tech to win close games. But he didn't force shots. He worked without the ball to get himself open. And he could take a pass and launch himself and the ball in one motion. He was hell to guard.

"He did this with no show of emotion. Defenders ran into him as he was going up and/or coming down. I never saw him retaliate with a wicked elbow, or even acknowledge a deliberate foul. But on defense he did not relax, as many shooters do. He stayed with his man. His ability to launch himself directly up made him a force against opposing jump shooters.

"Quiet. His public personality. On the court. In the locker room being interviewed. He was plenty confident. He was in no way cocky. It was a treat to see him play."

What does it say about Roger Kaiser, the player and the person, who, after all these years, is so vividly and admirably remembered by former sportswriters who have long since gone on to careers far removed from the Georgia Tech basketball beat?

There is a lot more to this story than Ws and Ls, records set and honors received. He is married to Beverly, his high school sweetheart, an old-fashioned marriage that endures, a love story and a partnership. They lost a beloved daughter to cancer, and twice he has won battles against cancer, proving he has the courage and grace and faith to carry on.

As I wrote this introduction, it occurred to me that much of the Roger-Beverly story seems almost too good to be true. I queried my preacher cousin, Doctor Don Harp, who has been close to the Kaisers since Roger coached and Don preached in Carrollton, Georgia. The two families celebrated New Year's in each other's home for thirty years until the time came to share holidays with children and grandchildren. They remain close and Roger still ushers at Peachtree Road United Methodist Church, where Don is pastor emeritus.

My question: "Athletics aside, is Roger as good a person as I think he is?"

Don's Answer: "Yes. He is as good as they come. He has a quiet confidence. I have seen him in almost every situation, from joy to sorrow. I went to Indiana with him on a recruiting trip, and he was a hero everywhere we went. He is a dear friend and a great person.

"I married all three of his children and baptized all of his grandchildren. I flew to Florida to see his daughter Jill and to Tallahassee to do her funeral when the tragedy of her cancer broke all our hearts, one of the most difficult days of my life. Their kids are like our kids and our kids are like theirs. Yes, Roger and Beverly are as good as they come."

Roger's time at Georgia Tech and my time in the *Atlanta Journal* Sports Department, I'm afraid, will never come again. Alexander Memorial Coliseum was new, a palace among poverty in the basketball SEC. It wasn't against the rules to cheer for the home team—and for hometown heroes. College athletics wasn't all about money and personal aggrandizement.

Growing up in the 1930s and 1940s, we read books about coaches and players and formed certain ideas of what they were like. After you got to know some of them in real life, you discovered all were not quite up to fictional standards.

Then you met John "Whack" Hyder and Joe Pittard at Georgia Tech. Whack, the humble mountain man Coach Adolph Rupp could never figure out. Coach Joe, who coached the Tech baseball team and taught Sunday school at Atlanta's First United Methodist Church. (We tend to forget that Roger was an all-SEC baseball player in addition to being a two-time basketball all-American.)

Whack and Coach Joe were much beloved. I recall interviewing Coach Hyder a few days before he was to take his basketball team for a big game in New York. I couldn't get him to talk about the game. He was more worried about the cold weather. One of his players didn't have a topcoat and had no money to buy one. That tells you something about Whack Hyder and the size of basketball budgets in those days.

The new Alexander Memorial Coliseum. Whack and Coach Joe. The kid from Dale, Indiana, and his band of brothers. Georgia Tech and Bobby Dodd (who never missed a Kaiser basketball game) at high tide. Coach Hyder was a puzzle that the Man in the Brown Suit from Lexington, Kentucky, could never solve.

They all came together to form what lives in memory as Camelot on the Flats, a time unmatched, unforgettable, inspirational, and unlikely to reappear. It is a story overdue in the telling. Reading it will benefit both today's athletes and today's athletic officials, including those at Roger Kaiser's alma mater.

Both readers and subject are fortunate that Richard Hyatt took on this prodigious project. An award-winning columnist for the *Ledger-Enquirer* newspapers in Columbus while becoming the acclaimed author of books on Georgia governor Zell Miller, President Jimmy Carter, and Tom Murphy—Georgia's legendary House Speaker, Richard was a youthful employee of the Georgia Tech athletic department before writing sports for the *Atlanta Journal-Constitution*.

With an amazing fifteen books in his portfolio, Richard is a true superstar in his profession. No one could be more uniquely qualified to tell this story. The story of Roger Kaiser is multifaceted and its telling is more than overdue. Richard Hyatt is the only person who can do justice to it. He knows the subject well, and if there is a better storyteller in the state of Georgia, I am unaware of it.

So keep reading. You will enjoy this story. You will be entertained and awed. And you will also be inspired.

Jim Minter retired as a newspaper executive but most readers remember him as a sportswriter. He wrote for the Atlanta Journal and became executive sports editor. He was managing editor of the Atlanta Constitution before being named senior editor of the Atlanta Journal-Constitution and a Vice President of Cox Newspapers.

1

Learning the Pick-and-Roll

"One of the best things in the world to hold onto is a friend."

Until Hurst Livengood pulled up in his spotless automobile, it was just another lazy day on Oak Street. Since his family moved into that house in town, Roger Kaiser and his pal Bob Reinhart had spent most of their waking hours playing ball on a regulation basketball court that Elmer Kaiser built for his oldest son. But when the coach of the Golden Aces got out of his car, the grade school boys stopped dribbling. He called them by name in his familiar high-pitched voice and they did not know how to act or what to say.

Livengood was coaching the Dale High School basketball team before those young fellows were born, and he helped put the tiny school on the map in a basketball-crazed state. They did not know why he was there, but in Indiana, even third graders understood that you treated the high school basketball coach with reverence, regard, and respect.

Strolling out on the dirt court next to Elmer Kaiser's homestead, he urged the boys on playing. Roger and Bob were too young to understand what was happening then, but they were auditioning for a man who would help chart the course of their respective futures.

Watching the young fellows move gracefully around that dusty court, the veteran high school coach offered an observation that neither of them would ever forget. "You little peckerwoods need to learn the pick-and-roll," Livengood said. "If you can master that play, you can make a living off it."

With that, he became the unpaid teacher and they were his pupils. For the next few minutes, the popular coach showed them the nuances of an offensive play that was almost as old as the game itself, and one that has aged with grace. It is two-man basketball in a five-man game, and it has never gone out of style. And Livengood was right. Roger and Bob would run the pick-and-roll themselves before enjoying long careers of sharing it with others.

When Livengood took up time with him that day, Roger knew in his heart that one day he would be a basketball player. He did not dream of being a star in college or hearing the roar of a crowd in a lofty arena. He never dreamed he would collect enough rings to wear a different piece of jewelry every day of the week. His dream was much less complicated, one that fit that particular time and place. He dreamed of wearing the black and gold uniform of the Golden Aces.

For a small boy in a small town, that was enough.

AROUND TOWN, HURST Livengood *was* basketball. He was a 1923 graduate of French Lick High School, a village that even before the emergence of Larry Bird was known for its hardwood success. The game was already on a pedestal in Dale when Livengood arrived in 1937, but he soon built one that stood much taller.

Under Coach Kenneth Carr, the 1934 Golden Aces won the first of the school's twelve sectional championships and also won the annual Spencer County tournament. They lost the opening game of the regionals by two points—a nasty habit that until the school closed in 1972 was never broken.

Three years later—before Roger and Bob were born—Livengood did something locals never forgot. His Aces and the Central team both claimed seats on the same bench at the regional tournament played at the Agoga Tabernacle because both squads thought they were entitled to it. And his arrogance was forever appreciated.

The mascot of that early team was Billy Livengood, the head coach's grade school son. The smiling youngster sat cross-legged on the front row in the official team picture. Twenty years later, Billy's role changed. He had the best seat on the Dale High bench, and the stars of his edition of the Golden Aces were seniors Roger Kaiser and Bob Reinhart.

Roger's childlike dream was shared by thousands of young boys around a state where high school gyms were holy ground and star players were small town gods. His birth on April 7, 1938, in Evansville, Indiana, was duly noted on the front page of the Easter Sunday edition of the *Dale News*. A column of local news events included a report that described Roger Allen Kaiser as a fine eight-and-a-half-pound baby boy.

On that same page of the newspaper was an article about Hurst Livengood's 1938 Golden Aces winning the sectional tournament by defeating Boonville 31–30 in double overtime, giving birth to a lifelong connection between Elmer and Louanna's son and the game of basketball.

This was Indiana. Unconfirmed family lore said Roger's father put a miniature basketball into his crib when he was a baby, and by the time the infant was able to sit up on his own, Elmer was rolling a ball toward him. On Christmas mornings, the largest gift under the tree at their house was often a regulation basketball.

Like generations of Hoosier youngsters, Roger learned the basics of the game on a hoop that his father nailed to the side of a coal bin. The ground was rocky and ball handling was an adventure. After they moved from the country, he pedaled his bicycle all over town looking for places to play, holding a basketball in one hand and the handlebars with the other.

Elmer came up with a selfish plan.

"You're nothing but a hound dog, traveling all over town playing basketball. I'll keep you home. I'll build you a full court," he said. It was a decision that would affect his son and the whole neighborhood.

David Dougan lived across the street from Roger. He never played on the varsity basketball team, but he spent many hours playing on Elmer's court rebounding the ball while Roger worked on his shooting. "It had two poles holding up the backboard, so you could drive to the basket. It quickly became a gathering spot for all of us," he said.

On that outdoor court, basketball was often a family game. Elmer, though he could not shoot a lick, played the game as a boy in nearby Santa Claus. Louanna, Roger's mother, was an all-state player in Huntingburg at a time when the state recognized girls' basketball as a varsity sport. Sharon was three years older than her little brother, and, while a cheerleader at Dale High School, she regularly joined the others for lively games of two-on-two or participated in highly contested family free throw shooting contests.

Roger teasingly called Sharon his "older and younger sister." She was a tomboy and an athlete way before Title IX opened doors for female athletes. Like her brother, she did not like to lose. "We were both competitive, which often created arguments," he says. "We played cards and found out quickly that our dad knew a great deal about card games. He and I played cribbage, and I earned every victory. That was a good lesson at an early age. You get what you earn."

Most days, the court was crowded with boys from school, and the starting lineup usually included Reinhart, Kaiser's close friend for as long as they can remember. With a brood of twelve brothers and sisters stacked into a small house, Bob was usually found at the Kaiser's.

Not even cold weather kept them from playing. When the ground froze, they brought in sawdust and went right on playing. After that, the court would freeze and thaw… freeze and thaw… and freeze and thaw. When others complained it was too cold to be out there playing, Bob did not let that stop him. He learned that if he cut the fingers out of a pair of gloves, he would not lose his shooting touch.

It was that court that the local high school coach visited. In a town as small as Dale, it was not unusual for Livengood to know boys like Roger and Bob by name. Young people—whatever grade they were in—had classes in the same two-story schoolhouse. Elementary school was on the first floor, and high school was on the second. Younger kids always complained that when Livengood was lecturing students in commerce class, they could hear his high-pitched voice all the way from upstairs.

Students of all ages played in the same well-kept gymnasium that had been around since 1927. In a town of less than a thousand people, at a high school where enrollment was less than 250, the gym seated 2,600 fans, and on Friday nights in the wintertime, it was filled with fans who were knowledgeable and rabid. Livengood had surely seen the boys at the ball games, for they were always around.

Livengood coached four of the older Reinhart boys, going all the way back to his earliest squads. Elmer Kaiser worked as a rural mail carrier, and his wife Louanna was a schoolteacher before they married. So just about everybody knew them. Besides, in Hoosier Country, it would be natural for a coach to stop and watch boys playing on an outdoor hoop, for they were everywhere. But what made the venerable coach decide to share his wisdom with those grade school boys on that particular day remains a mystery.

He was never their appointed coach, but what Hurst Livengood shared with Roger and Bob that afternoon was vitally important to each of them. It ensured that neither of them would ever have to hold down a real job—unless you count running the pick-and-roll as hard work. It introduced them to the finer points of a game that would finance their college educations and put them on the court with the legends of the game. It inspired them to be teachers and coaches, and allowed them to enjoy long careers doing what they loved.

And it started with the pick-and-roll.

2

Watchdogs Were Everywhere

"God gave us two ends to use—one to think with, the other to sit with. Success depends on which one you choose—heads you win, tails you lose."

Money was on the line when Roger Kaiser and Bob Reinhart dropped nickels into the Coke machine at Glenn's Restaurant, a popular spot near Delmer Harris Barber Shop. When familiar six-ounce bottles of Coca-Cola rumbled out of the bulky red dispenser, they provided a way for a young boy to win a wager and a way to dream of faraway places that he never thought he would see.

Looking for something to do, Roger and Bob often made bets on whose bottle came from farther away. It was a friendly competition that young and old enjoyed in Dale. Around their hometown were villages that were as small as their own, towns with names like Santa Claus, Huntingburg, Holland, Ferdinand, Buffaloville, Lincoln City, and Siberia—yes, Siberia.

Mostly, they got soft drinks bottled in Evanston, Illinois, or up the road in Jasper, Indiana. But occasionally, one of them got a bottle from an exotic spot like Fargo, North Dakota, or Cincinnati, Ohio. When they were not checking the bottoms of those contour Coke bottles, they were betting nickels on what color gumball would drop out of the barbershop's penny gum machine or trying to win money on pinball games they were not supposed to be playing.

Such was life in small-town Indiana.

A world war was being waged in places they could not locate on a map, but at home time stood still. Little had changed since the years that Abraham Lincoln roamed the fields of Spencer County. His mother, Nancy Hanks, was buried there, along with his sisters, and the nation's sixteenth president turned twenty-one in that area before his family moved to Illinois in 1830.

The county was named for Captain Spier Spencer, who was killed in 1811 at the Battle of Tippecanoe. The county was formed in 1818. Located in Carter Township, the town of Dale was founded in 1843, though there had been a log cabin school in the community since 1820. Initially known as Elizabeth, it was renamed for Congressman Robert Dale Owen of New Harmony. It was eighteen miles from the county seat of Rockport and thirty miles in different directions from Evansville, Indiana, or Owensboro, Kentucky.

Southern Indiana was settled by large numbers of German immigrants, as shown by the Germanic names found in local phonebooks. Many immigrated to that area because it looked like their homeland in Europe. The blending of various European backgrounds stitched a quilt of cultures that made life interesting.

Long ago, when they were teenagers and she was at Indiana University, Sharon Kaiser wrote the little brother she called "Rog" a letter about the simple childhood they enjoyed in a part of Indiana that often moved in slow motion. It could have described the lives of many others in that forgotten era:

> *Was just thinking about you and all the fun we've had together. Remember the old barn at the old house, the hayloft, where the cat always hid her kittens, the corncrib and the pigeons. Remember the walnut tree where we played tag, the pond that we and Daddy dug for the geese, and no one ever got near it but us and we got the whipping for it. Remember when we sold sweet apples for ten cents a gallon, buried our cats and dogs in the cemetery and rode down the honeysuckles on the fence. When David, you, and I played cowboy and I always got mad, when we slept together in the north room and always stayed awake and counted cars, and when we'd kick each other under the table and Daddy always got mad because we laughed, the game we played when we did dishes and how you hated to dry them. When Grandma lived at the old farm and we went swimming in the creek, hunted eggs under the barn, and played*

on the haystack. When Daddy used to hit us flies out in the old ball diamond out in the back lot, and I beat you in basketball because I was the taller. Then we grew older and Van and Joe came, and how scared we were when Mother had her operation. When Grandma Kaiser used to come up and we'd play chess, how I used to get mad and cry when I was beaten. Then we played cribbage, canasta, and now checkers together. When we built the new house, how we helped Daddy and Uncle Charlie. The first night in the house, it was after a football game, and how it came to mean home to us. Then you became the ball player of your dreams and I became a cheerleader. It was fun. It seems funny looking back at all the good times we had. It almost makes me wish I was that age and still playing with you and Wago and Dinny, Lady and Sandy.

His hometown had the measured simplicity of Mayberry, except that life in Dale was real, not fictional, and its lawman was Red Musgrave, not Barney Fife. As town marshal, Red was the designated crime buster. In his sleepy jurisdiction, going too fast and failing to stop at a stop sign were serious violations. So like Deputy Fife, the town marshal in Dale could have enforced the law with a single bullet

ROGER ENJOYED FREEDOMS boys living in big cities would never have imagined. He rode his bicycle all over town without giving it a second thought. He knew everybody and they knew him. Nobody was rich but nobody cared. It was a magical time, though no one paused to think about it. Dale was a simple place where folks went to church on Sunday and children went to the same two-story schoolhouse all twelve years.

Through his childhood, the town had eleven gas stations, six grocery stores, five churches, a drug store, two places to eat, and two barber shops, though places to entertain young people were severely lacking. In an innocent era before television, cable, the Internet, or four-lane highways, no golf courses or tennis courts were available, and no one had heard of soccer. There was a bowling alley for a while, but it was outside. If a young guy had a date with a pretty girl and wanted to take her to a picture show, he had to drive sixteen miles to Jasper and take her to the drive-in movie.

Roger and Sharon's father kept them entertained. He told them nightly bedtime stories and sometimes changed the names of the characters or invented new animals. Sunday mornings, Elmer read the funny pages out loud. They thought he could have been an actor, because he made them laugh by using a suitcase full of voices.

Sharon became a Golden Aces cheerleader, and her brother played whatever sport was in season. In a fading family snapshot, Sharon wore her high school cheerleading uniform and Roger was dressed for basketball. He held a ball that hid his number 7 for Mickey Mantle, his favorite baseball player.

Their parents were actively involved in their lives. By the time they were in school, two younger brothers had been born. Van was six years younger than Roger, and Joe was born when he was eight. Caring for younger children kept their mother at home, so Elmer made it a point to be on hand at the older children's activities..

Louanna was aware of what her children were doing, however. "If I had a bad day at baseball and didn't hit the ball well, she always made sure there were carrots on the table, to keep my eyes sharp."

Elmer was the head of the family. He controlled the finances and shopped for groceries. When Louanna needed money, she had to ask him for it. As the head of the house, he made most of the decisions, and if one of the children got out of line, he handled the discipline. Elmer was a private man who disliked discussing politics, religion, and money. He seldom went to church but made sure his children had a way to get there every Sunday. "He never showed or let on that he worried about any of us, but my mother worried about each of us continually," Roger says.

The Kaiser children were made to feel special. But though love was in the house, it was not a family that openly hugged and kissed. Sharon was their only daughter, and Elmer teasingly introduced her as his oldest daughter. Before Roger came along, the couple lost their firstborn son—a tragedy Louanna blamed on an old basketball injury. In their home, love was expressed in other ways as Sharon recalled when she spoke at her father's funeral service in 1992.

"I couldn't get him to tell me how he felt, but I guess he thought, if I couldn't tell by the way he acted, I wasn't very smart—and he had worked very hard to make sure that his children had a college education. My father had trouble saying 'I love you,' but when I would come in to the airport at Evansville, he would be one of the first in line. And when I left, the plane could be in the air, and he would still be there waving his arm."

The Kaisers were members of the Dale United Methodist Church, and while he was in college, Roger earned a pin for thirteen years of perfect attendance in Sunday school. His attendance streak continued while he was at Georgia Tech. On a road trip to South Carolina, the basketball team made a stop on the way home from a game at Furman University so he could be in church. His streak did not end until he was at the United States Olympic trials after his junior year of college.

But Roger would be the first to tell you that he did not always behave like an angel. Growing up, he and David Dougan seemed to learn everything wrong together, including cussing and smoking—two things Elmer Kaiser would not allow.

"We tried smoking and both of us got whipped," Dougan says. "It was just something to do. Sometimes, we'd pick up cigarette butts and smoke them, just like the grown-ups."

Roger admits stealing cigarettes from another friend's older brother, and he also remembers the last time he smoked a cigarette. "I was in a shed in back of our house sitting on a bale of hay with our dogs at my feet. The door flew open and my dad burst in. He whipped me hard. To this day, if I put a cigarette in my mouth, my butt hurts."

For boys like Roger, there was always something to get into. One Halloween night, Roger and some friends decided to play tricks instead of ask for treats. They were roaming around town having fun when they targeted a neighbor's outhouse. Instinctively, they knew what to do with it.

"We turned it over, of course," Roger confesses. "It had a heavy concrete base, and one of my buddy's feet got trapped underneath it. Most of the fellows ran, but me and two other guys went back to try and help him. We somehow managed to lift that thousand-pound piece of concrete, enough for him to get his foot out. Later on, when we told other people what we had done, they didn't believe us. They said we weren't strong enough to lift that thing. What they were forgetting was we were scared to death."

Most days, Elmer was done with his rural mail route by noon. In the afternoons, he and Roger played basketball or baseball out in the yard—something his father usually suggested. In his son's eyes, Elmer was not a gifted athlete. He shot layups off the wrong foot, and his two-handed set shot was crooked. But Elmer was always willing to rebound the basketball for Roger or hit him grounders for hours at the time. On one of those occasions, Roger learned more about foul language than he did fair balls.

"He would hit it, and I would lob it back to him. One time, the ball took a crazy bounce, and it got past me. I muttered some bad words and threw down my glove as I chased it down. My daddy heard what I said, and when I turned around to throw the ball back to him, he was gone. I assumed he needed to use the bathroom or get a drink of water. The bat was on the ground, and he had gone in the house without saying a word. I waited for what seemed like forever and finally walked to the door," Roger recalls.

Elmer was sitting in his usual chair reading the newspaper when Roger came inside looking for him. That was strange, his son thought. His father always read the paper in the morning.

"Where did you go?" the teenager said.

"I don't want to be around a guy like you," his father said. "I don't like being around someone with your attitude, and I don't want to play with someone that uses that kind of language."

That was Elmer's way of reminding his son not to swear and to keep a good attitude, and those were rules his son never forgot. Elmer seldom raised his voice. He did not have to be loud.

Roger did not wait for basketball season to practice shooting. He spent hours practicing his shot and getting comfortable shooting free throws. "My dad was my rebounder, and he never seemed to get tired. He spent hours just throwing the ball back to me shot after shot."

To Roger, he had the perfect parents.

"My mom told me how sweet I was. My dad could have had a master's degree in psychology. He never told me, 'You do this' or

'Don't do that.' He usually said something like, 'Roger, don't you think…'"

When his father did paddle him, his mother was around to pick up the pieces. She would tell Roger that his father loved him and that the whippings hurt Elmer more than they did him—a fallacy her son never accepted. Punishment often meant Roger could not go outside and play with his friends—usually, David Dougan. When Roger was on restriction, the two boys sat on opposite curbs and tossed the ball back and forth—a practice Elmer soon stopped.

In a community as small as Dale, Mr. and Mrs. Kaiser had plenty of help keeping their son in line, which Roger learned at an early age. It bothered him at first, so he asked his mother why nobody in town liked him. "They're always telling on me," he whined.

Watchdogs were everywhere. His uncle, Floyd Kaiser, ran the drug store, so he would hear details of his nephew's exploits. His aunt, Inez Kaiser, operated the telephone switchboard, and if she heard Roger's name mentioned, she eavesdropped. His father delivered everybody's mail, and his mother was a member of a bridge club—so they, too, heard things. His folks would know what he had done before he had time to get home.

IN AN IDYLLIC world like his, the troubles he got into were never that serious. You would not even classify them as misdemeanors. But to take away idle time, there were always chores and jobs—something Elmer Kaiser stressed. "He said if I wanted money to spend, I had to earn it," Roger remembers.

Before he could comfortably reach the handle to the lawn mower, Roger cut people's grass and sold apples. By the time he was nine years old, he was hauling coal for Cora and Nettie Heady, two sisters who lived down the street, for twenty-five cents a day. Those small jobs taught him big lessons.

"Selling apples taught me to deal with people, and it also taught me to count and to make change. When I was loading coal for those two sisters, I was late getting there one day, and one of the ladies told me they were afraid I wasn't coming. They said they thought they were going to get cold and freeze to death. For the first time, I felt like someone was depending on me," he says.

In his early teens, Roger learned first hand that you got money by sweating and working. During the summer, he worked on Charlie Niehaus' farm. When he was fourteen, his uncle Charlie—his mother's brother—was seriously hurt in an accident involving a posthole digger. Roger was not old enough to drive, but he got behind the wheel anyway and went for help.

For seven years, Roger served as his father's substitute mail carrier, and he was paid the same wages as Elmer. His father was tight with a dollar and he relentlessly taught his son the value of saving money. When Roger was paid, Elmer called him in and opened his safe. Inside was a ledger in which he kept an account of every dime his son earned. If Roger wanted to take money out of the account he had to convince his father it was necessary.

During his junior year at Georgia Tech, Elmer's tight grip on Roger's savings enabled him to buy a brand new 1959 Ford Fairlane two-door hardtop with chrome fender skirts. The college student was able to pay Ron Conner cash for the sporty car at Conner Motors in Dale. Back at school, fellow athletes teased him that the car was a gift from the athletic association.

"They really knew better than that," Roger says. "More importantly, I did."

As a young person, Roger spent many summers sweating on his uncle's farm, but there was always baseball. Uncle Charlie did not care for sports, and he could not understand why on Wednesdays his father picked up Roger and took him to a ball game.

Elmer was a lifelong fan, with the Detroit Tigers being his favorite team. He passed down that love to Roger. His father was a regular at his son's baseball games, and teammates took for granted that Elmer would keep the scorebook. But the rest of the year was reserved for basketball. "No one had to encourage you," Roger says. "That was just what you did."

When they were little, Roger and Bob Reinhart played with the bigger boys even when the older players would not pass them the basketball. They were always ready to pick up a loose ball or grab a stray rebound. They were in the fifth grade when they joined their first organized team. Their grade school coach was Gervase Hollander, a star on Hurst Livengood's first team at Dale High.

"We learned to play hard. I remember Coach Hollander asking us why we bothered to come out there if we weren't going to play hard. He said if we weren't going to play hard, then we might as well go home and sit in a chair."

Roger was a teenager in 1951 when Dale High dedicated its new gymnasium, and the facility was a point of pride for everyone. Trustee Charles Fuller ramrodded through an ambitious construction project that included $71,000 in school civil aid bonds sold specifically for the gym. Until this day, old-timers call it the "new gym."

Before long, Roger and the other young boys in town figured out that they could climb up on a ladder, walk across a ledge, and sneak inside to play ball on that sparkling new hardwood floor. More than anything, Roger wanted to be the one to make the first basket in that brand-new place.

"I made it, too," he says. "Someone held me up a rim so I could shoot it."

In a state that had sold its soul to basketball, gyms were often as important as the teams and the games that were played there. And that one with its polished hardwood floors would fulfill many dreams for many people—especially Roger Allen Kaiser.

3

A Game for Cozy Cathedrals

"God gives the meaning of victories and God takes the sting out of defeats."

Poets have failed. So have sportswriters, academic eggheads, and serious authors. None have been able to truly describe the burning passion that the people of Indiana have for the game of basketball.

Even James Naismith had to admit that in Indiana, it flourished like no other place. He created the game in Massachusetts in 1891 as a wintertime diversion, and three years later, a disciple from the Springfield YMCA introduced basketball to the people of Indiana. The lingering argument has been whether that contest between teams representing the YMCAs of Crawfordville and Lafayette was the first organized game played outside of New England.

Crawfordville is an obscure town located an hour west of Indianapolis, and even historians with impressive degrees have chimed in on the community's contention that it is the true birthplace of basketball in the state.

In 2008, Bill Pickett of the state's Basketball Heritage Project was commissioned to research questions about the town's place in history. His findings did nothing to dispute Crawfordville's importance in Indiana basketball history, but did take away some of its original bragging rights.

"Research found, first, that Crawfordsville was not, I repeat, not the location of the first game of basketball outside the state of Massachusetts and, second, that despite weak evidence to the contrary, the Crawfordsville YMCA was probably the location where basketball was first played in Indiana," Pickett wrote.

A 2014 ARTICLE in the *Indianapolis Star* wrote about that game and the hysteria that followed in a state where high school football had been left for dead. "It took hold on Hoosiers like nothing before and thrived in Indiana like nowhere else. Seldom was there symmetry between life and sports so seamless, and an undeniable truth remains rooted in Hoosier folklore," wrote reporter Zak Keefer.

Basketball became an escape from long dreary winters in a rural state where folks mingled only at church on Sundays and the high school gym on Friday nights. Rivalries between schools became competition between communities. Coaches were hired and fired based on how often they won and how often they did not. Ministers prayed for their boys on Sunday mornings, and every city wanted to have the biggest trophy case. Residents judged their town on how the team was doing, and every baby boy dreamed of one day hitting the big shot in the big game.

This grew out of a deep fascination with the yearly chase for the championship. In 1916, the state tournament consisted of 204 teams, and within eight years that number swelled to 564. In the 1950s, before schools consolidated, more than 900 Indiana high schools had boys basketball teams compared to 250 that played football. The tournament sold every seat for sixty straight years.

Until 1997 there were no classifications. Every school, every team, and every town competed for the ultimate trophy. Remember *Hoosiers?* In that classic sports movie, a team from a tiny town wins the big game. Though Hollywood sweetened the story, the ending is real. Milan High did win the 1954 state title, defeating big bad Muncie-Central. Roger Kaiser and Bob Reinhart can testify to that. Their coach, Jerry Kemp, suggested the high school sophomores go to the game, and they were in the arena that night.

DAN GRUNDHOEFER LIVED in Mariah Hill, a rural community of one hundred families five miles from Dale. His family shopped in Dale, and this was where he came to go to high school. He became a starter for the Golden Aces, and he soon learned that basketball was the topic of every conversation. "How far will we go? Will there be another Milan? We were all striving to be the next Milan, no matter how unrealistic that was," Grundhoefer says.

Alan Nass also grew up in that world. He was a star at Huntingburg High School and helped the Happy Hunters to the championships in the Southern Indiana Athletic Conference and the sectionals. As a senior, he was a member of the Indiana All-Star Team. Nass, a three-year starter at Georgia Tech, was team captain on the 1963 Yellow Jacket team that finished second in the Southeastern Conference. He is a member of the Indiana Basketball Hall of Fame.

Nass says high school teams were the lifeblood of their communities, and could rejuvenate a town when it was down. "You competed together from the time you were nine or ten years old. You grew up as a team, and the community knew you as a team. You became their sons."

Later, as his son became a six-foot-ten high school student, Nass would not push him to play, but he did encourage him. "'Andy,' I said, 'I don't know if you like basketball, but it would be easier if you played. In Indiana, if you're tall, they expect you play basketball.'" Andy Nass went on to play at Cornell University, where, like his father, he was a dean's list student.

Nass calls high school basketball a community lifeblood, but author David Halberstam described it as the state's connecting tissue. Bob Knight was at Indiana when he was a tour guide for the Pulitzer Prize-winning reporter in 1985. Halberstam was doing a story for *Esquire* and in the magazine article the author called basketball a sport for the lonely: "A kid did not need five or six other friends, he did not need even one."

Struggling communities found identity in their teams.

"It was what the state needed, for there was so little else to do, and because this was Indiana, there was nothing else anybody wanted to do. When the idea of basketball was bred into the culture, there was neither radio nor television. It became in those bleak years the best way of fending off the otherwise almost unbearable loneliness of the long and hard winters. There were few ways for ordinary people to meet with one another. The lights in a house went on very early in the morning and they were turned off very early in the evening… There was church and there was basketball," Halberstam wrote.

LIFE WAS THAT way in Jasper, a town of more than 5,000 people in Dubois County, fifteen miles from Dale. Mickey Sermersheim, one of Georgia Tech's first scholarship basketball players, came out of Jasper just after World War II. He remembers Friday nights and capacity crowds.

"Jasper built a gym in 1938 that seated five thousand people. The population was only five thousand and twenty, so if you put a few extra seats on the floor, you could have seated the whole town. Basketball players were heroes. If a player was walking down the street in Jasper, you moved out of the way. We loved our basketball."

Jasper High School celebrated a century of basketball in 2014, and John Hoffman was in the building. He played for the Wildcats ten years after Sermersheim and followed him to Georgia Tech. A member of a basketball family that both played and officiated, Hoffman is proud of the game's history in his home state, pointing out a few of its legends.

"John Wooden? Where did he come from? Oscar Robertson, the best player of all time, where did he come from? What about Larry Bird? Where did he come from? When every crossroads had a school and every town had a team, basketball was everything," says Hoffman, who spent thirty-five years as a successful patent attorney in Chicago. "It was so important that Huntingburg built a gym that seated more than six thousand in a town of less than four thousand, so it would get the sectionals away from Jasper."

THE CONSTRUCTION OF oversized gyms symbolized the grip basketball had on the state. An arms race to see who could build the largest arena eventually got out of control. School boards financed gyms and refused to hire librarians or teachers. At one time, fifteen of the sixteen largest gymnasiums in the United States were in Indiana.

College basketball has also been important. Indiana University has long been a fixture in NCAA postseason play. The Hoosiers have won five national championships and twenty-one Big Ten titles. Teams such as Butler, Indiana State, Ball State, Purdue, Notre Dame, and Evansville have also had their moments.

The Indiana Pacers were annual contenders in the short-lived American Basketball Association, and after the ABA folded, the franchise joined the National Basketball Association. Through the 2010 season, 152 Hoosier athletes had played in the NBA. Not bad for a state with a population of 6.4 million people. In 2014, there were fourteen players with Indiana backgrounds in the NBA, along with head coaches such as Gregg Popovich of the San Antonio Spurs, Randy Wittman of the Washington Wizards, Terry Stotts of the Portland Trail Blazers, and Brad Stevens of the Boston Celtics.

High school basketball is still a focal point of life in Indiana, though the early hysteria has waned. But the dream of a team from a backwoods town becoming another Milan is nearly forgotten. Dominance has shifted and teams from urban centers, rather than ones from rural crossroads, dominate the state tournament today. The cultural shift was magnified by desegregation, school consolidations, and the move away from a single classification tournament. But that does not keep small-town players from dreaming.

They are, after all, sons of Indiana.

4
Dale's Tower of Power

"Conduct yourself in such a way that your high school would want you to address the graduating seniors."

Arrangements were made. The wedding of Florence Woods and Vic Smith was set for Saturday, the fifth of March 1949, at two o'clock in the afternoon, at the United Brethren Church in Lincoln City, Indiana. And if anyone knows why this couple should not be wed, speak now or forever hold your peace.

Well, there was the matter of a high school basketball game. Not just any game. This one was big. The first weekend in March, Dale High won the sectional tournament in Tell City and earned a trip to the regionals for the first time in memory. As fate would have it, the Golden Aces would be playing that Saturday afternoon in Evansville, more than thirty-five miles away—the same day Beverly Hevron's aunt Florence and Vic were to take their vows.

From a distance, you would assume that the couple faced a terrible dilemma, but in Indiana, they knew what they had to do. This was not, after all, a high-society wedding. A small group of family and friends would gather at the church at the appointed hour. When the ceremony was over, the wedding party would walk down the street to Florence's parents for a simple reception of wedding cake and homemade punch.

So after the pairings were set for the postseason event, they changed the time of the wedding to 10:00 a.m. By late afternoon on Saturday, Florence and Vic Smith, as always, were in the stands at Central High School in downtown Evansville, ready to cheer for their beloved Golden Aces. The wedding was a happy event, but on the court, there was nothing to smile about as Dale lost to Central, keeping alive their dismal streak in regional play.

Win or lose, allegiance to the local team was in the DNA of home folks. It was part of their birthright as a citizen of Dale and the great state of Indiana. Bachelors came to the games and so did old maids. Families crowded into their seats and cheered as one. Late in the fall, people came to the gym to pick out their reserved seats and pay for their season tickets.

At sectional time, local stores closed early, and people formed a caravan of cars that would take them to the opponent's gym. Red Musgrove, the town lawman, led the parade. While he was gone, a marshal from a nearby community came to Dale to keep the peace. Those who could not get to the game pictured their radio dial as the basketball court and followed every play listening to an announcer who was as biased as they were. Whether you were in the bleachers or huddled by your radio, you studied every word and statistic in the local newspaper. It was a part of people's lives and part of the culture.

STAN GUTH WAS in elementary school in Dale when he came to understand the fervor people like Florence and Vic Smith had for their hometown team. His mother was a schoolteacher, and his father was the owner-operator of Glenn's, a popular restaurant with a large private room that was often the site of the basketball team's annual postseason banquet. Members of his family played basketball, baseball, and football at Dale. For as long as he could remember, Stan and his family spent Friday nights in a gym that was bursting at the seams.

"Basketball was the thing—the only thing," says Guth, who grew into an outstanding outside shooter on the 1963 Golden Aces. "Dale had an intersection, a caution light, and a gym—and that gym was packed out every Friday night."

Even young kids took the game seriously. When Stan got to high school, his coach was Del Harris, who still coaches in the professional ranks today. The Golden Aces were going through a rough stretch, and Harris gave the team a day off, hoping they would get their legs back. The boys ended up at someone's house, and, as good Indiana boys are wont to do, they chose up sides and had a pickup game. Harris was not happy but he understood their passion.

The school organized its first basketball team in 1914, playing games on an outdoor court. For a while, home games were played in a hall over Huber's and Elliott's store, and it was 1927 before the first gym was built. As the game's popularity grew around Spencer County and its six high schools, a county tournament was created. It was held in Dale in 1929, and the home team won the first of many county tournaments. Between 1929 and 1968, the Golden Aces also won twelve sectional crowns—including the one in 1949, the weekend before Florence and Vic's wedding.

In that crowded gym, Stan Guth and his brother Roger watched Roger Kaiser develop into a shooter with an unforgettable touch on a high school team that sometimes seemed to be on the verge of greatness. Youngsters singled out their favorites. "All of us little guys wanted to be Kaiser or Reinhart. Roger was an icon even though the word hadn't been invented," Stan says.

Stardom was not an accident. Hurst Livengood gave Roger important tips when he noticed him on that family court, and Gervase Hollander, his elementary school coach, developed the mental side of his game. But Livengood had one more trump card to play, and to do that he needed the support of the Kaiser and Reinhart families.

What Livengood did shows the absolute power of a basketball coach in a town such as Dale. Even moms and dads listened. He started coaching at Dale High in 1937 and directed the Golden Aces until he took a job at Converse in the northern part of the state in 1943. Livengood returned in 1948 and celebrated by winning his sixth sectional title in 1949 with his son Billy as his star.

His unorthodox proposal was that Roger and Bob repeat the eighth grade—not because of academics or failing grades, but because of basketball. "You guys are college material. You need to stay back a year," Livengood suggested. He was talking about their futures, but he had to be looking ahead to his own. He assumed he would be around to coach the two promising grade school stars.

His pitch was on target. By being a year older, they would be more physically and mentally mature. They would handle the pressure and be tougher. Roger's father liked the idea from the beginning, but Mrs. Kaiser at first said no. She thought it was a bad idea, so the coach focused on her concerns.

"He will make better grades and be socially advanced," he claimed. Later on, as a college freshman, Roger applauded that decision, for he believes that extra year of maturity helped him survive the rigors of math and science at Georgia Tech.

Back then, Roger looked at the maneuver through the eyes of a teenager. There were better athletes in the class behind him and more pretty girls, too, including Beverly Hevron—an attractive cheerleader from Lincoln City. The boys thought out every angle. Once the plan was in place, they quietly saved all of their tests. Exams they took the second time around were different, but those original quizzes were valuable study guides to the two young ball players.

Livengood must have planned to be their head coach, but that plan did not jell. For reasons never disclosed, he lost his job before Roger's freshman year. His successor was Jerry Kemp, a studious math and science teacher. No one knew it then, but in a quest for championship glory, the team would have four coaches in the next five years.

A graduate of Purdue University, Kemp originally thought he would become an engineer. When he was offered the job in Dale, he saw a town that was not too big with a population that lived the sport. He would find out that with that love of the game came intense pressures. Students soon discovered that their new basketball and baseball coach also took teaching seriously.

"My first year at Dale, I was teaching a mathematics class and some basketball players signed up for my course expecting grades. When I told them how the class would be run, they dropped the course," Kemp remembers.

Roger also had a brush with Kemp, the teacher.

"I got a test back in his math class, and I thought he had graded it harshly that I deserved full credit. I took the paper up to him and said, 'I deserved a better grade.' I wanted him to give me ten points. He looked over the test paper, and when he handed it back to me, instead of giving me ten points, he had marked off ten more points."

When he first saw Roger on the basketball court, Kemp saw a sturdy freshman with a shooting touch honed by hours on outdoor courts. "He had this wonderful work ethic. He would stay and shoot after practice more than any other player on the team. He had a unique combination of natural ability and a willingness to work hard."

Kemp started the season with the two freshmen hopefuls on the Deuces—which fans called the Aces' B team—but he soon brought them up to the varsity. Roger deferred to the upperclassmen but started two games, scored 91 points, and earned a varsity letter.

"There was a little resentment and jealously among the seniors during Roger's freshman year, until they saw how good he was," the former coach says. "By the time he was a sophomore, he was a team leader and the main scorer."

Teammate Dan Grundhoefer remembers Roger as well grounded even when they were young. "I heard about him when I was living out in the country and he was in Dale. When I heard he had done something special, it motivated me even though I had never seen him play. When we all got to high school, I could see he was always striving to be better. He was a good teammate because he was never negative. It was clear he had the talent. A star is often envied, but not Roger. Even when he was making headlines, he was never envied."

Friends knew how many hours he spent on the court by himself shooting jump shots and practicing his form at the free throw line. They also watched Roger and Bob go out for football at the suggestion of Jim Roos, a former Dale High football star, who believed playing football would make the two youngsters more aggressive. Bob was a quarterback, and Roger played end during his freshman and junior years. He was good, too, as a first team spot on the all-conference team indicated. Elmer ended that. He knew that football was a secondary sport in Indiana, and that his son's future was in basketball. He did not want him to get injured in a meaningless football game.

Roger started as a sophomore, but left the scoring to the upperclassmen. He averaged 11.9 points a game on a team that had an impressive 20–5 record and won the Pocket Athletic Conference title in Kemp's second season. But local politics was being applied more than basketball.

Hurst Livengood, recently removed as head basketball coach, had been elected the Carter Township Trustee—one of the most powerful officials in the county. He was in charge of elections and road repair in addition to overseeing local schools. He was also Kemp's boss.

"If he hadn't been my boss, I would have stayed," Kemp says.

Kemp quit and moved to nearby Loogootee, where he coached two more years before being succeeded by Jack Butcher, who would retire with more victories than any other coach in Indiana high school basketball history, compiling an 806–250 record in forty-seven years directing the Lions.

After spending six years at three different high schools, Kemp left teaching and coaching and took a civil service job as a mathematician, from which he retired after thirty-seven years. "I found coaching high school basketball in Indiana a fickle job. You almost had to live in a tent," Kemp says.

His successor at Dale High would also need a tent, though no one would have believed that when Roy Yenowine took the job. He had played at New Albany High School and attended Indiana Central and Huntington College before coaching four years at Harlan High and three years at Orleans High School.

Yenowine inherited a talented but young roster led by budding stars Kaiser and Reinhart. In a preseason interview, the new head coach praised Roger as a player and a person: "Roger is simply a wonderful all-around player and boy. He also has that intangible but important quality that makes for a leader. The other boys look up to him."

Roger began his junior season without his running mate. Bob Reinhart was declared ineligible for the first semester after conference officials discovered he had played in an independent baseball league that summer under an assumed name to help out one of his brothers. It was a foolish act in an area where everybody knew everybody else.

With Bob relegated to the bench, the focus was solely on Roger, and he picked up the slack offensively. Though that was hardly a secret, other teams found it difficult to keep him under control. Starting off the year as the Golden Aces' only serious scoring threat, he showed a hot hand as the team won its first five games.

Writers began to notice him, with one scribe declaring: "The redoubtable Mr. Kaiser is indeed a tower of power for his team and his early season showing has been Southern Indiana's best."

A newspaper columnist declared Roger a terrific high school player but said that despite his impressive numbers, he should be given more opportunities to shoot. "Potentially he could get 50 some nights if his coach would want to press things that far and work direct to him all the way. He is just that good."

The Golden Aces won the twenty-eighth annual Spencer County Tournament, and Roger scored 60 of the team's 127 points. After eighteen games, he was averaging 27.6 points a game, and he became the first player in Spencer County history to tally more than 500 points in a season. With games left to play, he broke the school's single-season record held by Billy Livengood, who scored 322 points in 1949.

Roger was in the chase to be the top scorer in the state until Crispus Attucks High School in Indianapolis arranged a special night for its star, Oscar Robertson. In a late season game against Sacred Heart High School, he took sixty shots and hit twenty-three en route to a dazzling 62-point performance, effectively wrapping up the individual title.

Though he did not win that mythical title, Roger was the proud winner of the final Allen Brooner Award. It was named for one of Dale's most popular athletes and the town's first casualty in World War II. Brooner lost his life at Pearl Harbor in 1941 and was a local hero, even for youngsters that never saw him play.

The Brooner Award was the brainchild of sportswriter Charlie Chinn and was sponsored by the newspaper in Rockport. Since 1944, it had been presented to a player that "showed mental attitude and the value to team." Roger was the fourth Dale athlete to win it, joining Dean Weller in 1946, Warren Stephens in 1951, and John Hedges in 1953.

In the 1956 sectionals, Dale beat Tell City 78–40 as Roger threw in 37 points, setting an individual scoring record at the Tell City Gym even though he sat out the final 150 seconds. The Aces defeated Rockport in the semifinals, with Roger scoring 22 and Bob chipping in 14. Dale won the postseason event by defeating the Cannelton Bulldogs 58–49, with Reinhart leading the way with 21. Kaiser had 17.

Success in the sectionals brought a handwritten letter of congratulations from Billy Livengood, the star of the 1949 champions, who by then was a student at Wake Forest University. It was strong encouragement from someone who had faced similar pressures on that very same court. Livengood pushed Roger to show them who he was and urged him to have no regrets when it was over:

> *I've seen them come and go since I was five or six and if you aren't already, you will be the best I've ever seen. I don't say that to paint a rosy picture or to build you up too high but really because I believe it and in you. But Rog, please try to listen and believe me when I say all of what has built up isn't worth a damn if you ever lose the sight of team play. Become too cocky and you know the rest ... I guess this sounds like a sermon but you know kid I like you and Bob like brothers.*

The week Roger received that letter from his childhood hero, the town held a parade and a citywide pep rally, setting the stage for the Golden Aces' eighth trip to the regional tournament in Evansville. But as they had done before, the team and the community came home wearing disappointment on their sleeves.

The favored Golden Aces lost 58–56 to Princeton, the eventual champion, and Roger was held to a season-low 12 points. The defensive play of Princeton's Leonard Nolcox made life miserable for Roger, and the junior guard also had to overcome a dangerous play in which his head hit the floor hard, leaving him dazed and unable to make the ensuing free throw.

Roger was never the same after the collision. Reinhart tried to pick up the slack by tossing in 20 points, and Larry Knott scored 10 to keep Dale in the game. After the season, Roger collected a slew of individual awards, but that performance continued to nag him.

A local writer pointed out the struggles Roger would face in his final year:

> We know Roger Kaiser is a great basketball player. Those in our area who have seen him play know that this is true. Yet

> Roger now has a challenge. To get the world to realize it he will have to make his senior year of competition something even more special than this one. For in being held to 12 points in the regional, Roger has given other teams' coaches ideas. They will now think they can produce like that in action with him. His regional showing was certainly below his regular form and therefore those who were seeing him for the first time but had heard about him often were disappointed. With another year of high school competition ahead of him the great Dale star can come back to even greater heights and make them forget the disappointment of last Saturday. But there is one thing more he will have to do so against aroused opposition. He will be a marked man next season. Everyone will have a new low to shoot at of 12 points. So history will not record the final verdict about his high school career until this time next year. He has that much time to prove that he can answer the challenge and beat off his pursuers.

Roger suffered, but not as much as his coach. In his first year at Dale, Yenowine's record was 17–7 and the team won the Tell City sectionals. He accomplished those things with a team composed mainly of juniors, and two of them were among the best players in the whole state.

Another sportswriter offered a postseason salute. "Yenowine, a newcomer on the Spencer County scene, did an excellent job and especially showed his wares by getting the Aces back on the beam after winding up the regular season in a 60–44 ditch at Boonville. His boys rebounded from that walloping with their best basketball of the year."

Despite those plaudits, after his team stumbled in the regional tournament Yenowine was out of work, though he soon found a job at Greenwood. He had Hurst Livengood looking over one shoulder and Principal Ralph Kifer—another former head coach—peering over the other. Even then, most people did not see his ouster coming.

Jerry Kemp did. "I had seen the handwriting on the wall when I was there. I predicted then that Hurst Livengood would make his son Billy the head coach for Roger and Bob's senior year."

How right he was.

5

In Search of the Big Prize

"Learn Patience! The people in front of you may know what they are doing and where they are going!"

With a whisk of a pen, Roger Kaiser's boyhood hero became his high school basketball coach. Years before that unexpected announcement in 1956, Roger anxiously met the bus when Billy Livengood came home from college. He served as his team's batboy during summer baseball games.

He had mentally recorded just about every play in every game when the coach's kid was the hometown star of the Golden Aces, and he learned to shoot a jump shot just like his mentor.

But when Hurst Livengood announced he was naming his twenty-five-year-old son head coach of the most talented high school basketball team in that part of Indiana, it took the air out of basketballs all over Spencer County. A few thought the decision reeked of nepotism, and some wondered how he could hand over such an attractive job to someone with no coaching experience. Devoted supporters remembered watching Billy grow up on the bench next to his father and that he ended up a hometown hero.

When Billy Livengood came home, he had been married less than a year. The week before his hiring, doctors at the draft board in Indianapolis rejected him because of a recurring bone condition in his ankle that had plagued the former high school basketball star and college baseball standout for several years.

Livengood, a speedy outfielder at Wake Forest, was second team all-ACC in 1954 after finishing second in hitting in the Atlantic Coast Conference with a mark of .376. He started his college career as a standout on the freshman basketball team at the University of Arizona, where it was hoped the dry climate would help him cope with asthma. He came home after one year to have an operation on his ankle, and then played at Central Junior College in Mississippi, helping the team to the National Junior College Tournament. He finished at Wake Forest, where he played basketball and baseball. After graduating, he earned a master's degree from the University of North Carolina.

Those credentials do not usually get you a job as a head coach in a basketball-rich state like Indiana—unless, of course, your father is the person who hires and fires. Hurst Livengood was the township trustee and had been out of coaching for several years, but he was still a revered figure after thirteen seasons as coach of the Golden Aces. He was deeply immersed in local politics, and he usually came down on the right side of volatile issues. He had accumulated the clout, and now he was using it.

Billy Livengood was hired to teach driver's education and to coach basketball and baseball. He had much to prove as a coach, but on the court, he would have a team that had the right ingredients to win a lot of basketball games. Hardcore fans prayed he might have enough juice to advance through the regionals—something a Dale team had never managed to do.

Yenowine produced a 17–7 record, though it was not good enough to keep his job. He was punished because he lost the game everyone expected him to win. But the key players from that talented team were returning—led by seniors Roger Kaiser and Bob Reinhart—young men who, whether they knew it or not, had been under the watchful eyes of Hurst Livengood since they were in the third grade.

Now he was turning over his protégés to his son. Grown-ups might have doubted his decision to hire Billy, but the sharpshooter his team would be built around was excited that his former idol was coming home. By then, Roger had worked under a number of coaches, but Billy Livengood had taught him more than most long before he became a star.

"He was the one I idolized when he was in high school. He said I needed a shot I could depend on. He helped me refine my jump shot and worked with me on perfecting the change of pace back when I was in grade school. So when I heard he was going to be our coach, I was glad. We always thought a lot of him," Roger says.

Even if he harbored concerns, he would have stayed quiet.

"Players didn't speak out on things like that back then. It wasn't our job. That was adult talk. My dad was a private man so he didn't speak out either. The Kaisers didn't believe in getting involved in such things."

Roger may not have shared his feelings publically, but the fact that Kemp stayed two years and Yenowine coached a single season was not lost on the quiet high school senior. "They won a lot of games, but they didn't win the last one."

Now it was Billy Livengood's turn.

Everything seemed to be in place for him to succeed. Players who had been together since grade school were now high school seniors. The team had talent, experience, and poise. They employed an explosive two-headed offense that featured jump-shooting Roger Kaiser and fast-breaking Bob Reinhart. They had ample size, balance, and rebounding strength in six-foot-five Larry Knott, six-foot-three Bill Bockstahler, and six-foot-one Dan Grundhoefer. They had someone who wanted the ball in clutch situations in Kaiser. They had a defensive stopper in the effervescent Reinhart. They had a shooter coming off the bench in Harold Huffman and a ball-handling whiz in five-foot-eight Mark Weller.

Roger's reputation was growing, and he had already gained the respect of his hometown classmates. "He never changed. He was one of us," neighbor and friend David Dougan says. "He was a good ballplayer, and we all knew it, but he was always Roger."

The Golden Aces and their new coach started the 1956–1957 season in style. Unlike the previous year when Reinhart was ineligible until after Christmas, Roger did not have to shoulder the entire load on the offensive end. His personal numbers suffered, but he felt more comfortable, and so did the team.

After an impressive early-season performance, a sportswriter looked ahead to tournament time, suggesting the Dale team might go all the way: "Are they really that good? If so, who will beat them? I honestly believe that if Dale were to play in the tournaments as effectively as they did Friday night, the Aces could win it all ... not just the sectional ... They could win the Big Prize."

People in town were looking ahead, knowing that a major test for their team might come when the Golden Aces traveled to Jasper for the Wildcats' annual holiday tournament. If the two schools met, it would be the first time they had ever clashed on a basketball court.

This was a date Dale supporters carefully marked on their calendars. Over the summer, Washington High unexpectedly dropped out of the yearly event, and the Aces received a last-minute invitation, probably because the big-city school thought their small-town neighbors would be an easy mark. Dale would play Paoili High School in the opener, with Jasper meeting Milan, darlings of the 1954 state tournament. The winners would meet in the nightcap.

Those first matchups were completely overlooked. All eyes in Dale were on Jasper. The towns were sixteen miles apart, but they lived in different universes. They played in different conferences, and their histories were not alike at all. Dale had never made it out of a regional tournament, while Jasper High had won the 1949 Indiana High School Championship—despite the fact that they went into the tournament with an unimpressive 11–9 record.

Coached by legendary Leo "Cabby" O'Neil, the Wildcats trailed at halftime in every tournament game but took home the big trophy with a 62–61 victory over Madison, surviving a field of 769 schools. Leading the way were Jerome "Dimp" Stenftenagel and Bob White, players on their way to stardom in the Southeastern Conference and the Indiana Basketball Hall of Fame.

People in Dale were aware of that heritage, and many were tired of hearing about it. The Wildcats had been a power since the 1920s when Bob Hoffman was playing and not officiating. Cyril Birge was their standout player in 1934, the year the 'Cats went 29–2. He, too, became an official and helped call the game in which Milan made history. Other Jasper stars included Bob Sakel, Tom Hoffman, and Paul Hoffman. This group also made it to the Indiana Basketball Hall of Fame.

These historic footnotes were on the minds of every fan who packed into cars and formed a caravan bound for Jasper. The game would be played in a 5,000-seat gymnasium that opposing coaches dubbed "Cabby's Cave," referencing their well-known coach. Another opponent remarked that going to that building to play was like coming into the Black Hole of Calcutta.

In the 1:00 p.m. contest, the Golden Aces beat the Ramblers 59–49, with Roger and Bob each scoring 17 points. That game was followed by Jasper defeating Milan in a meeting of former state champions. This set up the nightcap that everyone had been talking about. It was Dale versus Jasper.

At last.

John Hoffman had the natural swagger of a Wildcat. His father Bob and two of his uncles played at Jasper, and they were local legends. Decades later, he still remembers the night Dale came to town. "We were unbeaten, and we were crushing our opponents by more than twenty-two points a game … and they were a team we were supposed to beat."

John Hoffman knew Roger and Bob by reputation only, never imagining that the three of them would enjoy a lifetime friendship. Back then, they lived in separate counties, neighboring towns, and played in different regions, so playing a legendary team from the big city of Jasper was exciting to the Golden Aces. For the Wildcats, it was just another day at the office, and for years, Hoffman has needled Roger about how his teammates prepared for the game.

"I tell Roger that we prepared for Bobby Reinhart, not Roger. We thought if we slowed him down, we could stop Dale," says Hoffman, who now practices law back in Jasper after years in Chicago.

"Oh, yeah," Roger retorts. "Then why did you play a box-and-one on me?"

The Golden Aces did what Jasper fans thought was impossible. Dale upset the bigger school 53–51, and Roger's free throw in the closing moment made the difference. It was a night the people of Dale would never forget, and neither would Jasper.

Going into the fourth quarter, the score was deadlocked at 36. In that final period, it was knotted five more times. The nerveless Golden Aces wrapped it up at the free throw line. Grundhoefer hit the foul shot that put Dale ahead for good, and Roger hit three more at the line to seal the victory. He had 17 points. Grundhoefer finished with 15 and Reinhart had 10. Jody Geisler led Jasper with 21 and Hoffman had 10.

"The people from Jasper were devastated," Roger recalls.

Bitter feelings have not gone away. Hoffman bitingly recalls a tradition that he and his family followed after every Jasper game. His uncle Paul was all-Big Ten three straight years at Purdue and had a successful career in the NBA as a player and a front office executive. John's father was a legendary basketball official. The Hall of Fame brothers sat together at every Wildcat game.

"After every home game, I would look up at them, and they would give me a high sign. After we lost to Dale, I looked up there, and Uncle Paul wouldn't even look at me. 'Those cocky SOBs,' he always said."

Leaving the Jasper gym, the bus carrying the Dale team took a swing through town. Someone threw a bottle at the bus, and Reinhart wanted to stop and deal with the culprit, but the driver kept moving. David Knott, a reserve for the Golden Aces, remembers that bus ride and how sweet it was. "I'll never forget riding through Huntingburg on the way home after the game. We rolled the windows down and yelled: 'We beat the Jasper Cats! We beat the Jasper Cats.' Everybody on the streets cheered. It was a special evening."

THINGS WERE GOING their way, though no one was ever sure how the Dale team was doing until they checked in with the experts at Delmer Harris Barber Shop. His place was basketball central, and fans gathered there the next morning to dissect the finer points of last night's game.

Even when they did not need a haircut, players hung around the shop, hearing what grown-ups had to say. For several years, Bob Reinhart had a job there shining shoes for fifteen cents a pair plus tips. He did not make a lot of money, but the talk was rich.

Delmer Harris's ancestors had lived in that area since the 1820s. He and his wife had no children of their own, so members of the basketball teams were their adopted sons. He had a twin, and his brother Elmer, also a barber, named his son after his sibling. Del Harris later coached the Golden Aces for two seasons on his way to a respected career that took him to college coaching, to the NBA, and to international basketball.

Were the two barbers identical twins?

"When I visited Uncle Delmer every summer in Dale, it was like being at home," Del Harris says.

The Harris twins shared a passion for basketball and never let a lack of tickets stand in the way of seeing an important game. In the early 1930s, the Final Four of the Indiana State Tournament was played in Indianapolis. They went up there without tickets. They told somebody at the arena that they would sweep the floor to see the games. So there were identical twin brothers with matching brooms out there on the court sweeping the floor.

Evansville sportswriter Bill Robertson wrote about Delmer Harris's loyalty to basketball in Dale when the barber died in 1972. He compared his zeal to that of an excited high school sophomore:

> James Naismith never thought much about spectators, for the game he invented was strictly to fill a campus need during the long winter weeks when outdoor sports were in limbo. But the folks who follow the game and add to the excitement and perpetuate the legends are the ones who have translated the thrill of competition into a magnificent obsession. Indiana has millions of basketball followers but none were more loyal or dedicated or inseparable as Delmer Harris, who died Wednesday in Indianapolis … He followed his team with the zeal of a sophomore, the understanding of a coach and the concern of a father. Dale was the perfect community for somebody like that, for its citizens boast that it produces more than its share of outstanding boys and has enjoyed a remarkable stream of basketball talent … A basketball fan's allegiance and dedication could be minimized or lost in the impersonal vastness of a city like Indianapolis but not in Dale, where basketball long ago became a civic virtue and Delmar Harris was its most devoted and proudest standard bearer.

No one knew more about Dale High basketball than Harris, and from the beginning, Roger was a particular favorite of his. He set out to help the local kid get a major college basketball scholarship and a coveted spot on the Indiana All-Stars. Every year, that star-studded team played home-and-home games with the Kentucky All-Stars. No player from Southern Indiana—much less Dale—had ever achieved that honor, and Harris was determined that Roger would be the first.

"The politics of basketball was controlled by Indianapolis. My uncle knew how great Roger was very early, long before others discovered him. To spread the word about Roger's talents, my uncle wrote to every radio station and sports editor in the state," Del Harris says.

The barber diligently mailed out game reports, as if he were the team's press agent. He called sports editors and filled them in on the details of Roger's fairytale story. He invited big-city writers to Dale for games and introduced them to the shy high school star. He contacted college recruiters and bragged about Roger's performance on the court and in the classroom.

"I could ask my coach how I played last night, and I could also ask my dad," Roger says. "But I really didn't know how I played until I heard what the fellows at the barber shop had to say."

NO ONE HAD to ask what the home folks thought. They voiced their opinions at every game—something players would never forget. In their hometown, they were treated as semi-heroes, and they were remembered for how they played.

"My dad and I played cribbage before every game to help me relax. He never let me win either. Just like I never would let my son Chip win when we played cards. After my dad and I finished playing, the whole team met at my house and walked together to the school. The Deuces game would be going on, and we would get a standing ovation when we walked into the gym. We would get another standing ovation when we went from the locker room to our seats. Then, during the third quarter, we got one when we went to get dressed. Finally, we would get another standing ovation when we hit the court. That was four standing ovations before we ever scored a point."

His team was building a resume. "Dale's Reinhart-Kaiser combination is a tough nut to crack," one sportswriter wrote. "The team has a well-rounded war machine that is tough when they are clicking."

In late February, Dale rolled into Tell City for the sectionals. In the first round, Dale beat Cannelton, setting up a duel with Ferdinand. The Aces won 43–42.thanks to Kaiser's free throws in the closing seconds, moving a writer to dub him "a human icicle." The Crusaders held him to only two field goals, but he hit ten straight free throws to lead the way with 14 points. This set up the finals against Tell City, a longtime rival that Dale had never defeated in the deciding game of sectional play.

Dale defeated Tell City 40–38 on its home court for its seventh sectional crown. Like his father before him, Billy Livengood won that title in his first year as head coach of the Golden Aces.

Victory did not come easy, for the championship game was the Golden Aces' second contest of the day. It took three overtimes to determine a winner, and it came courtesy of Reinhart's sterling finish. "The Golden Aces, like all good teams should do, had the stuff when the chips were down and no could possible find complaint with the magnificent manner in which Bill Livengood's boys took over in the clutch," a reporter wrote after the nail-biting nightcap.

That put the Dale coach in the same position his father had been in and took him back to a time he vividly remembered as a player. His team had won twenty-one out of twenty-three games, and he was positioned to grab a moment of greatness.

THE YOUTHFUL HEAD coach was only five years old and the unofficial team mascot the first time he went to a regional championship. Wearing a miniature school uniform, Little Billy led the 1937 Dale team onto the court at the Agoga Tabernacle Auditorium dribbling a red rubber ball. He missed one shot but swished his second, and the crowd cheered.

It was his father's first year at Dale, and the flooding waters of the Ohio River forced the game to be moved from the Central High Gym to Agoga. After a pregame rift, both schools claimed the same bench, and Hurst Livengood refused to yield. But when the game ended, the Bears were advancing. As it had done before, Dale headed home without a victory in the regionals.

Two decades later, fans were much more hopeful. This would be their turn to celebrate, they believed. The Golden Aces were champions of the Pocket Athletic Conference for the second straight year and had a four-year record of 71–24 despite having three different head coaches.

Going into the regionals, the 1957 team had a sparkling 21–3 record, including that classic victory over mighty Jasper, and the Aces were among the top twenty teams in the state of Indiana, according to the Associated Press. In Roger Kaiser, they had the state's seventh best player and a player considered the greatest to ever play the game at Dale High School. They also had Bob Reinhart, who, on just about any other team, would have been a high-scoring leader.

This was the makeup of the team that packed up its gear for a trip to the state's third largest city. They left space in their luggage for the regional championship trophy—a souvenir no other Dale team had ever brought home.

The Golden Aces defeated Lynnville 67–45 in the opener. Roger led the way with 21, Bob added 15 points, and Dan Grundhoefer had 13. That set up the championship tilt with Lincoln, a team the Aces knew very well. Early that season—with starters Larry Knott and Bill Bockstahler injured and unable to dress out—Dale lost to the Lions 53–52 in overtime in a game played at Roberts Memorial Stadium in Evansville, with more than 8,000 people crowding the roadways leading to the building. Traffic was tough and so was parking, and many fans coming from Spencer County were late arrivals.

The second meeting would be played at that same stadium, and more than 11,000 fans came out to see which team would advance to Indiana's Sweet Sixteen. In the opening stanzas, Dale seemed in control, building up a twelve-point lead over the favored Lions. But in the last three minutes of the second quarter, Livengood inexplicably changed his game plan, something people still talk about today. The rookie coach backed off his aggressive style of play, as reported by Rockport sportswriter Charles Chinn.

"Only 3:23 was left on the clock when Dale changed tactics and began to play a delayed game and quite possibly this variance in attack was the impetus for the Lions as they took advantage of the Aces laxity to chip in three points as Dale missed their only effort which saw the halftime lead narrow to nine points," Chinn wrote.

Robertson had seen the Aces play many times, and the *Evansville Press* writer understood their futility. "It was a bitter disappointment, though certainly not a disgraceful one, for a Dale team that was probably the finest in its history. It was a team that had been preparing for three years for this one great assault on the stern regional ramparts and for nearly three quarters it seemed that success was going to crown the end."

In a follow-up, Chinn pointed a finger at Livengood's decision to slow down the pace in the second period. "It was with 3:23 left when Dale took time and it was at this juncture that we second guessers figure the strategy, minutely planned, backfired. Dale began to hold the ball, much to the chagrin of the partisan crowd ... Dale was unorganized when they started the third period while Lincoln, now smelling the fragrance of the Sweet Sixteen, was settled down and ready ... To the layman, Dale's delayed offense, regardless of the intent, was a replay of the straw and the camel's back."

Grundhoefer agrees with those comments. Even now, he wonders what might have been. "With the talent we had, a good coach could have done more. The team might have gone a long way with someone else."

Bill Emmons was not new to the sport. He saw his first Dale ball game in the 1930s when he was a child living in Buffaloville, where he still resides. "Someone in Santa Claus would take a bunch of us kids to games in Dale in the back of a truck, and it was a treat," he says.

Emmons graduated from Dale High in 1945. Until the school closed in 1972, he was one of its biggest fans. He saw most of Roger's games and that includes his last one. "When he and Bob were playing, you didn't want to miss one," he says.

Emmons also knew Billy Livengood. He had coached him in summertime baseball. "His dad was one of the greatest coaches Dale ever had. The young man was a good player, but he wasn't much of a coach. He lost his cool in that game against Lincoln. His substituting was poor and he changed his strategy. It was a sad night."

Lincoln earned a berth in the Sweet Sixteen, and once again Dale went home. In the next round, the Lions met, of all people, Jasper High. The Lions took the Wildcats to two overtimes but lost 69–67 when high-scoring guard Jody Giesler dropped in a pair of free throws. Jasper made it to the semi states before falling to Gerstmeyer Technical High School, a powerhouse from Terre Haute.

LATE IN THE school year, Dale athletes gathered for an awards banquet sponsored by the Kiwanis Club. Members of the football and basketball teams were honored, and Livengood singled out his star player. "Roger Kaiser is one of the best high school players in the United States," the head coach said.

Numbers did not tell the entire story, but Roger's were impressive. In four years of high school basketball, he scored 1,549 points, averaging 11.9 points a game as a sophomore, 26.1 points a game as a junior, and 23.8 points as a senior. (All without the benefit of the three-point basket.) For his career, he hit 49.2 percent from the floor and 82.3 percent from the free throw line. He scored a school-record 41 points in a game against Chrisney on a night he hit 18 of 21 field goal attempts in three quarters of play, and he once hit 36 straight free throws during sectional and regional play.

He and Bob were all-sectional, all-regional, made the Pocket Athletic Conference all-star team and were co-captains for two straight years. Roger also lettered four years in baseball, ran sprints on the track team, and was a unanimous choice for the all-conference eight-man football team in one of the two years that he played.

When Billy Livengood handed out letters to his players, his comments included an ominous statement that Robertson casually reported. The first-year coach bid the lettermen a fond farewell and offered the sincere hope that he would be serving as coach again next year.

A headline a few days later said it all: "Billy Livengood's Coaching Tenure Brief but Brilliant." The article indicated that the twenty-six-year-old coach had resigned after one season at Dale. This time his father had nothing to say.

Hurst Livengood served as township trustee until 1962. After forty-four years as a teacher and coach, he and his wife, the former Lena Rivers, owned and operated a tourist home called Santa's Slumber Land and later opened Livengood's Dog N Suds. They also built the Lincoln Motel, where their slogan was: "It is awfully nice to be important, but it is more important to be nice." In 1965, they expanded the restaurant into the Colonel Cafeteria, still standing today on United States Highway 231.

People still referred to him as "The Coach," and they applauded his successes. "It did not matter if Livengood was coaching, teaching, or starting a business, he always seemed to be successful. That's what made him special to everyone who knew him," columnist Randal Fischer wrote.

Lena Livengood, a retired elementary schoolteacher, died in 1968. Albert Hurst Livengood, by then a resident of the Huntingburg Convalescent Center, died in 1995. He was ninety-one years old. There was no visitation and no funeral service, though a graveside memorial was held two months after his death. He was buried next to Lena at the Dale Cemetery.

Del Harris, a world-class basketball scholar, still considers Livingood the best coach Dale High ever had. "When I was there, I was young. I wasn't as good as I wound up being, and one of the biggest mistakes I made as head coach was not involving Hurst. I should have invited him to practices and learned from him, but I was too insecure to do that."

Even now, Roger does not second-guess his childhood hero's strategy. "He got blasted pretty good," Kaiser says. "He must have felt like he was living in a glass house and everybody had rocks."

Members of that storied team have a special bond. They are scattered around the country, but they remain close friends. When they get together, they replay the fond memories of that 1957 season, and they dwell on the good times.

Billy Livengood has never joined them.

6
Saying No to the Hoosiers

"A person cannot teach what he does not know or lead where he has not gone."

Roger Kaiser signed with Georgia Tech because Coach John "Whack" Hyder said something no other college recruiter said. In simple terms, Hyder said he needed him. Pretty hokey in today's world where recruiting is a nationwide industry, but it was an accurate barometer of the insecurity of a small-town basketball star who was not as sold on his abilities as the big-time coaches who came to call.

Recruiters threw promises around like a bounce pass in heavy traffic. Hyder was different. There was something special about him and about Tech's portly baseball coach, Joe Pittard. These humble men talked about life and school and about being lifelong Methodists. Roger recognized that it was difficult for him to say no to people, and he knew that turning his back on these men would be very difficult.

Influential people pressed him to sign with Indiana University. He made a visit to the campus in Bloomington, and it was not a good experience. He spent the night in a fraternity house where the members left their windows open at night. "There was snow all over my bed," he laughs. "I decided right then that if went to Indiana, I would never pledge that fraternity."

Roger also considered Vanderbilt, Louisville, and Western Kentucky, and he visited Kentucky Wesleyan, but he sincerely liked the people he met at Georgia Tech. He also appreciated that they openly promised him an opportunity to play college baseball as well as basketball—a subject other schools skillfully avoided.

"I wanted a college of high scholastic standing, which was also a good basketball school, so I visited several. It was the attitude that brought me here. Several places had the scholastic rating and the basketball, but when I dropped in, they looked me over and said, 'Well, you can join these ten other guys if you want to.' At Tech, they made me feel that they wanted me and needed me."

The bucolic tactics Hyder used recruiting Kaiser were not out of character as *Atlanta Journal* sports editor Furman Bisher once described. "That was about the best recruiting spiel Hyder had to offer. When he first became head coach at Georgia Tech, basketball was played in a gymnasium, one of those old stone buildings that served a lot of purposes. Basketball was squeezed in between two sets of risers … Hyder came up in a time when coaches still taught classes on the side. Adolph Rupp was right—he was a country boy straight off the farm at Lula, Georgia."

Nass remembers those tactics. When Hyder was recruiting him in Huntingburg, he showed up at the Nass home in a station wagon with his wife Vera, his daughter Julia, and his son Tommy—something most coaches would never have done. "But in our part of Indiana, it was very effective," Nass says.

So was his choice of words. Even in the heat of a game, he did not curse. When he was riled, he would belt out, "Cheese and crackers"—a signal that something was bad wrong. When the retired coach died in 2003, Bisher wrote a column that concluded Hyder's trophies were the men who played for him and left with degrees in hand. He compared him to others in that profession. "He was the portrait of humbleness. Dick Vitale screeches and squawks. Gary Williams sweats and rages. Mike Krzyzewski colors the air blue. Bobby Knight rearranges the furniture. Whack Hyder maintained a somewhat pious calm."

His values were not always shared on the recruiting trail, but that did not bother Hyder. He was a staunch Methodist, and he did not drink alcohol, a belief that was hard for German Catholic families in Indiana to understand, Jasper's John Hoffman says. "Parents would offer him a cold beer, and Coach Hyder would turn it down. Then he would look across the living room and see that his prized recruit had a beer in his hand."

Byron Gilbreath handled the Germanic culture in his own way. On one trip to Jasper, the Tech assistant stopped off in a store that was a local hangout, and he was thirsty. When the owner offered him a "Dubois County Coca-Cola," he readily accepted it. The store had an old-fashioned soft drink dispenser where a paper cup dropped down and the carbonated water and the syrup drizzled into it.

Only this machine was specially rigged for special friends. When the cup dropped down, it already contained a shot of whiskey. Not knowing this, Gilbreath gulped down a big swig. He gasped and his bald head got red.

"What do you think?" the owner said.

"I think I'll have another one," Gilbreath said wheezing.

Roger's relationship with Hyder blossomed about the time he graduated from high school. Paul Fritch—the brother of a former Tech player and a tavern owner in Jasper—recommended Roger to Tech, and Hyder dispatched Gilbreath to see him play at a game in Evansville.

On the fourteenth of May in 1957, Hyder wrote his first letter to Roger. It was the beginning of a warm correspondence between them, and few of the letters talked about basketball. Unlike most of the mail Roger received, this one was typed on Georgia Tech stationary. The envelope had no street address, just Roger Kaiser, Dale, Ind.

It was more personal than business:

It was good to learn you are interested in coming to Georgia Tech on a basketball scholarship ... We won the Southeastern Conference Championship in baseball yesterday, beating Alabama 10 to 1. Buddy Blemker pitched a fine ball game. He certainly had a fine year in sports, and he is doing fine in his schoolwork, too. Roger, the scholarship I am offering you is for four years. We do not give one year scholarships, and we treat our students with respect while they are here ... It is not necessary for our scholarship boys to play other sports, but we encourage them to take part in a spring sport. I understand you are quite a baseball player. You should like our baseball program.

When Roger began to talk about visiting Atlanta and Georgia Tech, Paul Fritch offered one piece of unsolicited advice: "Have a firm handshake. Don't hand them a dead fish. And don't order your meat done."

A week after sending that letter, Hyder met Roger at the Atlanta airport. It was Roger's first flight on a commercial airline and his first trip to a city as large as Atlanta, where the airport seemed larger than Dale. He stayed at the historic Bilmore, a ten-story hotel that was the biggest building Roger had ever seen.

Once he checked in, there was a knock on his door, and there stood a familiar face from home. Buddy Blemker had been a summertime teammate of Roger's on American Legion baseball teams in Indiana. The Huntingburg native was Tech's leading scorer in basketball and an ace southpaw for the baseball team. He would introduce him to Coach Joe, the first college baseball coach Roger ever met.

"If you want to play both sports, come here," Blemker said. "This is the Sunny South. A lot of baseball scouts live right here in Atlanta, and we had sixteen of them at our game today."

That impressed Roger, who believed he was as good at baseball as he was basketball—maybe better. Besides, athletes in 1957 did not grow up with dreams of pro basketball. Like his father, Roger loved the historic purity of baseball, and he could imagine himself in a big league uniform.

Tech's friendly approach even emerged on a recruiting trip he made to a game in Nashville, where the Commodores were playing, of all people, the Yellow Jackets. Vanderbilt was after both Roger and Bob, and their player-host was Don Hinton from Rockport whom they had competed against in high school. Hinton showed them how he raced through red lights in downtown Nashville. He took them to a nightspot in a hotel where the visiting team was staying and left them so he could go see his girlfriend.

"There wasn't a vacant seat in the place until this fellow I didn't know tugged on my sleeve and said he had seats for me and my friend. It was Al Ciraldo, the Tech radio announcer who would become a dear friend. Al invited us to sit down with him and the Tech people," Roger says.

Pressure was building for him to go to Indiana. Branch McCracken, had never seen him play, but an assistant coach had. Even people close to Roger could not understand a local kid not wanting to play for IU. When a long black car parked in front of his house, and the president of the only bank in Dale walked across the lawn, Roger knew why Albert J. Wedeking was there. He was Spencer County's premier Hoosier fan, a major donor and a key supporter of the basketball program. He came to close the deal for McCracken, and he was not used to being turned down.

"You go to IU and I'll help you," the businessman said.

"What does that mean?"

"I'll help you."

An eighteen-year-old kid who had never lived anywhere but Dale and had never made a major decision on his own in his whole life sensed he was being pressured. Roger took it on himself to bring that conversation to a close.

"No, thank you, sir. I'm going to Georgia Tech."

It was the first time he had said that out loud.

College was not always an option for young people in Dale, but times were changing even though none of the girls in their class of fifty-one continued their studies. Roger was not the only Golden Ace player on his way to college. Bob Reinhart was going to Kentucky Wesleyan and later transferred to Indiana, where he played baseball and basketball; Dan Grundhoefer went to Kentucky Wesleyan; Larry Knott went to Louisville; Bill Bochstahler attended Indiana State; and Mark Weller went to Indiana.

Between Atlanta and Dale, there was a steady stream of mail that summer. Roger was getting correspondence from the other schools, but most of those letters were flat, impersonal boilerplate letters that could have been mailed to any prospect on their list. Hyder's letters talked about how hot it was in Georgia and asked about Roger's parents. The coach often included comments about Roger's girlfriend, Beverly Hevron. But Hyder's letters were most concerned about a high school math course that Roger needed and his College Board scores.

Hyder's letter of August 15 focused on Roger's freshman year of college:

Right now the only thing missing is the ½ unit of algebra. So let me know about it as soon as you can. We are certainly happy that you are coming to Georgia Tech and since I have seen your high school grades there is no doubt in my mind but that you will do well here in your studies.

On September 11—five days before freshmen were to report—Hyder finally wrote Roger to tell him that questions about the high school algebra course and his College Board exam were answered at last:

Congratulations! You have been accepted by Georgia Tech. Come on in, everything is set for you to start on opening day. I'll have reservations for your parents and girl friend. You will be able to stay in your dormitory room. You will be in Room 210 of Tower Dormitory. Coach Gilbreath lives in the dormitory next to yours ... Roger, you will have to study some here. I am certain you are ready. I want you to know that studies come first at Georgia Tech. This is how it should be everywhere.

Roger has preserved many of Hyder's letters in family scrapbooks. Their folksy, affectionate attitude is so different from the streamlined, artificial approach to college recruiting today. The Tech coach wrote lengthy letters in longhand and signed them John Hyder. He was as interested in the person as he was the player, for his letters never suggested that Roger should work on his basketball skills. Hyder talked about algebra and chemistry, warned him he would need to study, and, without proselyting, casually mentioned that he had mailed Roger a letter on his way to church.

Hyder's appreciation for the state of Indiana did not begin on the recruiting trail. His affection might be traced to World War II when he served in the United States Navy. "For two years, I was stationed on the U.S.S. *Indiana*, and every time we ate a meal, I was appreciative to the taxpayers of this state for providing the silverware."

His small-town approach might have been laughable to someone from a big-city high school, but it worked on a player from a town the size of Dale. No one in Southern Indiana even blinked when they heard that people called him Whack. Had they asked, they would have discovered that he was given that nickname by a favorite aunt and that his brothers were called Den, Jim, Bunk, Rat, Jet, Snooks, and Skeezix.

His letters are also a timeline of a budding friendship between two men—a relationship that started when Roger Kaiser was eighteen years old and continued until he offered a loving eulogy at John "Whack" Hyder's funeral in 2003.

A FORGOTTEN YELLOW Jacket pioneer named Jim Fritch helped lead Whack Hyder to Roger Kaiser. His brother Paul owned a questionable tavern in Jasper, where people could put down wagers on ball games while enjoying adult beverages. Jim Fritch told his brother about this hot prospect in the next county over from Dubois. The bar owner—known as "Wop" in an era that did not practice political correctness—passed his name on to Hyder.

In the summer of 1948, Jim Fritch had been one of a trio of ballplayers from Indiana who received the first full scholarships for basketball given at Georgia Tech. Until then, it was a program coached by members of the football staff and was built on football players and guys who just showed up to play.

Fritch and Mickey Sermersheim were from Jasper and had played together since grade school. Joe Keener hailed from Evansville. Assistant coach Bob Polk, a Navy V-12 instructor at Tech, and a native of Tell City, had rounded them up.

It was the start of a Southern Indiana pipeline. Over the next twenty years, Tech was blessed with small-town Hoosiers: Roger Kaiser and Stan Guth of Dale; Buddy Blemker and Alan Nass from Huntingburg; John Hoffman, Gary Phillips, Mickey Sermersheim, Bob Lukemeyuer, and Mick Stenftenagel of Jasper; Joe Keener from Evansville; Frank Landrey from Vincennes; Bill Nigg from Loogootee; Dave Clark from Tell City; John Partin from Columbus; and Jim Caldwell and Pete Caldwell from Lawrenceburg.

Rosters of Southeastern Conference teams in Roger's era also were stocked with players from Indiana. The list included Gene Tormohlen (Holland), Bob Perigo (Lafayette), and Dalen Sholwalter (Loganport) at Tennessee; Gary Stoll (Princeton) and Vic Klinker (Princeton) at Tulane; Jack Waters (Madison) at Ole Miss; Joe Hobbs (Sheridan) at Florida; and Jim Henry (New Albany), Don Hinton (Rockport), Larry Banks (Sandborn), and Bill Depp (Edinburgh) at Vanderbilt.

A player at Vanderbilt remembered a game at Ole Miss, where twelve of the twenty players on the two teams were raised within fifty miles of each other in Southern Indiana. "It was like a homecoming," he said.

The state was also well represented among SEC head coaches. In addition to Polk at Vanderbilt, Tulane's Cliff Wells and Tennessee's Emmett Lowery were from Indianapolis, and Florida's Norm Sloan was from Anderson.

The migration of Indiana talent to Tech began with Polk. He was an assistant coach at Tell City High School, his alma mater, when he enlisted in the Navy in 1943 and was assigned to the Navy V-12 Program at Tech as a physical education instructor. What does a Hoosier boy do when he has time on his hands? He starts hanging around a dark gym at the northern end of Grant Field, where Tech's basketball team is practicing.

During the war years, Tech's basketball coach was Dwight Keith, a backfield coach on the football staff who also worked in the athletic department's business office. Polk was a part-time assistant for two years while he was still in the Navy. Then in 1947, he was a full-time aide under Keith, who later edited a magazine that was popular with high school coaches in Georgia.

Behind the scenes, Tech athletic director Bill Alexander was planning a revamp of the school's floundering basketball program. He was impressed with Polk and offered him the head job. Instead, Polk suggested he be allowed to spend a year as an assistant coach looking for players before taking over the team. He asked for seven scholarships, and Alexander countered with three.

With that, Polk hit the road for Indiana.

"We caught his eye, and it was life changing for us," Sermersheim says. "His big pitch was for us to enroll by July 1. NCAA rules were changing. After that date, freshmen would not be eligible for the varsity. Come on down and play right now."

They had been in Atlanta about a month when Polk called Sermersheim, Fritch, and Kenner together in a dorm room. He told them Vanderbilt University had offered him their head basketball job and that it was an offer he could not refuse. Before choosing Polk, Vandy interviewed a slew of candidates, including Hoosier native John Wooden, then the coach at Indiana State University.

"Bob Polk offered all three of us a chance to come to Vandy with him. We'd have to sit out that year, he told us. After he left, we talked into the night. We decided we had a pretty good start where we were so we stayed at Georgia Tech," says Sermersheim, sharing a forgotten chapter in Yellow Jacket history. Ten years later, Polk unsuccessfully recruited Kaiser for the Commodores.

After Polk moved on, Roy McArthur became the coach, and it was not what the recruits expected. Games were played at Heisman Gym on Third Street. It was a quaint facility built by the Civil Works Administration, a program created during the Depression. It replaced a previous gym that burned and brought the team back to campus after years of bouncing around Atlanta.

Only the top teams in the SEC attracted fans. For other games, the place was empty, particularly embarrassing in a barn that only seated 1,200 people. It was so small that only students and faculty could get tickets. The old gym did earn a mention in the history books, though. In 1948, a game between Tech and UT-Chattanooga was the first college basketball game televised in the South just a few months after WSB-TV went on the air. And the Jackets won the game, 81–45.

Despite its shortcomings, in eighteen seasons, Tech was 98–61 at the Heisman Gym compared to a dismal 72–151 on the road. But to guys from Indiana, McArthur's style of play was totally foreign.

"It was four years of tough going for me. Jim and I had come up under Cabby O'Neil at Jasper, and he was great with strategy," Sermersheim says. "We knew the gym wasn't what we were used to, but I felt like Polk would make us the pioneers of a program that would be successful. I got my kicks from being an active student, and a degree from Georgia Tech was a life-changer for me. It gets more valuable every year."

THAT OLD GYM is gone now, but memories linger. Teeter Umstead entered Tech as a freshman in 1948. He had been a high school teammate of Naismith Hall of Fame member Frank Ramsey in Madisonville, Kentucky. Umstead ended up at Tech. Ramsey played at Kentucky and spent nine years in the NBA with the Boston Celtics, where he was the league's premier sixth man.

Umstead played his entire career in Tech's crackerbox gym, and he remembers how hot it could be, even in wintertime. "They would open the front doors, and if you shot a layup, you could keep on going outside and cool off."

Umstead says Tech sometimes produced decent teams and often had good individual talent. But like other schools in the SEC, Kentucky always stood in its way. "I remember Jim Nolan, a big guy from Macon, Georgia. He was a good player. And when Tech played Kentucky, he always outplayed Alex Groza, their all-American center. The Wildcats would win the SEC Tournament. Jim would make the all-tournament team, but Kentucky would go to the NCAA Tournament and Georgia Tech would stay at home."

Bobby Dodd succeeded Alexander as athletic director and head football coach in 1950, and he began raising money to build a true basketball arena on campus. During his junior year, Sermersheim accompanied assistant coach Whack Hyder on a PR tour of Atlanta high schools. Listening and watching, he rediscovered hope for Tech basketball.

"At one stop, he brought up the idea of Alexander Memorial Coliseum. It was the first time I had heard details about it. It was a dream of Coach Hyder and Coach Dodd. The more he talked, the more interest grew. People were starting to buy into it," says Sermersheim, who is still an active alumnus of Tech.

Alexander Memorial Coliseum opened in 1956. It cost $1.6 million to build. Its capacity was 6,966, and it was one of the largest in the SEC. Hyder became head coach in 1952, and Buddy Blemker and

Terry Randall soon formed an exciting backcourt that brought electricity to that new arena..

And an even greater reason to cheer was about to arrive.

PLAYERS WERE STRAGGLING in for fall quarter. A team meeting was scheduled for Sunday—after church, of course. Players reported September 15, and the first freshman basketball game was nearly three months away

The newcomers were an interesting mix. Among the 1957 freshmen on scholarship were six-foot-one Roger Kaiser of Dale, Indiana; six-foot-seven Wayne Richards of Augusta, Georgia; six-foot Bobby Dews of Edison, Georgia; six-foot-three Bill Poteet of Glasgow, Kentucky; and six-foot John Hoffman of Jasper, Indiana.

The unknowns of a new school year and the prospects of a new basketball season made that an unsettling time. For Roger, it was particularly uneasy. He was an excellent student in high school, but this was Georgia Tech, and he had waited all summer to be formally accepted. This did not leave time to mentally prepare for the drastic move from small-town Indiana to a metropolitan area like Atlanta.

He left behind his girlfriend Beverly, and he had not received a strong endorsement about choosing Tech from her or his family, neighbors, and friends. That included his high school principal who privately warned him that Tech was an engineering school.

Roger knew Blemker and Phillips, and during the summer, he became acquainted with Hoffman, who would be his college roommate. Hoffman's family drove him down from Indiana that weekend. So did Kaiser's parents, accompanied by Beverly, a former Dale cheerleader. Hoffman remembers his arrival, and Roger remembers his own. Years later, their recollections differ greatly, and neither will budge.

Says Hoffman: "They let me off at the curb. Our dorm room was small. There was room for one suitcase, and there was one metal cabinet for two guys. When my folks pulled away from the curb, I cried. I went up to our room, and Roger was sitting there with tears flowing down his cheeks. Two cocky jocks just sat there crying."

Says Roger: "John's story is wrong. John was in the dorm room when I got there. He was sitting there crying, and I was ready to cry."

When classes started, there were more reasons to cry. Roger had graduated from high school in a class of fifty-one students, and now he was going to classes that were larger than that. Adjustments did not come easy. He quickly found that college professors did not care if you learned or not. Learning was up to you.

In mechanical drawing, the instructor glanced at the roll book and asked for AA guys to raise their hands. Roger kept his hands on the desk. He assumed AA meant Alcoholics Anonymous until a classmate told him to raise his hand because AA meant Athletic Association. Finding a classroom dominated by athletes, the teacher was unhappy and he made them a promise.

"Either I won't be back tomorrow or you fellows won't be back," he said.

The students returned, but the professor was never seen again.

In another class, a professor said something about Abraham Lincoln that irked Roger, who thought he knew a lot about Honest Abe since the sixteenth president had grown up in Spencer County. He listened to the instructor, and then he spoke out, which was uncharacteristic of him and something Tech freshmen were not supposed to do.

"He was a crook," the instructor said.

"I didn't hear it that way."

"Well, who asked you?"

Then there was ROTC. Roger had never heard of the program, and honestly did not know what those letters stood for. He had never worn an Army uniform or marched in a military unit, but as a young man driven to be the best, he did what he had to do to get along.

Hyder gave the two freshmen time to settle into some kind of routine before he dropped by Roger and John's tiny dormitory room. Freshmen had been issued their ROTC uniforms, and they were preparing for their first serious inspection. With a can of Brasso in hand, Roger was polishing his belt buckle.

"You don't have to do that. They don't look at belt buckles," John said.

Roger went right on rubbing.

"Well, if they do, it'll be shined."

Hyder often repeated that story and what it told him about his star freshman. "I put the boy high in my book right then, and he always lived up to it. Regardless of what comes up, he is ready for it, and always tries to do more than is required," the coach said.

But in many ways, Roger felt lost.

He did not understand a tradition that called for freshmen to wear silly little Rat Caps wherever they went on campus, even to basketball practice. Roger was rushing to Alexander Memorial Coliseum one afternoon when some upperclassmen stopped the shy freshman and ordered him back to his dorm room to get that infernal cap.

"I was so naïve that I didn't even know who Bobby Dodd was. If the Evansville newspaper didn't have it then, I didn't know about it, and they never wrote much about Georgia Tech football. After I got to Tech, his name would come up because Coach Dodd was what everybody measured things by, and I wouldn't even know who they were talking about. Someone took me by to see him, and I still didn't know who he was," Roger admits.

Roger was struggling with more than shiny belt buckles. In high school, he never learned how to study. It was not because he was lazy, but because learning came natural to him. He did not feel prepared in any subject he was taking, particularly math. He was beginning to believe that folks in Dale might have been right. Maybe he should have gone somewhere else. Hoffman was doing well so Roger watched how he studied and worked every night and tried to emulate him. That would be his salvation.

Preseason basketball drills finally began and Roger was relieved. He felt comfortable on the hardwood. Freshmen were not eligible for the varsity so the first-year guys practiced in a smaller gym upstairs at Alexander Memorial Coliseum. When it was time for uniforms to be handed out, a team manager asked Roger what number he wanted. In high school, he wore number 44, and that was the number he wanted to wear at Tech. But the student manager declined.

"What position do you play?" he asked.

"I'm a guard."

"Then you can't be number 44. That number is for forwards."

"That's football malarkey," he told the student manager.

Hoffman, his roomie, was eventually given number 44.

This was no time to argue. Besides, he was thinking that he was not going to come back after Christmas. Without giving it a second thought, Roger looked up at the number over the locker where he was sitting.

"Give me number 21, so I can remember my locker number." Later, he found out that no player at Tech had ever been given number 21. That became his number, and it was number 21 that eventually hung from the rafters of Alexander Memorial Coliseum.

The first Baby Jackets' game was against Young Harris, a powerful junior college team from the mountains of North Georgia that was coached by Luke Rushton, an old friend of Coach Joe's. Tip off was 4:00 p.m., hardly a suitable time for a basketball game on a busy campus like Georgia Tech and a bustling city like Atlanta. As they dressed in Tech uniforms for the first time, Kaiser and his teammates anticipated big things.

"When we came out on the court, it was quiet. The only person in the building other than the two teams was Dan, a heating-and-air man. We knew he was there because we heard him clap one time. It was a shock for someone used to getting standing ovations in a crowded high school gym," Roger says.

The freshman team won its opener. In the weeks that followed, Roger made himself even more at home on the basketball court. Points came easy and the Baby Jackets were winning handily.

Gordon Darrah, a freshman at Georgia, arrived in Athens as a standout guard on a state championship team at Baker High of Columbus. He and Roger would play against each other most of their college careers. The Bullpups knew about Roger even before they saw him in uniform.

"We had heard about him, and we knew we were playing Roger Kaiser," says Darrah, now a businessman in his hometown. "Part of it was where he came from. He came from Basketball Country, and besides that, he was a natural athlete."

What Roger saw on the road to play other SEC schools really made him rethink his decision to come South. Woodruff Hall at the University of Georgia and the Sports Arena at Auburn were dilapidated bandboxes.

It was a world he did not understand.

"I would call home, and I would get no sympathy there," Roger says. "My folks just reminded me that it would be worse if I was in the Army; they sure wouldn't let me come home. But nobody ever said 'I told you so.'"

WHEN FALL QUARTER ended, there was more on his mind than Christmas. Roger did not tell anyone, but he packed for his trip home with the idea that he would not be coming back. He had quietly contacted Indiana University and talked about transferring, but the coaches in Bloomington were not very encouraging.

Back home in Dale, he shared with his parents and his girlfriend Beverly that he did not want to go back to Atlanta and that he intended to transfer. He thought they would be overjoyed, but to his surprise they were not.

His mother called Ike Blemker, the father of Tech's varsity co-captain. He lived in Huntingburg but worked at a factory in Dale. He told Mrs. Kaiser how to reach Coach Hyder, who was in Detroit where the team was playing in the Motor City Invitational. To everyone's surprise, the Yellow Jackets won that tournament. Hyder had reasons to celebrate, but he was upset at the news about his freshman star.

The team was flying home and he was suffering from the flu, but Hyder rented a car and drove unannounced to Dale. He showed up at the Kaisers and offered Roger a ride back to campus.

"You ready to go back?" Hyder asked.

Once again, he could not say no.

7
Father Knew Best

"People will forget what you said. People will forget what you did. But people will never forget how you made them feel."

His name is almost forgotten now, but in 1955 Joe Helms hit a jump shot that was heard around the world of basketball. It resonated through the Commonwealth of Kentucky, where the Wildcats 129-game home winning streak came to an end. It echoed through the Southeastern Conference where teams believed Adolph Rupp was unbeatable. It vibrated through a dreary gym at Georgia Tech and gave the Yellow Jackets hope for the future. It reverberated all the way to Indiana, where Roger Kaiser first became aware that the Atlanta school had a basketball team.

It was a puny shot really, from eleven or twelve feet out, and the shooter was the smallest guy on the court. Helms, only five-foot-eight, had 23 points, but his shot with eleven seconds to play made a crowd of 11,000 zany Wildcats go mute. Many of them had never seen Kentucky lose. It had been thirteen years after all since the 'Cats lost to Ohio State in Alumni Gym—an arena that no longer existed.

Describing the outcome, *Atlanta Journal* sports editor Furman Bisher wrote: "It was the most incredible event in basketball since Dr. James Naismith discovered the peach basket."

Never one to understate a story, Rupp told his players that from that day forward, until history was no longer recorded, they would be remembered as the team that broke that string. "Even if you go on to win the NCAA championship, you must carry this scar with you the rest of your lives."

Twenty-three days later in Atlanta—with a film crew hired by Rupp recording the action—the Yellow Jackets did it again, defeating the Wildcats 65–59 in Heisman Gym, a multipurpose building that dated back to the Great Depression. It was named after John Heisman, who, before World War I, coached football and basketball at Georgia Tech.

Those losses were the only blemishes on Kentucky's record going into the postseason where, in the NCAA Tournament, the Wildcats lost to Marquette, giving them a 23–3 record for the season. Tech, meanwhile, had lost to unheralded Sewanee a few days before they shocked Kentucky the first time and finished the season 12–11. Two years before that, Kentucky was 25–0 and Tech was 2–22.

So when word reached the Evansville sports pages that Tech had defeated mighty Kentucky—the nation's number one team—a basketball junkie like Roger Kaiser took notice. Huntingburg's Buddy Blemker, a teammate in summer baseball, was on the Tech freshman team, and Gary Phillips from Jasper was also there. Roger remembered these things when he heard the Yellow Jackets were interested, and he understood the sincerity of their head coach when he said they needed him.

When Kaiser reported for the first day of practice as a freshman, his coach was a Naval ROTC instructor named Sonny Stevens. But when someone introduced the team's graduate assistant, Roger's curiosity was piqued and later he had opportunity arose, he had a question for him.

Yes, it was that Joe Helms.

"He was a volunteer coach. He worked on campus in Tech's Research Center. One day at practice, he pulled me aside and said Coach Hyder wanted him to work with me on some new moves. The main thing he showed me was a jab move that would be very valuable to me. I'm still teaching it today. As simple as it was, I wasn't using it then. I probably didn't need that move in high school, but it sure did help me in college."

HERALDED VICTORIES OVER Kentucky were pieces of the foundation on which Tech built its program before the team moved into Alexander Memorial Coliseum in 1956. The first year in the new building, with sophomore guards Buddy Blemker and Terry Randall joining veteran Bobby Kimmel, the team set a school record with eighteen victories in twenty-six starts.

Hyder still did not get proper respect. Bisher wrote that his salary was the size of a Methodist preacher. He taught a full load of classes in physical education—which he would do even after he retired from coaching. He had little help and was unable to hire a full-time assistant until 1956, when enough money was added to his budget for him to add broad-shouldered Texan Byron Gilbreath. Little time was wasted. The former Austin College head coach went right on the road scouting talent all over the country.

In the 1957–1958 season, Blemker and Randall played in the main event alongside colorful Dave Denton, but the team limped to a 15–11 record that could have been better. The Jackets played four overtime games during that up-and-down season and lost three of them. But even diehard Tech football fans were starting to notice the talent assembled on the freshman team where Kaiser scored 22.4 points a game, Wayne Richards chipped in 18.4 an outing, John Hoffman added 13.2, and Bobby Dews was a promising field general and pesky defender.

There were new faces when the 1958–1959 season began, and the retooled Jackets lived up to expectations. The team was once again built around the diminutive backcourt of Blemker and Randall, which forced Roger to play out of position. That did not concern him, for in high school he played a hybrid position that effectively made him a center on offense and a guard on defense.

Roger adapted to playing on the wing opposite Denton, with Frank Inman and Richards sharing the post. His problems came on defense where he usually had to match up with much bigger players. Despite his size, Kaiser pulled down a team-leading 182 rebounds that season, an average of 7.0 a game.

Blemker and Randall had dominated the basketball, the shot chart, the scorebook, and the headlines, and now they were asked to share the ball and run plays for an unproven sophomore. The two all-SEC guards could have been resentful, but that would not have fit their personalities.

"They were true student athletes that were intelligent enough to know their strengths and weaknesses. They were also smart enough to know what I could do and couldn't do. Defenses in the SEC had seen them for two years, so teams were catching up to them. They knew that to win, they had to do some things differently."

Playing on the inside led Roger to a rough-and-tumble play involving Kentucky all-American Johnny Cox. It occurred at Alexander Memorial, in Tech's first sellout of the season. The incident came in the aftermath of a situation that caused the gentlemanly Hyder to jump to his feet, storm down the floor and wag a finger in Rupp's face. The legendary Wildcat coach had left his seat and got in Roger's face after Cox went high in the air, hit the floor with a thud, and did not get up. Words were exchanged and the language was not pretty.

Hyder defended his sophomore star but after the game, when reporters asked what happened, his answer was calm. "It was nothing. Kaiser told me they had not cussed him, and I forgot about it."

Roger says otherwise. Rupp called him a dirty S.O.B., and he told Hyder that. However, at that moment and time, the Tech coach did not choose to get into a war of words with the outspoken Wildcat mentor.

Cox recovered and ended up with 23 points in Kentucky's 94–70 win. Kaiser scored only 11 points and fouled out of the game—his only disqualification that entire season. Reporters crowded around Rupp and asked him what happened, and afterward he, too, was calm.

"Oh, that Cox spill," Rupp said. "We make it a point never to criticize. Kaiser was playing aggressive basketball and in the effort laid wood to Johnny. But that's part of the game."

In seasons to come, Roger Kaiser would have the last word.

LAPS AROUND THE conference reminded him that he was in football country where basketball was only an afterthought. To bear that out, in 1958, Auburn football coach Ralph "Shug" Jordan held the single season record for Georgia basketball wins with eighteen in 1948. Even today, he is fifth in wins among Auburn basketball coaches. During his tenure, Jordan funded Auburn's first basketball scholarship by giving all-SEC player Shag Hawkins proceeds from a Coca-Cola machine in the gymnasium.

Georgia Tech had a new place to play, but most SEC gyms were relics that were smaller than the high school gyms Roger played in back in Indiana. Conditions were deplorable. The lights were so bad at Woodruff Hall that when his team was about to play the Bulldogs in Athens, Joel Eaves dimmed the lights at Auburn practices. Circumstances at Ole Miss were so backward that visiting teams dressed in a classroom upstairs. At halftime, players stood in line at a public bathroom if they needed to urinate.

Auburn moved into the Sports Arena in 1948, and playing in a refurbished airplane hangar was a unique experience for Roger and generations of visiting teams. Benches were at either end of the court, and opponents sat among Tiger fans. Sidelines were so close to the court that fans on the front row had to move back when a player was inbounding the ball.

Roger laughs about a game at Auburn that typically went to the wire. As the seconds ticked away, he dribbled the ball and watched the clock with his back to the stands. "Coach Hyder had instructed me to hold the ball until they came out of their zone defense, which you could do in those days. I held the ball for six to eight minutes when this one fan started giving me trouble. He was so close that I could hear every word. He started saying how hard it must be for me to hold the ball. 'You know you want to shoot it,' he said.'"

THIS WAS THE SEC Roger Kaiser came to know. Alexander Memorial Coliseum was the most modern arena in the league, but it was also a long way from family and friends. Before four-lane highways, the trip from Indiana to Georgia was long and tedious, so his girlfriend and his family could not see him play very often.

On nights he was playing, Beverly tuned her radio until she found the score on WSB out of Atlanta. His parents discovered they could pick up Al Ciraldo's trademark play-by-play on WGST on their car radio. When their son was in action, they drove around town until they found a spot where they had good reception.

"They even got accused of parking," Roger says.

Though playing out of position, he led the team in scoring right up to the final game. Roger endured an uncharacteristic late-season slump, but like the team, he recovered nicely. The Jackets won their last seven games to close with a 17–9 record.

Roger scored 382 points, six behind Blemker, who led the team in scoring for the third consecutive campaign. Firing from the hip as he always did, Blemker averaged 14.9 points a game and became the school's all-time leader with 16.2 points per game. Kaiser recorded 14.7 points a night and Randall had a 14.0 average. The enigmatic Denton fell to 9.4 points a game.

By his sophomore year, his shaky start in the classroom behind him, Roger settled into a routine. He learned to work on academic assignments as hard as he did his jump shot and his improved work habits might be attributed to his roommate. Hoffman was an excellent student, so good that he would finish sixth in his graduating class at Tech.

"He put me on a guilt trip, and all of a sudden I was studying like he was."

ON THE BASKETBALL court, the graduations of Blemker and Randall, as well as Frank Inman's unexpected decision not to return for his senior year, the team effectively belonged to Kaiser. For all his talent, Denton was not a player you could build around, for his performances in the classroom were as chaotic as his drives to the basket, often leaving him ineligible for important stretches of time. That left it up to Roger and a committee of Richards, Dews, Hoffman, Riley, and Poteet, joined by sophomores Josh Powell and John Gher. Teammates recognized Roger's leadership traits and elected the upcoming junior as their team captain.

But the true team leader was always Hyder. A former outfielder in the New York Yankees' minor league system, he did not have big-city charisma or the endless chatter of a used-car salesman like many in his profession, but players could always trust him.

An article in *Sports Illustrated* described him well:

> He is a man of genuine warmth and generous spirit, who treats his players with the affection and trust of a father—and this is an incalculable asset in persuading the good high school

> players to come to Georgia Tech. It is instantly clear to the most cynical observer that Whack Hyder believes basketball to be an activity provided by the university for the benefit of the students and not to serve the ambitions of the coach.

In 1955, the year Helms shocked the Commonwealth, Rupp asked Hyder if they could talk after Kentucky practiced at Heisman Gym. When Hyder showed up, the Wildcat team surrounded Rupp, who posed two questions: "What's your aim in basketball, and what do you expect to accomplish in a gym like this?"

If Rupp thought this would rattle Hyder, he failed. His answer was typically folksy. "My first aim is for our kids to lead a good moral life. Next, I want them to graduate. And third, when it comes time, I want them to concentrate on basketball."

"You can't do that," Rupp replied. "Boys aren't that way anymore."

Roger Kaiser was—which Adolph Rupp would soon learn.

8

Pulling the Trigger

"Our greatest weakness lies in giving up. The most certain way to succeed is always trying one more time."

Shuffling back to the dugout on the first base side of Rose Bowl Field, Roger Kaiser was dejected and confused. The ball got to the plate faster than it did in high school, and the Louisville Slugger on his shoulder might as well have been a ship's anchor. The promising freshman watched five or six pitches sail past him without taking a swing, and now he was on his way back to the bench.

"I struck out and I never swung the bat," he says.

Lane Akers played basketball, was an all-SEC shortstop, and captained Georgia Tech's first SEC baseball champions in 1957. Now he was coaching the Yellow Jacket freshman team, and he did not pass up a chance for a teaching moment.

"What happened? Couldn't you pull the trigger?"

The first-year player did not know what to say.

"Go over to the side, get in your stance, and swing the bat ten or eleven times until you're comfortable pulling the trigger."

"It must have worked, because the next time up, I pulled the trigger, and I hit the ball out of the park," Roger says.

That was the way it was supposed to be. His basketball trophies could already fill a museum. He had been one of the top high school players in basketball-rich Indiana, and now he was playing in the Southeastern Conference. But in his dreams, Roger saw himself wearing spikes instead of Converse high-tops. Baseball was the game his father loved, the one that he faithfully scored from behind the backstop when his oldest son was playing.

Among Roger's boyhood treasures are two keepsakes. One is an autograph from Cincinnati Reds slugger Ted Kluszewski. Another is a scorecard from a Major League Baseball exhibition game in the spring of 1952 at Bosse Field in Evansville. The New York Giants played the Cleveland Indians. Leo Durocher was the manager of the Giants, and Al Lopez led the Indians. Each is enshrined at Cooperstown. The rosters of the two teams included future members of the Baseball Hall of Fame, such as Bob Feller, Bob Lemon, Early Wynn, Larry Doby, Willie Mays, Hoyt Wilhelm, and Monte Irvin.

The shy fourteen-year-old baseball fan found the courage to collect autographs on his scorecard from a number of the big league stars. Mostly faded, they survive as a testimony to his love of a game he dreamed of playing.

Roger played high school baseball in the spring. In the summertime, he played in independent leagues all over Indiana, facing teams from places like Holland, Huntingburg, and Jasper. On the school team, he hit over .400, attracting Major League scouts who told him he ought to be in the outfield. He arrived at Georgia Tech as a promising shortstop, but once he saw his basketball teammate, Bobby Dews, gliding around the infield, it confirmed that he belonged in the outfield.

Dews was a skinny kid with glasses, whose father, Bobby Sr., had been a journeyman catcher—who sometimes played barefooted—in the Brooklyn Dodgers organization. Young Bobby grew up around bush league ballparks all over the country, giving him an education that others never received.

Coach Joe Pittard saw the same things Roger did. He watched Dews chew up ground balls during one of their first infield drills and told him to take it easy. "I want you to relax and enjoy the game, because I can tell by looking at you that you're gonna be my shortstop," Coach Joe said.

Kaiser eventually moved to the outfield where he spent the rest of his college career—a switch Coach Joe tried to explain. "When you're a sophomore, you'll play right field. When you're a junior, you'll play left field, and as a senior, you will get to play centerfield. That's the way it is."

Despite those antiquated quirks, baseball was a welcome change from the rigors of basketball, and Roger discovered very quickly how much more enjoyable baseball practices were. "Basketball is serious. Baseball is fun," he says.

The freshman baseball team was an interesting mix of abilities and backgrounds. Baseball was not blessed with a big budget for scholarships, so to fill out the team, Coach Joe invited members of the student body to join a squad built around athletes on basketball and football scholarships. Very few of the other guys were getting financial help, so they were impressed when Coach Joe asked Roger what size spikes he wore.

"You must be good," one of his teammates said.

"Why would you say that?"

"Because he asked about your shoe size."

That would not be the last time a baseball teammate commented about his friendship with Coach Joe. The subject also came up during his sophomore year when older teammates asked Roger to go to the coach and ask about letting Blemker play first base when he was not pitching.

"He'll listen to you," the teammate said.

Roger agreed that Blemker was the best hitter on the team and that they could use his bat in the lineup every day, so even though he doubted Coach Joe would listen to him, he said he would go see him.

The opportunity came at practice.

"I got a suggestion for you," he said.

Coach Joe listened and gave a brief answer.

"Kais, I have a suggestion for you. Go back to the outfield and let me coach.."

Despite that awkward conversation, the bond between them went beyond sports. Soon after he arrived on campus, Pittard and basketball coach Whack Hyder invited the young freshman to their respective churches. He was a Methodist and so were they. Roger found a Sunday home at Coach Joe's church, the First United Methodist Church on Peachtree Street, which was pastored by the Reverend Pierce Harris, a former minor league baseball player.

"Coach Joe didn't have a son, but he loved me like a son," Roger says. "Later on, he asked me what kind of glove I liked. I said I used a Mickey Mantle model glove. He bought me a new Roger Maris model glove and made sure that I had fat bats to use in cold weather and skinnier ones for warmer climates. When the other guys realized that, they said I was his pet."

THERE WAS A lot to love about Coach Joe—literally and figuratively. Julian Howard Pittard joined Tech's football staff in 1943 after twenty-two years as head football coach at Gainesville High School, where he won two state titles. During World War I, he was an athletic officer at Fort McPherson, an Army base in Atlanta, where he taught German prisoners of war the game of baseball.

Athletic director and head football coach Bill Alexander hired him as a B team football coach and head baseball coach. There was no baseball team during the war years, so he had to recreate the program from the ground up in 1946.

In sixteen years as head baseball coach, he won the SEC title in 1957 and took home a division crown in 1959. He retired from coaching in 1961 but remained on the Tech athletic staff until his death in 1972. He was inducted into both the Helms College Baseball Hall of Fame and the Georgia Tech Athletic Hall of Fame.

No one in the athletic department during the Bobby Dodd era was more loved than Coach Joe. He was proud of his role at Georgia Tech but just as proud that he was a Sunday school teacher at First United Methodist Church, where his pastor loved baseball and the Lord.

Coach Joe found in Roger a young man who knew how to play baseball and knew how to behave. He played the game hard but was in church on Sunday mornings. If Roger ever doubted his decision to come to Tech, all he had to do was remember the coaches he played under. They were the primary reasons he came to Atlanta, and they never let him down—on or off the playing fields.

"I knew they both cared about me—and that was important," he says.

Loyalty to his coaches is one reason Roger never seriously considered an offer from the Cleveland Indians in January of his sophomore year. John Schulte, a journeyman catcher for five big league teams, had turned to coaching and scouting. He wrote Roger a letter inviting him to Daytona Beach, Florida, to work out for other Cleveland scouts. The club had been in contact with him while he was in high school, but baseball's bonus rules had changed, and they would be able to sign him without having to keep him on the big club.

Schulte pressed him to come to Florida all expenses paid, but Roger never responded. Later on, he received a call from his father's favorite baseball player, Hoot Evers. A member of the Indians' front office, Evers also wanted Roger to sign with Cleveland.

And again he said no.

COACH JOE WAS in the twilight of his career and at the same time he was enjoying some of his finest years. An SEC championship and a division flag were good indicators, and so was his team's school record eighteen victories in 1957. It is not a coincidence that Buddy Blemker was on the mound for those important seasons.

The resounding thud of his fastball into the catcher's mitt was about the only noise Blemker ever made, so it is natural that Roger remembers a moment when the hurler came out of his shell. "He clapped his hands and said, 'Come on, Rog, get a hit.' It was something totally out of character. So with that encouragement, I went up to the plate and hit a triple."

Blemker's quiet demeanor on the court and the diamond helped the Hoosier pitcher mask the turmoil swelling inside, which, years later, he shared with his neighbor and teammate.

"I came into a game at Fenway Park, got one man to fly out, and Ted Williams was the next batter. My knees were shaking," Blemker said.

"How did you do?"

"I hit him on the elbow," the left-hander said.

That was not the whole story. That outing turned out to be the former Tech hurler's only appearance in the Major Leagues. He got five outs, gave up three hits (including a grand slam home run), had two walks, one wild pitch, and hit that one batter.

Roger was a sophomore and Blemker a senior in 1959. Mike Tomasovich was a highly sought-after high school senior in Weirton, West Virginia,. Ohio State University recruited him as a football player, but Hyder and Pittard promised him he could play basketball and baseball if he came to Tech. On April 1 of that year, on a recruiting trip to Atlanta, he toured Alexander Memorial Coliseum and was escorted to the cozy baseball park where he wanted to meet some Tech players.

"Roger was pitching batting practice when I got there, and they asked me if I wanted to hit off him. I'll never forget hitting a couple of balls out of the park in my street clothes," Tomasovich says.

Tomasovich became one of Roger's teammates in both basketball and baseball. He was third team all-SEC in basketball as a senior. The burly Polish youngster—whose younger brother Ted followed him to Tech—says Roger's baseball skills are often underappreciated. "Mostly, he played centerfield for Coach Joe. He wasn't the fastest guy around, but he always covered a lot of ground."

When the 1959 season began, Blemker was joined by two of his basketball teammates, and the two sophomores made a difference. It was a year the three of them would not forget. Tech went 17–9–2 and made it to the NCAA District 3 playoffs in Gastonia, North Carolina—the first time a Yellow Jacket baseball team had ever advanced into postseason play.

Tech had a chance to win the SEC title outright, but it came down to a final series in Atlanta against Ole Miss—and unfortunately, Blemker was unable to pitch every day. Behind their senior ace, the Jackets won the opener 4–3, but the Rebels came back to win the second game. In the rubber game, Ole Miss jumped on the scoreboard for six runs in the first inning and held on for an 11–7 win as Tech contributed six errors. Roger had a good day, though, with a double, two singles, and an RBI.

Ole Miss got the trophy, but Tech got the invitation to Gastonia, for the Rebels were forbidden by state law to participate in any event that might lead to them playing against African Americans.

Roger enjoyed an eye-opening season. He flittered around .400 at the plate for most of the year and finished with a .388 batting average—tops in the SEC. He made the all-SEC baseball team and was named the most valuable player in the conference. He was also voted the most outstanding player in the NCAA regionals.

"Every time I hit the ball, there was nobody there. I could hit it off the end of the bat, and it would dribble over the first baseman's head for a hit. When you're going good and your team is winning, everything goes well and everyone is focused," he says.

Roger never got into that zone again. He hit .318 and .324 his other two years in college; as a junior, he had a game against Georgia in which he slugged two home runs and batted in five runs. But he never had another season like the one he had his sophomore year—and neither did the Yellow Jacket team.

As a junior, he missed preseason baseball drills and several nonconference games in Miami because of the United States Olympic basketball trials. He also started that year with an annoying thumb injury that hampered him most of the season. Scouts came calling nevertheless, but the deals they offered were not that impressive.

Professional basketball offers were also on the table, though this was 1961 and contracts were not as lucrative as today's million-dollar packages. Salaries averaged about $10,000 a year, and unless a player was drafted in the first round, there were no guarantees.

Roger eventually chose basketball over baseball, and mostly it came down to timing. "If I had had the statistics in my senior year in baseball that I did as a sophomore, it would have been very different."

But he didn't, and he has no regrets.

He saw the struggles that Blemker—with all of his gifts—had in professional baseball. If the talented left-hander could not survive, Roger silently wondered how he would fare.

"I don't know if I made the right decision or not, but the deals were not lucrative when you compared them to the corporate offers that were floating around. I heard about the bus rides in the minor leagues, and in basketball—you flew. You would get on a plane in Pittsburgh and get off in Hawaii, which was quite an experience for a boy from Indiana. If I had it to do over, I would do it the same way."

9

That Little Girl from Lincoln City

"May you always have love to share, wealth to share and friends who care."

Roger Kaiser was a hometown hero, a boyish basketball star embraced by neighbors who felt they had an investment in his future. Beverly Hevron was his high school sweetheart, a vibrant cheerleader who never stopped cheering for her favorite player. They had classes together in the eighth grade and married when he was a college all-American. They have held hands through joy and heartache, and after more than sixty years their partnership is so seamless that even their oldest friends cannot remember when they were not a couple.

Dan Grundhoefer is one of those people. He was a classmate at Dale High School, and to him they are the best things that ever happened to the other.

"They have been a team all these years," he says. "He was the player and she was the cheerleader. They deserve each other. He was shy but Beverly would talk to everybody. My dad, the coal miner, always talked about how friendly and nice she was. 'She even talked to me,' he said."

Beverly would admit she seldom stops talking, and Roger Allen Kaiser will always be her favorite player and her favorite topic. Shy and reserved, he does not comfortably wave his own flag, but she constantly carries one of his banners in each hand. She keeps his scrapbooks and is his official photographer. When he is playing or coaching, she keeps his scorebook up to date and speaks her mind to fans or reporters whom she deems critical. They graduated from high school in a class of fifty-one, and thirteen of them went to school together in the same building all twelve years. These things might indicate that their bond was instantaneous, that it was love at first sight, but that was not the case.

Roger lived in town, and she grew up in Lincoln City—Abraham Lincoln's old stomping grounds. Roger was a city boy, and she was a country girl who had to ride the school bus every day. They were aware of each other in elementary school, but they really met when Roger repeated the eighth grade and became a member of Beverly's class. The older man was suddenly in her life every day.

"I thought he was stuck up," Beverly confesses, "but as I got to know him, I realized he was really just shy."

Roger and Bob Reinhart joined her class in school for basketball purposes, not because they were struggling students. Even at that age, Roger was immersed in basketball and baseball, but she was a girl who understood such things. She had been a regular at Dale High basketball games, since she was an energetic little girl. Aunt Florence took her to the games, Uncle Vic shared the finer points of basketball, and Beverly was forever hooked.

"I also started listening to Indiana University games on the radio back then. Chesty Potato Chips was the sponsor. I was in elementary school, and I can still sing their jingle…" which she will do on cue.

DALE AND ITS inhabitants were thoroughly washed in the blood of basketball, so it was not unusual for a young lady to get wrapped up in the game. There was not a girls' basketball team, so Beverly did everything she could do to support the Golden Aces. She edited the yearbook, was a high-stepping majorette, and was drum major of the school band. She was one of the perky cheerleaders who showed up on the front row of every team picture taken after a big victory.

Roger was a high school sophomore and a full-fledged basketball star before he and Beverly's future began to unfold. The team had gathered for a postseason banquet at Glenn's, one of the few restaurants in Dale with a dining hall large enough for such an event. What happened that night is hard to describe. It was as if the shy ballplayer with the flattop haircut noticed the beautiful dark-haired cheerleader for the very first time. Roger and Beverly have told this story over and over again, and years ago he preserved it by writing it out in longhand.

The words that follow are his:

This particular incident points out how a member of the so-called weaker sex prevented me from getting my nose flattened. It was my junior year in high school and I had gone to a basketball banquet. We were all seated and ready to eat when I noticed one of our attractive cheerleaders was sitting next to me. I had never noticed her to be so attractive before so therefore I tried to carry on a conversation with her as much as possible. She seemed rather friendly and since I knew that she lived three miles from the school I asked to take her home.

At the time I did not know that she had been dating rather steadily the biggest and I'm sure the roughest player on our football team. He was 6-foot-4 and weighed 240 pounds. If only someone would have told me this my next few days would have been much more pleasant. But since I knew nothing about her former dates I took her home and asked her for a date the following Sunday night. She accepted and I was in high spirits. I had found a new love until the Saturday before the Sunday night date when this monster of a man advised me to break the date. Rather bravely I informed him that when I wanted a date I usually asked the girl. Sunday came and since I didn't give his advice much consideration I didn't break the date.

We went to the show and were enjoying ourselves laughing when I happened to glance over my shoulder and there he sat. He was not laughing at all and the look on his face ruined the show for me.

When we left the show he did likewise and the rest of the night was like having a huge bloodhound following me. Everywhere we went he followed although he did take time out for a few beers, which I knew wouldn't help matters if he decided to get me. After we had eaten it was time to take her home and when I drove into her driveway he followed. By now I had lost all my acts of bravery.

Now since it is customary to walk a girl to her door I finally got up enough courage to get out of the car and when I did there he stood. He looked bigger than ever. He promptly demanded that I get back in the car and leave. He would see that my date reached her house safely.

When I didn't react to his order he immediately informed me that he was going to put me in the car. He probably would have if this girl wouldn't have bravely walked up to him and slapped him good a couple of times. The look on his astonished face caused me to do two things. First I couldn't help but cough and then I hurriedly walked the girl to her house.

After that night I dated the girl rather steadily without interference from him. This Christmas we became engaged and are planning a summertime wedding. So I should have good protection for a long time.

As a couple, something was different about them. They could be silly and playful like their teenaged friends, but they had a serious side that made grown-ups treat them like grown-ups. Roger became a member of the Hevron family, and Beverly was part of his. Beverly took over his mother's chore and clipped every article about him she could find. She pasted them in bulky scrapbooks. When one book was finished, she started another. It is a job she has never finished.

They were as together as a couple of high school kids could be. Roger had his life and Beverly had her own, but when they talked about the future, it was one. Their lives were intertwined. He was the basketball star and she was the cheerleader, but she began to cheer for only one guy. If Roger hit the big shot and Dale won, she was as excited as he was. If the Golden Aces lost and Roger was disappointed, then so was she.

When college recruiters started hounding him, Roger invited Beverly to join him and his parents for the adventure. They talked over his campus visits, and she went along with him and his family on a few recruiting trips. When the Georgia Tech basketball coach started writing Roger on a regular basis, he often asked Roger to tell Beverly hello, indicating that Whack Hyder sensed she would be part of the process.

But she could not convince Roger which school to choose.

LIKE JUST ABOUT everybody else in Dale, Beverly Hevron originally wanted him to go to Indiana University. That included her boss at the bank where she worked part-time. She knew Roger was interested in Tech, but Atlanta was so big and so far away. She feared they would not survive the time apart and the distance between them.

But on a Saturday in September, several months after graduating from high school, Beverly joined the Kaisers on the long drive to Atlanta and Georgia Tech. She said good-bye to Roger on a busy campus sidewalk and watched him go into the dormitory alone.

From that day forward, she was the school's biggest fan. She followed the football team the best she could back in Indiana, and she learned all she could about Tech basketball and baseball. She and Roger stayed busy writing letters and whenever he could, Roger and some friends from back home piled into a car and took a hurried midnight trip home.

"We would leave for Indiana on Fridays, after we all got out of class," teammate Alan Nass remembers. "There would be four of us in the car, and it was a ten or twelve-hour trip. It was usually me, Roger, John Hoffman, and another Indiana boy, Wade Rademacher. I remember this one trip where Coach Hyder was going to be up there on a recruiting trip. He cancelled his flight back to Atlanta and rode back with us. That was Whack for you."

The couple and their love survived. Beverly kept up with the scores of Roger's basketball games by tuning into WSB radio late at night all the way from Atlanta. She made it to Alexander Memorial Coliseum as frequently as time and money would permit. They settled into a routine, and nobody was surprised when at Christmas of his junior year they announced they were officially engaged.

THE COUPLE TALKED about having Del Harris officiate at their wedding ceremony in Dale, but their childhood pal ran into complications. Harris had just graduated from Milligan College, a Churches of Christ institution in East Tennessee. He had taken his first coaching job at a high school in Tennessee on his way to a career in basketball that included being the head coach of the Houston Rockets, Milwaukee Bucks, and Los Angeles Lakers in the NBA. He even spent two years coaching the Golden Aces.

In 1960, Harris was a newly ordained minister. When he was not coaching, he was serving part-time at a small church near the Milligan campus. "Roger and Beverly wanted me to marry them, and I wanted to be there for them. But an epidemic of hepatitis was spreading through Johnson City. I caught it and I stayed in bed all that summer," Harris says.

Then came the traditional invitation:

Mr. and Mrs. Benjamin Romine Hevron request the honor of your presence at the marriage of their daughter Beverly Aquilla to Roger Allen Kaiser on Sunday the nineteenth day of June, nineteen hundred and sixty at four o'clock at the Evangelical United Brethren Church in Dale, Indiana. Reception following the ceremony at the Dale American Legion Home.

Beverly wore a traditional white gown with a flowing train that she bought on sale at a store in Louisville for $65. Sharon Kaiser, her future sister-in-law, served as maid of honor. Roger wore a white dinner jacket with a smart little bowtie, and so did his best man, Bob Reinhart. Bridesmaids wore dresses and hats made by Hazel Cooper, one of Roger's aunts.

With Harris still bedridden back in Tennessee, the Reverend Glenn Porter presided. It was a sultry summer afternoon, a beautiful setting in a church that was not air-conditioned. The traditional ceremony moved flawlessly until the minister either lost his place or forgot the vows.

"Guess who took over?" Roger laughs.

Beverly, of course.

The efficient young bride had memorized every part of every person in the ceremony, and she quietly took charge, feeding Reverend Porter every cue until he gathered his wits.

After a photographer took the usual round of black-and-white photographs, the newlyweds left for the reception at the American Legion Hall in a white hardtop convertible owned by Mark Weller, a member of the wedding party and Roger's former high school teammate. After sampling cake and punch and posing for more pictures, Roger and Beverly followed tradition and patiently unwrapped every single wedding gift.

At the reception, there was one minor glitch. Reinhart, Roger's best man, made some inappropriate noise by lighting a firecracker that almost went off in Beverly's sister Bonnie's face. "He got one of Ben Hevron's famous looks for that," Beverly says, still remembering her father's stern expression.

When Bob's unscheduled fireworks display ended, Roger and Beverly left for their honeymoon in Chicago. It would be a brief trip, for he was due back at Georgia Tech for summer school in a few days. The American League baseball schedule altered those plans. While they were in Chicago, they discovered that the New York Yankees were playing the Tigers at Briggs Stadium in Detroit. They could not miss an opportunity to see Mickey Mantle play in person, so they rerouted their trip to the Motor City.

It was unseasonably cold that June, and Beverly needed a heavy coat to wear to the ball game. They found their way to Marshall Field's so she could shop for something warm. Roger said he would park outside the department store and wait on her. Such a plan might have worked in a town the size of Dale, but it would not work in a congested place like Chicago. One of the city's finest ordered Roger to move along, and the newlywed naively thought he would circle the block and come back for his new bride.

Easier planned than accomplished.

"I bought my coat and went out the door I had come in just like I said I would. No Roger. I waited and waited and waited, and still he didn't come. I didn't know what to do. I was near tears and I finally said to myself that I could always call my daddy," Beverly says.

Fighting traffic and one-way streets, Roger made it back to where his anxious bride was waiting. They drove to Detroit, went to the baseball game, and by the next day, they were on their way to Atlanta.

After their brief honeymoon, they moved into a small apartment on Tenth Street, not far from the Tech campus. Beverly went to work at Delta Airlines, and her husband started back to class.

It was a simple time for young people from small towns who were far away from their families for the first time. Several of his Tech teammates had also married girls from home—including John Hoffman, Alan Nass, and Mike Tomasovich—and the couples spent their free time together.

The fellows got free movie tickets, and they saw every new film that came to the Fox Theater. They walked to the Fox and other downtown movie houses and never gave it a second thought. Other nights, they got together and played Canasta or Bridge. They did not know it then, but they were forging friendships that would never end.

WHEN FRIENDS THINK of those years, they remember Roger and Beverly as a matched set—a match made in heaven as well as Dale. When they got married, they partially fulfilled a whimsical prophecy made in the yearbook their senior year of high school: "The well-known socialite, Bev Hevron has just returned from Los Vegas with her sixth husband, the Reverend Roger Kaiser."

His former high school coach believes Beverly has always been a good influence on Roger. "She will always tell the truth," says Jerry Kemp, who returned to Dale for their wedding and has shown up at many of their class reunions.

College teammates laugh about those times when their captain had to follow his wife's instructions. Tomasovich remembers a short shopping trip that he and Nass took with the Kaisers to the Hubbard Manufacturing Company in Bremen, Georgia.

They were supposed to ask for L.C. Guice, a Young Harris College friend of Coach Joe's. Guice did not give away clothing, but he sold athletes suits, sports coats, and slacks at discounted prices. "We were on our way to pick out some new clothes when Roger and Beverly got into an argument. I sat in the backseat and thought to myself, '*You can't talk to my captain that way*.' He was an all-American and a big basketball star, but Beverly didn't back down. He was just Roger to her."

Members of that team still get together frequently, and Tomasovich describes a more recent trip to Plains, Georgia, that they made to hear President Jimmy Carter teach Sunday school at the Maranatha Baptist Church. Hoffman was driving a Lincoln Navigator, and he hooked up a new Garmin GPS to help them find their way to the church.

"Hoffman kept complaining and cussing that 'lady' on the GPS machine that was telling him where to turn. Beverly finally took over. She said you go this way or you go that way. She seemed to know every back road in rural Georgia. Turned out she had been the navigator that helped get Roger's basketball teams to all of those small colleges," Tomasovich says.

Roger and Beverly grew up together, and they have grown old together. They graduated from high school together and had three children together. She was the cheerleader and he was the star player, but when they came home after ball games, they were a loving couple that has somehow survived. They have celebrated the joy of championships, and together they somehow found the strength to bury a daughter.

Roger is not sure when he decided Beverly would be his wife. "She had already proved her love for me. She stayed in Indiana and worked until I could take care of my time at Georgia Tech. After we married, I had schoolwork, athletics, ROTC, and the responsibilities of being a husband. She's the best thing that could ever have happened to me."

Through it all, their roles have not changed, Del Harris says.

"Roger was a consensus two times all-American as a player, and as a coach, he won four national tournaments. For a guy who has done all of that, he's humble. If you were in a room with three janitors, two firemen, two filling station operators, and two burger flippers, you couldn't pick Roger out of the pack—unless Beverly was there. She would point him out."

Theirs is a magical relationship built on friendship, love, and faith, and the Reverend Don Harp—their pastor and friend of more than forty years—says they are in sync like few couples he has ever known.

"They have been together forever, long enough that they have become one of those couples where one starts a sentence and the other finishes it. They seem to know what the other one is thinking," Harp says.

When the Harps and Kaisers lived in Carrollton, they were high-profile families. One of them was the pastor of a church, and one of them coached the local college basketball team. They played lots of card games, and their families spent New Year's Eves together, a tradition that endured until their children grew up and moved away.

Roger is notorious for going to bed early, but at those gatherings, Don says he always stayed awake long enough to eat several bowls of boiled shrimp. Weather permitting, Roger and Don liked to go out in the backyard and compete in two-on-two basketball games. Like others, the reverend does not remember Roger being on the second place team very often.

"He does not like to lose," Don says.

Teeter Umstead played on Whack Hyder's early teams, and while Roger was on active duty, he worked at the scorer's table at Alexander Memorial Coliseum. Later in life, his son played at West Georgia College under Roger, the coach. They developed a close friendship, and their families often shared meals together. It was Teeter who introduced Roger to a new game.

"I built a horseshoe pit in my backyard, and I played all the time. I was pretty good. When Roger came over, we had always played a game of H-O-R-S-E, and he always won. But after I got the pit, I asked him if he wanted to play some horseshoes. I won every game at first, but we had to keep playing until he started winning. Games he played in the backyard were just as important as hitting a winning shot in the SEC."

Their roster of friends is varied and ageless. This is not a new phenomenon. Jenny Buntin, their oldest child, remembers when she and her sister Jill were in high school in Carrollton. Neighbor boys would flock to their house on Lakeshore Drive on Sunday afternoons, not to see the girls but to play basketball with their father.

"And they never won either," she says.

One of their friends today is Doctor David Jones, a pediatric surgeon in Atlanta., He came into their lives when he was a young person from Macon attending the Roger Kaiser Sports Camp. Jones talks about Roger's influence on his life and of his love for Roger and Beverly. "They are so young mentally," he says. "I don't think they'll ever grow up. They'll probably grow up when they take their last breaths."

Roger and Beverly collect friendships like the Hall of Fame basketball player and coach collects awards, and the Harp family continues to be among their army of close friends. They now attend Peachtree Road United Methodist Church in Atlanta, a congregation Harp once served. Even after he was no longer their pastor, Harp was there for them in moments of need that both families cherish.

More than once, Harp waited outside hospital operating rooms when Roger faced serious surgery and frightening biopsies. He married their three children and also baptized their eight grandchildren. When their oldest daughter, Jill, was overcome with breast cancer at a much too early age, Harp flew to Florida to officiate at her funeral on one of the most difficult days he endured as a pastor.

The two families have cried together, but mostly they have laughed together, something Roger and Beverly do so well. That is why Don Harp cannot help but smile when he talks about the good times they have shared together.

"Beverly has always been a Mother Hen about Roger. I've read some of the long letters she wrote to people that she believed had wronged her Roger. I always tell them that I hope Roger goes first, because the rest of us can't care for him like Bev. More than anything, I believe that without each other, Roger and Beverly would be lost."

Roger knows that. He says his greatest accomplishment in life was finding her and keeping her. To him, marrying Beverly Hevron was greater than any of his star-studded feats in sports. He is reminded of that whenever he reaches into his jewelry box.

Spending a lifetime as a player, coach, and administrator, he has amassed a glittering collection of rings. Individually and collectively, they are impressive. Roger wears them on a regular basis, not because he wants to impress other people, but because he is proud of them.

Each keepsake ring represents hard work, the rewards those labors brought him, and more than anything reminds him of the people who made those special moments possible.

"I have conference championship rings, national championship rings, class rings, Hall of Fame rings, and best of all—a wedding ring. My greatest accomplishment has definitely been getting and keeping my wife. It was my best decision, and one of the first I made on my own. Many years ago, a person that shall remain anonymous asked me, are you really going to marry that little girl from Lincoln City? I thought to myself, what a stupid thing to say and also how very little he knew about Beverly."

To this day, she amazes her husband.

"She is multitalented, a wonderful mother, cook and organizer. She is also a real people person. She loves people and she never meets a person who stays a stranger for very long. We're told how much we need a college education. She doesn't have one. So how in the world did she become so wise and capable?"

10

An All-American Hero

"If you lie in practice, you will be found out in the game."

John Logue is a better writer than he was a college basketball player. In a likeable self-deprecating manner, the author of twenty-five books will tell you that when he played for Joel Eaves at Auburn University, he was the fourteenth man on thirteen-man teams and that he spent more time sitting on the bench than he did on the court.

His description is reasonably accurate. He wore number 20, though he seldom played enough for his jersey to need washing or for him to earn a varsity letter. But two seasons studying under Professor Eaves gave the journalism major valuable insights into a game he would later write about.

After graduating from Auburn, Logue was a reporter for United Press International, *The Montgomery Advertiser,* and *The Atlanta Journal* during an era when college basketball was finding its rightful place on Southern sports pages.

Eaves is best remembered as the athletic director who, in 1964, hired Vince Dooley as head football coach at the University of Georgia. But during the preceding decade, he had been a coach that was ahead of his time. He graduated from Auburn with honors in 1938, and after a stint at Atlanta's Murphy High School, he became head basketball coach at his alma mater in 1949. Eaves treated the gymnasium like a classroom. It was the same way in football. As head scout for Shug Jordan's football team his weekly reports were as detailed as a graduate school thesis.

"To be a successful coach, all you need is to get a baseball cap, a whistle, and know how to use a projector," Eaves once said, and those were components when he installed the shuffle offense at Auburn. It was process as much as style. Players were in constant motion setting screens and patiently looking for layups. His teams were always prepared, and Logue remembers the Tigers preparing to play Davidson College just after Christmas in 1951. Eaves showed the team film of a game between Davidson and Duke.

Dick Groat, the only player ever named to both the college basketball and baseball halls of fame, was the leader of the Blue Devils. He went on to play shortstop for four National League teams, mainly the Pittsburgh Pirates. He was most valuable player in 1960 and led the league in hitting with a .325 average. He also played a season in the National Basketball Association.

As a two-time all-American at Duke, Groat averaged 26 points a game and was second in the nation in scoring, so he was all over the floor when Eaves flicked on the movie projector. What Logue saw in that darkened room left a lifetime impression.

"Nobody I had ever seen before shot a jump shot," he says. "In my day, everyone was married to the floor. But there was Groat, making other guys look silly, shooting the ball while in midair. It was amazing to us."

He remembers the first time he had an opportunity to observe Roger Kaiser in action. He was just a freshman and his best years were still ahead of him, but the Atlanta sportswriter left Alexander Memorial Coliseum talking about his jump shot.

To a writer, his form was poetry.

"He had an ability to climb into the air like I had never seen before," says Logue, who later was managing editor of *Southern Living Magazine*. "He was perfectly in balance when he kicked his legs, and when he got up the air, physics kicked in."

To Roger, this was the payoff for the lonely hours and cold days he spent perfecting and practicing, starting on that outdoor court his father built for him. His legs were sturdy and his hands were large. He was blessed with unusual hand and eye coordination and an unyielding confidence that made him hungry for the basketball when clocks were rushing to zero. He was a shooter and a scorer, like few before him, in a conference built for fall and made for football.

He did his best to change that culture, wrote David Moffitt, the Atlanta sports editor of United Press International: "While Roger prefers to have his basketball do the talking for him, he has played no small role in elevating basketball to a place of eminence at football minded Georgia Tech. He has one of the most exciting jump shots ever seen in the Southeast. He's a shooter, not a gunner ... He is confident but not cocky. Off the court, he gives the impression he wouldn't harm a fly, but on the court, he's murder to the opposition."

HIS FELONIOUS ASSAULT on SEC teams cranked up during his junior year when Roger teamed with flashy Dave Denton to take the Yellow Jackets on a magical ride to places they had never been before. They were a pair of aces that no one would have ever imagined showing up in the same hand.

Roger was focused and organized. The helter-skelter player known as "The Duke," was a polar opposite with movie star looks. Denton could do everything but shoot, and his hyperkinetic style kept him around the basketball. How else would you explain a guy six-foot-two pulling down seventeen rebounds in a single game? His reckless play would fit in well today. But fifty years ago, he was someone you had to notice. He was different than the other nine guys on the court. Unfortunately, he was also remembered for his antics off the court.

Denton's biggest headline came when Roger was a sophomore, on a Monday evening before Kentucky came to call. Denton was a product of Bowling Green, a town about 150 miles from Lexington, so matching up with the Wildcats was especially big at his house. So how did he prepare? He mingled in with an overflow crowd of 7,348 fans outside and tried to make money off the tickets he had been given.

"Need tickets?" he asked two fellows he did not know. "I've got two reserved tickets for $20." Once a price was set, they nabbed the Tech star for scalping.

"Oh, no," he cried. "I've only got a few minutes to get dressed for the game."

The undercover lawmen set him free in time for the big game. A few days later, a kindly judge also turned his head on the player's ill-timed salesmanship. He only fined him a dollar. On the basketball court that night in 1960, Denton recovered nicely—as reported in the next edition of *Sports Illustrated.*

> 'The worst team I ever had,' grumbled Kentucky's proud Adolph Rupp. And The Baron had good reason for his disgust. He had just watched Georgia Tech tame his Wildcats 65-44. The eager Yellow Jackets, seeking their first Southeastern Conference title since 1938, forced Kentucky into its poorest shooting performance of the season (16.3 percent) with a harrying half-court press, received an added bonus when little Bobby Dews held the Wildcats' Bennie Coffman to one point. Sophomore Roger Kaiser produced 24 points, and Dave Denton, who had been nabbed for ticket scalping before the game (he later was fined $1 by a sympathetic judge), got 18 and dazzled the confused Wildcats with his dribbling.

Memories of his late teammate make Roger smile.

"Dave was an original," he says. "Ticket scalping was the worst trouble he got into, but he was always into something. I remember one road trip where we were ready to get on the bus at our hotel and he was nowhere to be found. Everybody was looking for him. He played the piano like Jerry Lee Lewis, and someone found him in the hotel ballroom pounding the keys and forgetting the time."

If someone got caught breaking a rule, it was usually the free-spirited Duke of Bowling Green. Others might push curfew but he was the one that got caught. Academically, he was never able to color inside the lines, as Roger relates. "He had to hand in a paper one morning by nine o'clock. He turned it in at 9:30 and the professor wouldn't accept it."

When it came to basketball, Denton was a showman in short pants, especially when it was time to distribute the basketball to his sharpshooting teammate. By the end of Roger's junior year, observers were calling the Tech duo the most exciting tandem in college basketball.

They were not alone.

Dews was a swirling ball hawk that columnist Jesse Outlar described as "quicker than a jackrabbit." Richards understood that his job was to stay down low and rebound. Riley, though not a gifted offensive player, knew his role was defense. Hoffman, Poteet, Gher, and Powell provided depth when they were called upon.

Opponents focused mainly on Roger, who, from the beginning of the season, was a force that demanded respect. Georgia's Darrah saw the changes in Roger's game before numbers were posted or awards were presented. As a sophomore, Roger deferred to upperclassmen Blemker and Randall. As a junior, his own gifts bubbled to the surface.

"He wasn't the attraction when we were sophomores, but our junior year, it was all Roger Kaiser," the former Bulldog captain says. "He was disciplined and very serious. He knew what he was going to do and when he was going to do it. He was a tremendous shooter, but he knew the game and could get the shot. He did the whole game."

ADOLPH RUPP LEARNED that firsthand. Whack Hyder was always a thorn in Rupp's hide and Roger helped keep that habit alive. His performances against the Wildcats were a subject of folklore throughout his career.

After Rupp escaped with an 89–79 victory over the Yellow Jackets on national television, The Baron said, "It makes me shudder to think what a helluva shooter that Roger Kaiser is. He's murder." That day he almost single-handedly slew the 'Cats. Blood dripped from a cut above his eye as he poured in a career-best 38 points—more than any opposing player had ever scored against mighty Kentucky.

A year later, Roger delivered the decisive blow in a 62–60 upset of Kentucky before a packed house at Alexander Memorial that included members of Georgia's General Assembly. The score was tied at sixty when he made a quick move, darted left to elude three defenders, and put up a twisting one-handed shot from fifteen feet out, floating above the outstretched arms of Kentucky's Billy Ray Lickert. The ball dropped through the net as time expired.

To humble Wildcats fans even more, Roger did all of this with a fractured thumb on his shooting hand or, as he told someone after the game, it was "just a little-bitty fracture" that he had suffered in the final minute of Tech's previous game.

"Everyone in the place knew Kaiser was going to shoot," lamented Rupp. "But what could we do about it. Our boy had him covered, but he got it off. It was a difference of one second and two points."

Veteran *Atlanta Journal-Constitution* photographer Charles Pugh captured that memorable moment on film. It is an unusual frame, for it does not show Roger Kaiser at all. It does show the scoreboard with one second remaining, and it does show the ball coming out of the net. It also pictures Georgia Tech players Alan Nass and Josh Powell already starting to celebrate, and beside them is the helpless body language of Kentucky's Ned Jennings, Carroll Burchett, and Lickert. Later on, when Roger asked Nass why he was not going for the rebound, the big guy's answer was honest: "Because I knew you would make it."

Writing in the *Atlanta Journal*, Logue described this monumental play. "Perhaps never in the history of the big bowl on The Flats has one man done so much to win a game as did Kaiser in this tense struggle."

THE NATION DISCOVERED Georgia Tech and their star shooter in 1960. It had been twenty-two years since the Yellow Jackets won a Southeastern Conference title, and behind Kaiser and Denton, they jumped into the fight for the SEC championship. Kentucky, as usual, was in the hunt. So was Auburn. But for most of the season, the attention was on Hyder's crew.

That meant Roger, for he enjoyed a dream season of memorable moments. One came in February when, with games to spare, he set the school's single-season scoring mark, moving past fellow Hoosier Buddy Blemker by scoring 30 points and grabbing 10 rebounds in an innocuous game against Louisiana State University. To mark that moment, press row was filled with local heavyweights, and they were impressed:

• Furman Bisher—"Dale has a population of 850 Hoosiers and is largely agricultural in its economy, except for one furniture factory. On this Monday evening, Dale won a degree of fame rather Georgian in scope when 9:21 p.m., this Roger Kaiser took a jump shot that scored two points and broke a record set by the son of the manager of the town's lone furniture plant. Last season young Ray Blemker, who registered from Huntingburg, nine miles north of Dale, scored 452 points for the Georgia Tech basketball team. This broke the season record set by Bobby Kimmel, who came from Louisville, Ky., just up the river."

• Jesse Outlar—"Some Tech scholars may be having trouble with calculus, but they're downright hep on arithmetic. Mr. Bob Wallace hadn't revealed the fact on the PA that Kaiser was on the verge of authoring a new scoring mark. But his historic shot hadn't cleared the net when the tumult and shouting started. Even Kaiser knew that he had carved a bit of athletic history at Tech ... A man asked Kaiser how it felt to become the sharpest shooting Engineer of all time. 'Great!' Kaiser summed up in an outburst of originality."

Tech beat Kentucky twice, but Auburn always seemed to be between the Jackets and the top spot. The Tigers were known as "Snow White and the Seven Dwarfs," referring to Joel Eaves's white mane and the fact that no one in their lineup was taller than six-foot-four. In most places, a shortage of size would lead to problems, but in the Auburn Shuffle that Eaves adapted from Bubba Ball—a high school coach in Columbus, Georgia—interchangeable parts were welcomed.

In a nonconference game in Atlanta, Auburn defeated Tech 66–59 and held Roger to 16 points. A month later in February, at the Sports Arena, the Tigers handed the Yellow Jackets their first SEC loss. Roger had 19 points, but the rest of the lineup was ineffective. There was still hope that Tech could finish on top, but a 62–57 setback at Vanderbilt in the final regular season game ended those dreams.

Auburn was regular-season champion. But the Tigers were on NCAA probation and were ineligible for the NCAA tournament. A sizzling performance in Gainesville that saw Roger score 28 points en route to a 69–55 victory over Florida clinched Tech's first postseason appearance. The Engineers outscored the Gators 15–1 in OT.

Auburn (19–3) and Tech (22–6) finished in the top fifteen nationally after the Engineers climbed as high as eighth. This relegated

Kentucky (18–7) to third place in the SEC, two games in front of Ole Miss and Tulane. Roger averaged 22.8 points a game and hit an amazing 86.3 percent of his free throws. He and Denton were first team all-SEC, and Roger was SEC player of the year and Tech's first consensus all-American.

The Jackets looked ahead to the Mideast Regionals at Louisville's Freedom Hall. The first order of business was finding out their opponent. It came down to Notre Dame or Ohio University, and smart money was on the Fighting Irish. Only, the Bobcats pulled an upset out of the hat. With a TV audience back in Atlanta looking on and 18,000 fans in the arena, it would be Tech versus Ohio U.

Their flight to Louisville for that game provided an extra added attraction for Roger. To pass the time in the air, he picked up a copy of Look Magazine, which included a big spread on the 1961 all-American basketball team.

"To my surprise, I read the list of players and saw my own name," Roger says. "Al Ciraldo heard me talking about it and he said I was not supposed to know, that it hadn't been announced yet."

Delta Airlines had received an advance copy of the magazine, which explained the unintended announcement. "So there I was, with no radio or television, sitting on an airplane with my roommate. What a way to learn of the honor."

When the game began at Freedom Hall, the unknown underdogs started with a flurry, building a 19–6 advantage. The lead was twelve with thirteen minutes to play, and when the clock stopped ticking, Roger had 25 points and Tech had the 57–54 victory, earning the right to meet powerful Ohio State.

"We couldn't hit anything in the first half, but I thought we were going to win after we cut their lead to six points and were getting good shots. Our full-court press deserves a lot of credit. It was our bread and butter again. And Wayne Richards was a big part of it," Roger told an *Atlanta Constitution* reporter.

Howard Joliff shredded Tech's zone in the first half and put up 16 points. During the break, Richards asked coaches to put him on the big fellow, and his only basket in the second half was a tip-in. "I don't think I'll be as nervous against Ohio State," Richards said, "but when I walked out there Friday, I felt like I was playing on Grant Field. Have you ever seen so many people?"

That set up a meeting in the regional finals with the third-ranked Buckeyes. Ohio State's lineup included Jerry Lucas, John Havlicek, and Larry Siegfried—a trio on its way to greatness. Lucas had 25 points and 16 boards, and Havlicek had 15 and 10. But the sharpest dagger belonged to unheralded Joe Roberts. His 19 points hit Tech where it hurt the most and sparked the Buckeyes 86–69 victory. This vaulted them to the Final Four in San Francisco and eventually the national championship.

Tech put up a fight, though. Roger led all scorers with 27 points, and Denton—playing his final college game—had 15. Jim Riley, in the game of his life, pulled down 15 rebounds to go with 8 points. A Tech team would not get that far in post-season play again for nearly twenty-five years.

The prose of John Logue captured the moment:

"A Georgia Tech team of incalculable courage refused to recognize its own human limitations here Saturday night in meeting the greatest offensive machine in the nation head-on, and emerged beaten, but unbowed."

Decades later, the sportswriter turned mystery writer still paints a colorful picture of that game. Logue's seat at Freedom Hall was at the end of the press table. After all this time, he needles the person sitting closest to him on the Buckeye bench.

"Bobby Knight played as much as I did," he says laughing.

Knight played long enough to pick up one personal foul. It was his only mark in the scorebook. Logue and the Hall of Fame coach laughed about that memory when Knight brought his Army team to play against Tech many years later. Of course, most of the General's legendary career was spent at Indiana University.

But Logue's most vivid memory is of number 21. "The best player on the floor in Freedom Hall that night wasn't Jerry Lucas or John Havlicek. As good as they were, the best player was Roger Kaiser."

EVEN PRINCE CHARMING has setbacks and Roger's first public disappointment as a basketball player came at the United States

Olympics trials in 1960, weeks after he took his team to the NCAA Tournament for the very first time.

His invitation to try out came late in the regular season and left him in a quandary. Even if he did not make the team, he would miss the early part of the baseball season on the heels of his outstanding sophomore year. One of the reasons he went to Tech was its baseball program, so he did not want to let down Coach Joe or his teammates.

Hyder helped him make up his mind.

"Roger, this may be the only chance you ever have to represent your country," he said. So he accepted the invitation, getting there later than most of the other players. When he arrived, United States Olympic officials greeted him with a question.

"There's a problem with housing," an official explained. "We know you were supposed to room with Jerry West, but he came in early and has become friends with someone else, and they want to room together. Would you mind rooming with Oscar Robertson?"

At a time of racial turmoil they must have thought a player from the Deep South would have problems living that close to a black player, but they did not know Roger. They were relieved when a broad smile covered his face and he told them rooming with Oscar would not be a problem. "We're both from the state of Indiana, so I know what a great player he is. That will work out just fine."

Assembled in the Mile High City was what many still consider the greatest array of amateur basketball talent this country ever put on the court. Included were West of West Virginia and Robertson of Cincinnati, along with Lucas and Havlicek of Ohio State, Walt Bellamy of Indiana, Terry Dischinger of Purdue, Bob Boozer of Kansas State, Adrian Smith of Kentucky and the Armed Forces, Darrell Imhoff of California, and Kaiser of Georgia Tech.

Behind the scenes issues forced Coach Pete Newell to make the toughest decisions an American coach had ever made. With so many stipulations and so many roster spots being dictated to him, he had to cut players who, under other circumstances, might have been issued red, white, and blue uniforms. Havlicek was an alternate, and talented players such as Lenny Wilkens of Providence, Satch Sanders of New York University, and Roger were among the well-known players sent home.

"Like most players, I blamed the coach," Roger admits.

He had never been cut from a basketball team in his life, and he was an all-star at every level of play. He also thought he had let down Coach Joe and his teammates who had been on the diamond for weeks while he was in Denver. Back home, rushing to get in shape for baseball, he hurt his hand. It gave him pain throughout that season when he gripped a bat and hit the ball.

Time healed his wounded ego.

One of the youngest U.S. teams ever assembled, the 1960 squad won the gold medal in Rome, putting on a clinic every time it took the court. Five players averaged in double figures. As a team, they averaged 102 points a game and held opponents to less than sixty—and they did these things with grace and dignity. They manhandled Brazil in the medal round 90–63, with Lucas scoring 25 points. Nine of the Olympians played in the NBA, and four were rookies of the year. Fifty years later, the Naismith Hall of Fame and United States Olympic Hall of Fame inducted them as a unit.

"I realized there were guards who were better than me. West and Robertson are two of the greatest that ever played the game. I offered scoring, but they could do it better than me. I might have had a better chance if I had been a point guard. But look at the great experiences I had. I got a chance to room with Oscar and to find out that not only was he a great player but a fine person. I was on the same court with some of the greatest players of all time and had a chance to work under a coach like Pete Newell. Most important of all, years later, I consider Jerry and Oscar in my treasury of friends."

11

Bedlam and Basketball

"We are all alike. We have ears, eyes, arms, legs and a heart. The difference is in the heart."

It was a day filled with history, hoops and hysteria.

History was made when William Augustus Bootle, a United States district judge in Macon, swung the doors open wide for Charlayne Hunter and Hamilton Holmes and forever ended racial segregation at the University of Georgia. His actions set up a clash of wills in Atlanta where Governor Ernest Vandiver had pledged to close state schools before he would allow the races to be educated in the same classroom. That Wednesday in 1961, with federal court orders in hand, Hunter and Holmes went to classes with white students for the first time and tension on that rolling campus was thick.

Hoops probably would have been rescheduled in today's world given the great potential for violence. But this was another era, and at 8 p.m., on the eleventh of January, another round of clean old-fashioned hate began as teams from Georgia Tech and Georgia met for the third time that season.

On the night of the basketball game, a game clock that should already have been scrapped led to hysteria inside ancient Woodruff Hall, but more serious was the turmoil on campus and in the state at large. John F. Kennedy had been elected in November and rumors were flying that Vandiver would join the president-elect as Secretary of the Army. Wally Butts had recently stepped aside as Georgia's head football coach after twenty-two seasons and longtime assistant Johnny Griffith was his successor. There were also headlines concerning possible construction of a Major League baseball stadium in downtown Atlanta and a modern basketball arena on campus in Athens.

A few days before Tech and Georgia met, Vandiver sent a telegram to JFK withdrawing from consideration for a cabinet position. That same week the Georgia Legislature convened and Bootle's decision to end 175 years of racial segregation was the primary topic.

Hunter and Holmes started to class on the morning of the game and demonstrations continued throughout the day. That night, hooded Klansmen in full regalia marched past the Varsity on College Avenue. During the game, an angry mob roared across campus yelling racial taunts, throwing bricks and looking for trouble. Before that night was done, authorities escorted the two black students back to Atlanta and expelled eighteen others who had resisted them being there.

There was also a wild-and-wooly basketball game, one that fans of both schools still argue about. At the core of these discussions is Roger Allen Kaiser, the most controversial field goal he ever made and a time piece that took a beating but kept on ticking.

WOODRUFF HALL WAS built in 1923 and by 1961 the Bulldogs record in basketball was as bad as the condition of their home court. Harbin "Red" Lawson had been in charge since 1952 and since taking over he had not enjoyed a winning season. Over all, a Georgia team had not had a winning record since 1951 when Jim Whatley went 13-11. To make matters worse Lawson had not defeated his rivals from North Avenue since 1957 when his squad pulled out a 69-68 victory.

Already that season, the Engineers had prevailed 74-56 in Atlanta before squeaking out a 54-51 decision at the Gator Bowl in December. The Bulldogs had lost star guard Gordon Darrah to a siege of ulcers but loyal fans earnestly believed the guys in Red and Black had turned the corner since that holiday meeting. Georgia enjoyed a modest three-game winning streak defeating Mercer, Tulane and LSU in the week leading up to the important meeting in Athens.

Tech was struggling to find scoring support for Roger. Leading up to the rematch junior forward Josh Powell had begun to emerge as a scoring and rebounding threat. With a boost from Powell and sophomore Alan Nass, Roger really began to shine. As was often the case, he saved his best for Kentucky.

In a nationally televised game from Lexington, he scored 38 points pouring in buckets from every angle. He hit 13 of 25 from the floor and was a perfect 12-for-12 at the free throw line. He had 21 in the first half alone. His was the most points an opponent had ever scored against the Wildcats bettering 37-point performances by Alabama's Jerry Harper in 1956 and Mississippi State's Bailey Howell in 1957.

Despite Roger's heroics Kentucky prevailed 89-79. "We figured he was going to get 23 or 24 anyway, so why knock ourselves out trying to stop him … But by golly we didn't count on that man getting 38 points. Hell, he came close to beating us by himself." Rupp said.

That set up the return bout with Georgia and though the campus and the community were in chaos, the game was a sellout. Athletic Business Manager Howell Hollis urged fans not to come to Athens without a ticket. He said ticket windows would not be open and that only students would be admitted. "We just don't have any space in Woodruff Hall for anyone but students. If anyone comes over hoping to see the game they will be disappointed," Hollis said.

Lawson tried to be positive leading up to the non-conference game, harkening back to the Gator Bowl loss to that same bunch of Yellow Jackets: "We had just been wallowing around in that old stuff called bad luck and we finally got out of the wallow."

Or so he thought.

THE RED HEAD'S team started off the game like it was finally going to break its losing streak. Unheralded Joey Miller put the clamps on Roger and the Bulldogs took command early. During the first twenty minutes the Jackets never led, trailing by five points at the break. Roger seemed out of sync and was held to 11 points in the first half.

This excited the hopeful crowd and ratcheted up the volume in Woodruff Hall. This was the first time Beverly Kaiser had been to a game there. She went with John Hoffman's family and they were among a handful of Tech fans in the building. Beverly was standing under the bleachers when Bulldog faithful started to stomp their feet above her filling her hair with dust and trash.

The second half was a seesaw affair. Tech did not grab the lead until Nass hit a free throw to make it 59-58. Seconds remained when Wayne Richards pushed a basket through from the foul line to put Tech on top 73-71 only to have Georgia's Don Keiser hit a jumper from that same spot.

Tech took a timeout but the play Hyder called did not result in a basket and with forty-five seconds remaining Keiser pulled down a rebound. It was the Bulldogs' turn to call time and the team huddled around Lawson. When play resumed, Georgia ran twenty seconds off the clock before tiny Allan Johnson got the call. His fifteen-foot jump shot could not have been better, giving Georgia an apparent victory.

This is when things got crazy.

A jubilant Lawson ran out on to the court to embrace Johnson, ignoring the six seconds showing on the clock. Fans joined him and officials had to push the celebrators back into the stands. After getting tied up by Georgia's Phil Simpson, Frank Landrey retrieved the jump ball and called time with two seconds showing on the clock.

Hyder looked down the bench at Roger, who he had uncharacteristically pulled out of the game after his lethargic performance in the second half. "Go in and make it," the coach said.

The play was simple. John Gher, a baseball player with a strong arm, would throw the ball to Roger around midcourt. He would turn and shoot. Johnson had other thoughts. He tangled up with the Tech captain and to this day Roger claims the Bulldog defender fouled him. As he stumbled, Roger somehow got off the shot. It was not one he practiced and was mostly a two-handed effort. Somewhere in the pandemonium the buzzer sounded, but the ball miraculously swished through the net.

Tech reserve Mike Tomasovich carries a mental picture of what happened next: "Coach (Red) Lawson came running out on the court, thinking his team had won. It was a huge upset. Everybody was screaming and jumping around, and fans came running out of the stands to celebrate. The referee ruled the shot was good, and then I saw the Georgia coach cry."

Attention turned to the scorer's table where Colonel Ernest B. Smith operated the official clock. Smith, a United States Army Air Corps officer in World War II, had been head of Georgia's physical education department since 1946. Technically, he was Lawson's boss.

Officials, coaches and students rushed the table. Smith stood firm. He gave referees his honest opinion that Roger's shot had been made before the buzzer. He said the buzzer was automatic and that it would sound after twenty minutes had expired. If it went off, he said he must have brushed it accidentally.

Order was restored and with the score knotted at 75, overtime began. Tech totally dominated the extra stanza, going on to post an 89–80 victory, with Roger scoring eight points in five minutes.

Lawson was inconsolable. How could anyone move the ball that far in that short a time? He talked about filing a protest but changed his mind since it came down to a judgment call. It was a loss from which he never recovered.

In a written report to SEC Commissioner Bernie Moore, the timekeeper said a malfunction of the clock caused the game to run a few seconds longer than it was supposed to and that Roger Kaiser's shot was made as the buzzer went off.

> A great number of people, especially those sitting on the clock end of the gym, have sworn that when Georgia Tech took time out with approximately a second to go, the horn sounded simultaneously as Tech signaled for timeout. Apparently, people around the clock heard it, but we at the bench did not. Neither did the officials. No one told us it had sounded and the officials came over and said the game was not over. As I had not heard a buzzer start, I did not dispute what they said.
>
> The clock sounds automatically only at the end of 20-minute periods. I expected it to go off later as I had not heard it at that time. In such a case, expecting the buzzer to sound automatically, I never watch the clock …
>
> Apparently there was a malfunction of the clock. After the Tech timeout, I started the clock when the ball touched the Tech player's hand after being thrown in. When the clock went off again,

the hand was over in the white section. Apparently, the game continued one or two seconds longer than it should have according to the time presumably shown on the clock.

A few days later Hyder praised the retired colonel for making such a pressurized decision but he refused to be drawn into discussions about the clock. He said his team spent that time out planning strategy not worrying about how much time was left. "We knew we had to do something quick … Whether it took one second or more to get off the tying shot we will never know. I do know we got it off before the buzzer sounded."

Several years before that, a vote was taken at a league meeting that would have required modern clocks to be installed around the conference. Waivers were given to Georgia and another school that were planning new arenas. "I voted to waive the new clock at Georgia," Hyder said. "If that clock helped me win a ball game as some people feel, then I'm happy I voted the way I did."

An embittered Lawson said his team did not deserve such a fate. "They played a great game and shouldn't have lost like that. I just can't figure out how Tech could do so much in one lousy second."

Hyder's joy was diminished by events after the game. A Bulldog football player punched Powell in the head and Roger was hit in the stomach while he was talking to Georgia's Don Keiser. "Without thinking, I started to go after the fellow that hit me but Don took me by the arm and cautioned me against that. I'm glad he did too."

Through the years Powell needled Roger about why he was the one that was punched. "Why didn't he hit you? You get the shot and I get slugged."

Why memories of that unusual game and Roger's last-second shot have lingered so long is unexplainable. Some stories claim Roger's basket won the game and others say the timekeeper suffered a seizure. People still approach Roger with questions and comments and many claim they were there that night, which is not very likely.

Popular Bulldog athletic department official Loren Smith has his own opinion. He even draws a crude diagram of how that old clock operated. Smith was sports editor of the *Athens Banner-Herald* and was at Woodruff Hall to present awards at halftime to Bulldog football stars Fran Tarkenton and Pat Dye. He was seated at the scorer's table near the timekeeper.

"I am probably the only living person who knows what actually happened. I used to go to basketball practice a lot so I understood that clock. It always started two seconds early so it finished its cycle two seconds early. That meant when Tech called its timeout, the game was actually over. Red Lawson should have known this and should have informed the officials before every game. But he didn't," Smith says.

He says he heard the buzzer sound when the timeout was called which reminded him what was going on. Two-tenths of a second later and it would have buzzed normally. Smith also questions how, in two seconds, the ball could be inbounded to Roger, and how he could dribble down court and get off a shot. "But if any Tech man should become a hero at Georgia's expense, I'm happy it was Roger Kaiser. He broke our heart but he is a gentleman and a longtime friend."

For Roger, coming back to hit such a memorable shot after such a bad night was a blessing. All he knows is that the ball went through the basket. Other people can believe what they want to believe. No video of the game exists so there is no way to prove what did or did not happen. When fans want to talk about the events of that night after all these years it makes Roger smile.

"Whatever people say about it, we still won."

ILL-TEMPEREDFANS pushed through the doors of Woodruff Hall and spilled into a night filled with protest and anger. The atmosphere was still out of control when *Atlanta Journal* sportswriter Jim Minter left the gym. Years later, he wrote a column describing what occurred on and off the court.

"Ordinarily, the basketball game would be my main memory of that night in Athens. It would, except that when the game was over, I walked out of the gymnasium into the rioting. Rocks thrown, torches burned, threats shouted. The dean of students was hit in the head by a brick. I've never known how much was 'outside agitators' or students raising mindless hell. It wasn't Ole Miss, but it was enough."

Most Georgians were embarrassed, regretting that such a lawless event took place in their state. Not everyone felt that way, including *Macon Telegraph* sports editor Harley Bowers. He actually defended what happened at his alma mater. In a column published after the game, he blamed Roger Kaiser for everything.

"News analysts have not given Kaiser proper credit for his part in the postgame activities. There is every reason to believe the students attending the game would have gone home without a thought of Charlayne were it not for Kaiser's shot."

Bowers was in the minority. This script was read on WSB Radio's Five Star Final. Sports Director Phil Schaefer put Roger in a different light than the Macon columnist:

> Last night Georgia led Georgia Tech by two points with five seconds to play in their non-conference basketball game. All-American Roger Kaiser got the toss from out of bounds and with a combination of a stumble and a push sent the ball through the hoop from over forty feet away with one bare second on the clock, to tie the game. A fired up Tech jumped the gun on the Bulldogs in the overtime and walked away with an 89–80 victory … the ninth in a row over Georgia. It's not the final score that was important in this case … but the terrific example set by Kaiser … the example of never giving up until the game is over. To give that last ounce. This is a fine example of the Georgia youth of today who show sportsmanship … and fortitude in everything they do. To All-American Roger Kaiser of Georgia Tech goes tonight's WSB Radio 7-50 Award … for his fine example first … and second for the thrill he gave Tech fans last night.

Dramatic shots and meaningful moments were common and sometimes taken for granted throughout Roger Kaiser's career. He was an effective shooter early in games, and he had a killer instinct that allowed him to erupt at any time. Late in a game, friend and foe alike knew that if the contest was on the line, Roger wanted the basketball.

Billy Livengood planted the seed.

"He was our coach when I was a high school senior, but long before that, he told me I had to have a shot I could fall back on, one that was hard to stop and one that I had confidence in. I spent hours practicing that jump shot in the yard and in the high school gym. That's all I ever did," Roger says.

That unwavering mind-set continued in college, and Alan Nass said it wasn't selfishness. "I only got to play with him one year at Tech, but we knew that the best shooter on the floor was Roger, so we wanted him to take the shot. You just knew it was going in. His ability to score the basketball and his ability to score when the game was on the line was like no one I have ever seen. Back home I got to play a little with Larry Bird and Jimmy Rayl, and they had that same sense of confidence that they could do it. Gifted players like them are able to take charge and react to the situation—whatever it is. But I'll say this: the finest shooter I ever played with or against was Roger Kaiser."

12

Retiring No. 21

"YOU are responsible for what you are and what you will become."

Georgia Tech football was a well-oiled machine. Playing in a big city that had not yet attracted a professional sports franchise, the Yellow Jackets were the primary headline makers. Practice sessions in the fall were almost as important as Saturday afternoons at Grant Field, which seldom had an empty seat. Reporters hung on Coach Bobby Dodd's every word, and the man affectionately known as "The Sly Gray Fox" was a master at colorful quotes and unusual angles.

Going into the 1960s, Tech was usually around the top ten in the country, was on network television more often than most of its Southern neighbors, and was invited to major holiday bowl games (which they always seemed to win). An audit of their accounts would have shown they had plenty of money in the bank.

The skills and national contacts of Sports Information Director Ned West produced a constant flow of all-conference and all-American stars in football and made Georgia Tech a national brand. One of his preseason media guides became a conversation piece outside of sports. It featured a cover picture of Marilyn Monroe nicely filling out a tight-fitting Tech sweater.

Basketball was often an afterthought. But the opening of Alexander Memorial Coliseum in 1956; the upsets of Kentucky; the recruitment of talents such as Blemker, Randall, Denton, and Kaiser; and the sellouts that followed forced Tech's athletic department and the sports departments at the Atlanta newspapers to rethink old priorities.

Forsyth Street in downtown Atlanta was a breeding ground for this breakthrough. Housed in one building were the news operations of the *Constitution* and the *Journal*, the city's two major newspapers. Reporters from the two papers rode in the same elevators, and papers were printed on the same noisy press, but they worked on different floors and went toe-to-toe for news. It was the same in sports where two staffs only came together on Sundays.

Sports editors coddled the unions that dominated composing rooms that produced the morning and afternoon papers. For years, Tech football tickets were used to keep back shop workers on their sides. With free tickets in their pockets, union members often ignored the clock and helped get late scores in the paper. Dodd and West did their part by supplying hard-to-get tickets in the West Stands at Grant Field.

That began to change.

"All of a sudden, guys in the composing room wanted Georgia Tech basketball tickets. They wanted to see Kaiser," says Jim Minter, the executive sports editor of the *Journal*.

"And why not?" John Logue says. "When he was playing, the place was electric."

To Minter, Roger was the right person in the right place at the right time.

"His was just the opposite of the perfect storm. Instead of bad things coming together at the same time, good things came together, and he was the principal good thing. He was the best college basketball player we had ever seen … the perfect example of a student athlete … a character out of an old-fashioned storybook on and off the court … a superstar who didn't act like one. People came to be awed by grace and humility and ability and effort they had never seen before."

Tech was an SEC contender and Kaiser was an all-American. Sellouts were common and the papers responded. Editors assigned more than the beat writers who covered Tech and sometimes sent along additional photographers. Columnists Furman Bisher and Jesse Outlar showed up more often, and between games the sports sections produced big spreads on Tech basketball.

In Roger they saw a hero, a leader, a performer of miracles, and a living, breathing clone of the fictional student athlete found only in sports mythology. With him on the scene, basketball became a front-page sport, and Alexander Memorial Coliseum—one of the newest venues in town—was ill prepared. Courtside seats were a premium, so West doled out press tickets like items lifted from Fort Knox. But the most valuable commodity was a parking pass.

Reserved spaces in a tiny lot next to the studios of WGST Radio were few and before the season only West could dole them out. If editors wanted additional spaces, they had to beg. During the Kaiser years, when the two papers assigned as many as three writers and three photographers each to big games, that got tiresome.

Wanting to make a point. Minter took an official Tech parking pass into the print shop at the newspaper and asked them to print up several hundred counterfeit passes. They looked like the real thing, and before a particularly important game, Minter passed them out to people he knew would use them.

Logue still laughs at what happened. "Coach Dodd had to park by Grant Field, and Whack Hyder couldn't find a place in the lot. Ned West was furious, but we accomplished what we wanted to accomplish. We got more passes."

SUCH SEISMIC CHANGES followed the emergence of Roger Kaiser. Fans wanted to see his classic jump shot, and even in an era before the three-point basket, they wanted to see him score—sometimes at the expense of their favorite teams.

Football was the main event, but he helped basketball reach a level of parity. As always Rupp was in charge, but coaches like Hyder, Eaves, Babe McCarthy, and Norm Sloan were fielding good teams. Attendance around the league picked up dramatically, and other schools began to discuss larger, more modern places to play.

Roger became a celebrity and earned more ink than any college basketball player in the region ever had. But his image would not have been complete without the unmistakable artistry of Alfred Joseph Ciraldo.

A native of Akron, Ohio, Al Ciraldo graduated from the University of Florida in 1948 and came to Atlanta to broadcast University of Georgia basketball and Decatur High School football games. At the age of fifteen, he announced minor league baseball games for the Akron Yankees where he befriended a young outfielder named Whack Hyder. When he heard his friend was in town, Hyder introduced him to people at WGST.

Ciraldo started describing Tech basketball in 1954, and his legend began to grow. He also sold advertising, and for years, he sold more radio time than any salesman in town. He was on Tech's football broadcasting team for a long time but is remembered most for basketball. He had a unique style that should have been trademarked. His staccato rhythm and colorful catchphrases were identified with the Yellow Jackets for thirty-eight years.

Games were not just close. They were "barnburners." Baskets were not good; they were "goot." If a ball rolled around the rim before dropping through the net, it had "a lot of iron but goot." If a player broke away for a layup, it was "a bunny." In Ciraldo's vernacular, a player crossed the time line, not midcourt. Alexander Memorial Coliseum had "overtaxed capacity crowds." And of course, no Tech football game could begin without toe meeting leather.

Watching him work made a person nervous, for while he was talking his feet were dancing. In an era where words told the story, his work at the microphone sold Tech basketball to fans who never bought a ticket. Games had drama and listeners felt part of the action. He knew the game and the players, and because he was Hyder's friend and confidante, he even knew the game plan.

Jimmy Carter was in his circle of friends. They met when the one-time Georgia Tech student was running for governor in 1966. Ciraldo boosted his campaign by inviting him into the radio booth at Grant Field. One of Ciraldo's favorite stories involved Carter when he lived on Pennsylvania Avenue. It came in Annapolis at the 1977 Tech-Navy football game.

Behind the microphone, Ciraldo was usually immersed in the game, but on this afternoon, his mind wandered. He was wondering if the

President of the United States would really make it to the visiting radio booth.

"He said he would come, but he was having trouble persuading the Secret Service. When he walked in, I motioned him to sit and pointed to the mike. He knew what to do." So for seven minutes, Al Ciraldo did the commentary, and Jimmy Carter did the color. It was preserved on tape and prized by Ciraldo.

His health failing, Ciraldo retired in 1992 after broadcasting 1,030 Tech basketball games. He died in 1997. He is a member of the National Radio Hall of Fame, the Georgia Tech Athletic Hall of Fame, the Atlanta Sports Hall of Fame and the Georgia Sports Hall of Fame.

Until the end, number 21 was among his favorites. When Ciraldo was selling Tech basketball, he was also selling the players, and he introduced listeners all over the state to Roger Kaiser. Roger played his last college game in 1961, and Ciraldo broadcast hundreds of games after he graduated. But for many fans, they remain inseparable.

Fans like Walter Banks.

To call him an usher at Turner Field demeans him, for the effervescent Banks is more like an ambassador. He has been the host of the owner's box since 1965, right after the Atlanta Braves got off the plane from Milwaukee. He shows dignitaries to their seats and makes sure he has peanuts waiting for Jimmy Carter, a frequent visitor to the box.

When Banks met Roger and Beverly Kaiser, he knew him immediately, even though African Americans were not welcome at Alexander Memorial Coliseum when Roger played at Georgia Tech.

"Never got to see you play," explained Banks, who uses numbers to make his point in just about everything, "but Al Ciraldo told me everything I needed to hear. You were the first 21. Deion (Sanders) wore 21 and Dominique (Wilkins) wore 21, but you were the original 21."

RETURNING FOR HIS senior year, Roger Kaiser had a portfolio rivaled by few players that had ever taken the court in the SEC. And in Tech circles, he was respected like no other basketball player who had worn the White and Gold.

On a quaint campus that stretched from Frank Gordy's Varsity to Lester Maddox's Pickrick, he was a student leader even in Army ROTC, which in the beginning was such a mystery. Professors admired his natural work ethic, his serious approach to academics, and the fact that he was due to graduate on time in the spring of 1961.

He was also popular around an athletic association that was run like a small family business. Players went in and out of the offices on Third Avenue on a regular basis, so everyone knew their names. Staff members adopted Roger and when he and Beverly were expecting their first baby ladies in the business office chipped in and bought a high chair.

Teammates elected him captain for the second time, and in his final season, Beverly was in the stands to lead his cheers. As a junior, he set the school's all-time single-season scoring record and was the SEC's top point producer. His assault on record books continued, and he was on his way to setting career standards in every offensive category. In his first two varsity years, the team went 17–9 and 22–6—two of the best seasons the Yellow Jackets had ever had consecutively—but there were fewer celebrations during his senior year..

Dave Denton and all his dizziness was gone. So was Jim Riley, a willowy but important role player. Their departures were expected, but no one planned on losing Bobby Dews. With a year of eligibility remaining, the slender guard signed with the St. Louis Cardinals. He seemed on his way to a promising career as a middle infielder when he suffered a serious leg injury that cost him his legendary quickness.

The South Georgia native has jovially described his role on the basketball court at Tech as that of a non-shooting guard. "I almost had a heart attack during one game when I passed Roger the ball and he threw it back."

Dews graduated from West Georgia College and became a published author. Mostly he worked in baseball, retiring in 2006 after thirty-five years as a minor league manager, roving instructor, and bullpen coach with the Atlanta Braves.

Joining Roger and his returning teammates in 1961 was a group of talented newcomers. Nass and Tomasovich brought muscle to the frontcourt. Red-shirt Keith Weekly flashed the potential to take up some of the scoring load, and Frank Landrey was a promising ball handler. But the loss of Dews was never overcome, especially when it came time to play a pressure defense—a trademark of the 1960 club.

"We just weren't as good," Roger says, looking back at his final college season. "We never came close to replacing Dave and Bobby, and the rest of us didn't get that much better."

The Rambling Wreck suffered a streaky season of ups and downs and finished with a 13–13 record. They were preseason favorites in the SEC, won three in a row to start the year, and then lost four straight. The Jackets rallied to win four of their last five outings and needed a win at Vanderbilt to finish with a winning record.

The Commodores did not cooperate and coasted to a 79–59 victory, which was not the proper way for Roger to end his spectacular career. He scored 21 points but hit only 7 shots in 20 attempts. His teammates hit a paltry 13 of 44, emblematic of a year in which Roger averaged 23.4 points a game and no other player averaged more than eight.

His body of work impressed Tech football coach Bobby Dodd. Late in the season, he called Roger Kaiser the greatest all-around athlete in Yellow Jacket history and said he was prepared to debate football fans on that belief.

Dodd delivered that message in an insider newsletter written by retired *Atlanta Journal* sports editor Ed Danforth that was usually reserved for football news. This was one of the few times it ever dealt with basketball. "Kaiser is not only the finest basketball practitioner we have seen at Tech but he is the greatest competitor I have seen in action in recent years in any sport. He comes up with the big play under pressure," Dodd said.

Roger's awards were many. He is Tech's only two-time all-American in basketball and—along with Kenny Anderson—is the only Yellow Jacket ever to be a consensus all-American. He finished his career holding eighteen of twenty-five individual school records and was Tech's all-time scoring leader with 1,628 points and an average of 20.4 points per game. More than fifty years after his last game, he holds the SEC record for free throw accuracy with an uncanny 85.8 career mark.

Basketball aside, he was elected to Who's Who in American colleges and universities, was voted into ODK (an honorary society whose members were chosen for leadership and scholastic ability), was a member of Koseme, the Rambling Wreck Club, and was student council representative for the Industrial Management Department. In Advanced ROTC, he held the rank of captain, was a member of Scabbard and Blade, and was one of five students to receive the Distinguished Military Student Tactics Award.

These recognitions underscore why Roger was praised as an all-American boy as well as an all-American basketball player. His reputation as a student athlete moved people to pay tribute to the image and the person. Opposing coaches joined the chorus and admitted they were glad they would not have to defend against him anymore.

EVEN THE SCHOOL newspaper joined in the accolades. *The Technique* could be irreverent and did not always walk the campus line, but an editorial writer marking Roger's departure played it straight.

"Roger Kaiser is ending his college career and thus will end one of the longest streaks of record-breaking Tech has ever witnessed ... Yet throughout all this hullabaloo, he has remained the same humble, modest man that all know and respect. He does not profess his greatness, but all around sense it. We proudly pay tribute to a great scholar, leader, athlete, and man whom Tech will never forget."

His pending graduation moved Georgia governor Ernest Vandiver to declare the twenty-seventh of February in 1961 as "Roger Kaiser Day." A ceremony was held after his final home game against Florida. The Gators made it interesting despite the fact that Coach Norm Sloan had just dismissed four of his starters. Tech held on for a 52–50 victory, and then it was over. Number 21 had hit his last jump shot, and after a brief intermission, wife Beverly and his parents, Elmer and Louanna, joined him at courtside.

Public address announcer Bob Wallace introduced the special guests. Assistant Athletic Director Tonto Coleman read the governor's resolution, alumni officials offered appropriate comments, and Whack

Hyder poured out his heart as he announced that for the first time in school history, Georgia Tech was retiring a basketball jersey.

There would never be another Roger Kaiser, and there would never be another 21. He joined Clint Castleberry—a spectacular halfback who died in World War II—as the only Tech athlete to be so honored.

That night was memorable, but the event that grabbed their hearts took Roger and Beverly back home. Delmer Harris—his barber and unofficial press agent—put together a celebration where Roger's hometown could show its love.

It came in June, a time that could not have been busier for Roger and Beverly. They were awaiting the birth of their first child; Roger was about to graduate from Tech; they were getting ready to move out of their apartment on Tenth Street; he was trying to decide between a business career and professional sports; and on the thirteenth of June, they were expected to be in Dale for "Roger Kaiser Night."

The week of the celebration, pulling a rented U-Haul trailer, the couple made the twelve-hour drive to Indiana. They arrived, and to everyone's shock, Beverly went into labor early and was taken to a hospital in Huntingburg, where she gave birth to their daughter Jenny. Her birth was announced on the sports page of the Evansville newspaper, above the Milwaukee Braves box score and below an article about Yankee-killer Frank Lary's 2–1 victory over New York.

Once Jenny was born, Roger, his brother Van, and his brother-in-law David Hevron rushed back to Atlanta for his graduation. His diploma in hand, the three of them moved the couple's belongings out of the apartment and drove back to Indiana. Roger ended up in Huntingburg and Harris needed him to be in Evansville, where a motorcade in his honor was due to form. Chester Nass, Alan's father, offered a private plane and flew Roger to Evansville.

Everything worked out fine.

"I even fit into that dress," Beverly says laughing.

Grace Brown, a folksy columnist for the local newspaper, doubled as a justice of the peace. She had known Roger since he was a child. She joined him in the motorcade bound for Dale and wrote about the experience:

> I rode in the police car, driven by Town Marshal Leroy Musgrave and we were escorted to the Evansville city limits by two motorcycle policemen. At each intersection they flew up their hands as if to say, 'Look Ma, no hands!' … Roger Kaiser, Keith Conner and Mark Weller were second in line in a white convertible. On the police radio, we heard Jasper Post tell Trooper Frank Cook, 'the convoy is leaving Boonville' and he joined the parade at Lincoln Tavern. So did the fire truck and another string of cars … One lone sign along the route indicated that somebody knew what was going on. On a lawn in Boonville was the message 'Congratulations Rodger Kaiser. Good Boy.'

Poor spelling did not diminish the feelings, feelings that in a matter of days made it possible for a humble guy from a small town to became a father for the first time, graduate from college, fly on a chartered plane, ride in a motorcade formed in his honor, and nervously sit through the reading of laudatory comments from the vice president of the United States, the governor of Indiana, members of Congress, Coach Bobby Dodd, Furman Bisher, Billy Livengood, and other dignitaries he did not know.

Newsmen who had been writing about Roger since he was a high school freshman enjoyed writing about that celebration. One described him as "the boy who made Dale something more than a small mark on a map," and another said the local product had become the most famous basketball player in the history of Georgia Tech. A more ebullient writer called him "the Hoosier boy who became king of Georgia."

When the motorcade arrived at the St. Joseph's Catholic Church, Roger was only a few blocks from the house he lived in as a child. Scanning the familiar faces, Roger could feel the affection. It was a final gesture from Harris, whose letters and phone calls to reporters and recruiters first spread the news about a talented ballplayer in tiny Dale.

Jerry Kemp, his first high school coach, came back. "He's been an all-American since he was in the ninth grade," the former coach said.

High school classmates also returned. Teammates John Hoffman and Alan Nass, both Indiana boys, represented Georgia Tech. But the most emotional displays came from his college coach and his best pal from childhood.

"If I said what I feel about Roger, I couldn't talk at all," Hyder admitted.

Directing comments at Roger's mother, the homespun coach told about a call he got from her when her son was a freshman at Tech. She told him Roger was thinking about not going back to Atlanta after Christmas break and that he was talking about transferring to Indiana. "If you want to keep my boy, you better come down here and talk with him," she said.

Hyder rented a car in Detroit, drove to Dale, and invited his star recruit to join him for the trip back to Georgia. The humble coach protected his investment and made possible a career unlike any Tech basketball player had ever had. "Kaiser is the idol of every kid in Georgia," Hyder said. "It's been good, Roger, and we wish you well."

Stealing the scene was an old friend known for his sharp tongue and edgy wit. But in his hometown, Bob Reinhart was warm and caring. "I bring greetings to Mrs. Elmer Kaiser from Branch McCracken," he said, referring to the longtime Hoosier basketball coach who could not convince the former Dale standout to come to Indiana University

Then he addressed Roger's coach.

"I can assure you, Coach Hyder, that if Roger had gone to Indiana University, the only difference would be that he would been an all-American from IU instead of Georgia Tech."

As kids, they spent a lot of time playing ball on that family court in Elmer Kaiser's yard, so he was well acquainted with Roger's natural attributes as a basketball player and a person.

"Roger is smart. He has brains and ability. He has made the fullest use of his ability. He's sound and at his best under pressure. Remember how he beat Ferdinand in 1957? His leadership is outstanding. He's loyal to his mates, his coaches, and to Dale.

"He is the best friend I ever had."

13

A Tale of Three Cities

"How do you live your life when no one is watching?"

Around the struggling American Basketball League, the saying was that as Roger Kaiser goes, so goes the Tapers. That might have been so, but the former college star had nothing to do with the franchise going from Washington to New York to Philadelphia in less than two seasons.

No, this was not the league that used that red, white, and blue basketball. That was the American Basketball Association, and it came later. The ABL began play in 1961, started by Abe Saperstein, the ebullient founder and owner of the Harlem Globetrotters. Though the league did not survive, its innovations helped change the face of contemporary basketball. The ABL introduced the three-point play, opened up the lane, extended the shot clock to 30 seconds, hired pro basketball's first two black head coaches, brought George Steinbrenner into professional sports, and generally played hell with the basketball establishment.

Before choosing a career in professional basketball, Roger faced a library of tough decisions. He found himself at a crossroads not unlike the one he had as a high school kid trying to decide which college he would attend. Only now he was a grown-up with a college degree, a wife, and a new baby.

Corporate America offered promising opportunities, but companies wanted him to relocate, and Roger was determined to stay near home. He originally dreamed of a career in baseball, but baseball did not share his big league dreams. He was everybody's hero, a basketball player at the top of game, but if he played for pay, would pro basketball provide the kind of life he wanted for his family?

People he trusted warned him that firms would not allow him to dictate where he worked, that newcomers had to go where they were sent. Knowing how important basketball had always been, friends also suggested he ought to get the game out of his system before moving into the business world, reminding him he would not be able to choose where he played basketball, either.

"I wanted to work for companies like General Electric or Proctor and Gamble, and I was naïve enough to think if they wanted to hire me, I could tell them where I wanted to go, and they would send me. It wasn't like they were recruiting a basketball player. There were so many people looking for a job that would happily go to New York or Iowa for three years," Roger says.

Pro basketball was not the glamorous proposition it is today. The NBA had a good supply of superstars, but the average salary was less than $10,000 a year. Heeding the advice of Henry Lane of General Electric, Roger promised himself and Beverly that if the money was not there, he would give up pro basketball in three years and explore a career in business.

"Henry Lane told me I would fall behind in the business world if I stayed in basketball too long. He said if I wasn't at the top of the professional scale in three years that I ought to quit," Roger says.

The NBA was still suffering from growing pains, and it would be decades before it became a league of millionaires. There was no major television contract, and media coverage was spotty. The NBA as we know it had only been around since 1948, and by 1961, after a shuffling of franchises, it settled down to eight teams, but only the St. Louis Hawks were west of the Mississippi River.

That was about to change. For the first time in the modern era, the league expanded with the addition of the Chicago Packers. A special expansion draft allowed the club to add veterans from the other eight teams. When the college draft came along, the Packers were allowed to draft fifteen players, including six in the second round.

Jim Pollard, a teammate of George Mikan with the world champion Minneapolis Lakers, had been head coach at LaSalle

University and the Lakers before joining the expansion team. He chose six-foot-eleven Walt Bellamy with the first pick in the college draft, and the Indiana University star became NBA Rookie of the Year. With the last pick in the fourth round, the Packers selected Roger Kaiser—the forty-first player taken in the draft, the ninth taken by Chicago, and only the fifth Georgia Tech player ever drafted, joining Colin Anderson, Jim Nolan, Pete Silas, and Dave Denton on that list.

Training camp with the Packers was crowded and competitive, with prospective players coming and going every day. Practices were unorthodox with the squad usually being divided up for games of twenty-one. Roger soon decided that he did not fit into Pollard's long-range plans.

"I didn't like the coach," Roger says laughing. "When I grew up and became a coach myself, I learned that players always blame the coach. It was the same way at the Olympic trials when I blamed Pete Newell. In our next to last preseason game, I had my best game and scored 12 points, and then I didn't play in the next game. That was really discouraging."

His thoughts turned to the ABL. The Washington Tapers had drafted him, and they called regularly. It was intriguing when they talked about how Roger's deadly jump shot would be a valuable weapon in a league that would reward outside shooters by establishing a three-point line at twenty-five feet from the backboard and twenty-three feet, nine inches from the center of the hoop. It was 1979 before the NBA adapted such an arc and 1986 before the NCAA approved it.

The ABL was an eight-team league created by Saperstein after the NBA reneged on a promise to let him acquire a franchise in Los Angeles. When the Lakers moved to the West Coast, and he was not involved, he followed up on his idea of a new league. The veteran promoter believed many cities would support pro basketball, and he intended to use his ever-popular Globetrotters to support those franchises by playing frequent doubleheaders in their arenas. Though NBA officials dissed his ideas, they eventually enjoyed widespread expansion and thrived on his idea of a three-point field goal.

The new league was built around nineteen players that either jumped from the NBA or were cut by the older league, along with performers from the industrial leagues and the venerable Eastern League. The ABL also welcomed players who were banned from the NBA because of past transgressions, including Connie Hawkins, Bill Spivey, Tony Jackson, and Sylvester Blye. Draft choices such as Roger, Larry Siegfried, Bill Bridges, and others were seen as the future faces of the league. Even Denton, his former Tech teammate, played part of a season with the Hawaii Chiefs.

With an off day coming up in the Packer camp, the discouraged rookie arranged a private meeting in New York with the new owner of the Tapers. Roger met a stage full of characters in the ABL, and none was more memorable than Paul Cohen, a basketball junkie and the millionaire president of the Technical Tape Corporation.

"I remember he was wearing a dark blue suit, and that his hands shook so badly that he had cigarette ashes all over the front of his coat. I learned later that he suffered from a form of muscular dystrophy. I started to tell him who I was, and he said he remembered me from Georgia Tech and that he had seen me play on TV against Kentucky."

Cohen offered Roger more than he would make in Chicago and sweetened the deal with a $1,000 signing bonus. There was just one problem. Roger was under contract with the NBA, though he was not savvy enough to think about that.

Cohen wanted him to start practice immediately.

"I can't do that until I sign a contract."

"What do you take me for? A smuck?" the owner said.

Later, Roger had to ask someone what that word meant.

Back at the Packer camp, the NBA gave Roger his outright release, and he was on his way to the ABL. The only rap on him as a player was that he was too small and too slow. Picking up his family in Indiana, they drove to Washington, where he reported to his new club. They went to Uline Arena, a nondescript concrete building near Union Station whose only claim to fame is that it was the site of The Beatles first American concert in 1964. Today, it is a faceless parking garage.

When Roger pulled into the parking lot in 1961, promoters were preparing for a Ray Charles concert that night. Roger left Beverly and the baby outside while he went inside to sign his ABL contract.

There was no published ceiling on ABL salaries, but the acceptable range was between $4,500 and $15,000. When Roger signed with the Tapers, he was near the top of the pay scale. The Packers drafted him in the fourth round, but the Tapers offered a much fatter contract. He would be paid around $12,000 a year, the third or fourth highest on the club.

"The ABL took me out of my comfortable environment. "Coming from a small town in Indiana, going to Atlanta was an awakening, but going to Washington, D.C., and later New York City, was way out of my plans. But playing for the Tapers gave me an opportunity to meet more people and to continue to play a game that I loved."

WHEN JERRY LEWIS is one of the owners of the team, you know it will be whacky, and for the next three years, Roger Kaiser's life was a nonstop adventure of basketball and zaniness.

"I heard Mr. Cohen and Jerry Lewis were close friends, and when I told him I was a big fan, he said he would make sure I got to meet him. When I did, he autographed a picture to Jenny and Jill, and I thanked him for doing it. It was then that he told me he owned part of the team," says Roger, who still has that signed photograph.

Cohen's friendship with the struggling young comic began when he and partner Dean Martin were working in the Catskills. In a 2012 interview for one of Ted Turner's channels, Leonard Maltin asked Lewis about how an old Tuck Tape dispenser came to have a familiar caricature of Lewis on one side and Martin on the other.

"Because Paul Cohen, who was the chairman of the board of the company, was a dystrophic, and Paul Cohen was the man who gave me the idea to do a telethon. We were very, very close friends, and I struggled with his particular disease. He decided to give Dean and myself shares in the company. Those shares were very meaningful, but of course that became a conflict of interest, so I had to tell him, 'No, we will just be there,' as we promised to be for him, but with no remuneration."

Cohen fed his love of basketball by backing several semipro teams that were usually named for his company. When Saperstein offered him a chance to be involved in the startup league, he was excited.

After the demise of the ABL, it was discovered that Cohen shared in the ownership of other ABL franchises, which, to Roger, explained some of the goofy trades the Tapers made with teams that he was backing.

Before his team played its first game, Cohen made a bold prediction to the press in Washington that never came true: "We will start with the tallest, most powerful, fastest, and best-conditioned squad in the ABL. We've got a winner."

Not quite. But they were interesting.

The original head coach was Elmer Ripley, known for stints as head coach at Georgetown, Notre Dame, Columbia, Army, John Carroll and Yale. When ownership grew unhappy with Ripley, they had three head coaches. This confusing triumvirate was composed of Stan Stutz, Mario Perri, and Cohen himself. That curious ploy moved *Washington Star* columnist Francis Stann to compare the club to a ship without a rudder. "Individually, most can play on any club in the ABL and some apparently could make it in the NBA. But as a team, they haven't jelled," he wrote after the Tapers got off to a shaky start.

NBA great Bill Sharman was an ABL coach before he became the architect of the early Los Angeles Lakers. After seeing them play, he called the Tapers a prospective powerhouse. "They've got some real good men. Kaiser, Blye, Dierking, and Jackson can play this game."

Sharman was one of Roger's idols when he was growing up in Indiana. They were both baseball players, and their styles of play on the basketball court were similar, even to their amazing accuracy at the free line. Leaving Boston behind, Sharman started in the ABL as a player-coach with the Los Angeles Jets. When they played the Tapers, he guarded Roger. In that game, Roger made an interesting discovery about the way his childhood hero played defense.

"Every time the officials' backs were turned, he'd come up real close and pinch my nipples. I kept asking him, 'What are you doing?' He just laughed and wouldn't look at me and kept doing it every time he had a chance. He was trying to get into my head, and guess what, he sure did. I couldn't concentrate on anything else," Roger told writer Bob Lieb, the author of *Shooting Threes and Shaking the Basketball Establishment*, an entertaining history of the ABL.

Sharman started off as a hero, but around Roger in the ABL were eccentrics like he had never met before—starting with his owner. Cohen was scared of flying. As one of their coaches, he intended to follow the club on the road, so he purchased an elaborate bus with a crew of drivers so he could go on West Coast jaunts. Players who had big games were invited to travel with the boss, and several times Roger enjoyed those comforts. If Cohen did not make a road trip, an employee from the tape company sat on the bench and had a phone installed, so he could relay defensive strategy to Stutz. But the true characters were the quirky players who passed through the dressing room.

Dan Swartz, the team's top scorer that first season, later won a championship ring with the Boston Celtics. He came to the Tapers after playing AAU ball, where, as the league's leading scorer, he apparently had an unlimited license to shoot, Roger says. "We used to call him the 'dark hole.' He had no conscience … He was always hollering, calling for the ball, and you knew if you passed it to him, it wasn't coming back. One time he took a shot from the corner, got knocked down, and the rebound came back to him lying on the floor. Did he pass it? No, he took the shot while lying on the floor."

Gene Conley, Roger's roommate on the road, was a starting pitcher with the Milwaukee Braves and part-time basketball player with the Celtics. Roger was a diehard Yankee fan, so he and Conley had some interesting conversations. On a road trip to Hawaii, Conley got into an off-court altercation with Fred Sawyer of the Chiefs, broke his hand, and missed several weeks.

Connie Dierking jumped from the NBA to the ABL. He was a productive player in both leagues, but he had a morbid fear of flying, which meant he was usually not available when the Tapers went to Hawaii. He agreed to go on one road trip. Drinking heavily, he survived the flight, only to get into a fight with a local at one of the games in Honolulu. The other fellow, said to be a member of the "Hawaiian Mafia," threatened the Taper center, so Dierking and his wife only left their hotel room for the games.

Tony Jackson was one of the most exciting players in the ABL. The NBA barred the former St. John's University star because he did not report an alleged bribe when he was playing in college. He started the season with the Tapers and was among the league's top scorers and long-range shooters. But when the team reported for practice one afternoon, they found he had been traded to the Chicago Majors, owned by Saperstein.

Sylvester Blye was a playground legend on the streets of New York and a member of the Rucker League Hall of Fame. He went to Seattle University, where after just one game, the NCAA found he had played with the Harlem Clowns under an assumed name and declared him ineligible. The NBA also banned him. His unlikely connection to Cohen began when the businessman's car stalled in a questionable part of town and Blye helped him get it started. When Cohen found out he was a ball player, he signed him up for an industrial league team that he owned.

But the unconventional character Roger talks about the most wore a cape and a hood and sometimes heard bells in his ears. The team heard he was coming for weeks in 1962, and those who knew him kept saying, "Machine Gun's coming. Machine Gun's coming."

Then one day Cleo Hill did come.

"He wore a hood, and it wasn't a hoodie. He had a hood on his head and a long black cape that touched the floor and covered his body. I had never seen anything like it," Roger says. "I didn't know what to think, but when he got on the court, Cleo could play."

Hill attended Winston-Salem Teachers College, where the legendary Clarence "Big House" Gaines was his coach. It was the school that later produced Earl "The Pearl" Monroe. Harold Bell, a contributor to BleacherReport.com, described Hill's mystique:

> Cleo was a basketball icon and legend on Tobacco Road long before his pro career. To believe it you had to be there to see him. When Cleo played you would have thought the ACC Tournament was being held on the campus of Winston-Salem State. White folks traveled from all over the state to see him play. Cleo Hill was worth the travel time and price of admission. There were times when our own students could not get into the games. There was nothing Cleo could not do on a basketball court. His offensive arsenal consisted of left and

> right hand hook shots, set shots, a jump shot from any and everywhere, a great rebounder when he needed to be, he was fearless driving to the basket and he was a 80 percent foul shooter.

There was an aura about him, and it went beyond the game. In the 1960 NBA draft, he went in the first round to the St. Louis Hawks, the ninth player taken. He was only the fifth player from a historically black college to ever go in the first round.

What happened has been debated in books and on an ESPN documentary. Some people say the Hawks' veteran scorers—Bob Pettit, Cliff Hagan, and Clyde Lovellette—resented Hill taking away many of their shots. Some say he was the victim of racial quotas and that management was upset that he was involved in the boycott of a preseason game by black players on the Celtics, led by Bill Russell. Former St. Louis coach Paul Seymour, who was gone by mid-season, later confirmed some of these allegations.

In one season with the Hawks, Hill averaged 5.5 points a game in limited action, and then he was gone. He never went to training camp with another NBA team, and no other club ever called. "It wasn't racial. It was points," Hill said.

By the time Hill was picked up by the ABL, the Tapers had relocated to Philadelphia, after moving from Washington to New York during the 1961 season. There were still sparks of his enormous talent, but he was facing more serious challenges. He averaged 6.5 points a game in twenty-two appearances.

"People said he suffered from severe migraines, which made him hears bells ringing. That happened one day during practice, and he fell to the court holding his head. After that, when some of the guys wanted to get out of practice, they would say, 'Hey Machine Gun, you hear those bells?' He would hold his head and sit down. There wouldn't be enough guys left to scrimmage, so practice would be over," Roger says.

Stutz was the club's primary coach and he was unlike any other coach Roger had ever played under. His earlier coaches never cursed but Stutz certainly did. "Stutz was sure tough. He used to tell me I was his favorite player. Then he would turn around and say, 'I like you but do I have to punch you in the face to get you to play hard? He could out-cuss my granddaddy, and that took some doing. That was all new to me. I had a college coach who used to say 'cheese and crackers' when he got mad. I thought Stutz behaved that way because he was from New York," Roger told Lieb.

Playing in the Uline Arena was an adventure in itself.

"Our first game in Washington was really something. The building was also being used for ice hockey. They laid the basketball court on top of the ice, and they didn't do it right. We had a house full that night and it was hot. Moisture was coming up through the floor, and you could barely stand. Players were falling down all over the court, and nobody wanted to take jump shots or shoot on the move, because you were afraid you would fall down," Roger says.

Beyond the foolishness there were social lessons. Like many white players of that era, Roger had little experience with blatant racism. He played in an all-white Southeastern Conference, and though he enjoyed rooming with Oscar Robertson during the Olympic trials, his experience with black players was limited. With the Tapers, he saw glimpses of what his black teammates had to endure at a time when the Civil Rights Movement was at its peak in America. One of those teaching moments came at a restaurant in Washington.

"It was the first week of camp and we all went out to eat. One of our black players commented about the high prices at that restaurant. It didn't sound right so I looked at his menu. That's when I realized the waiter had given different menus to the blacks and whites. We got up and left," Roger says.

ROGER KAISER HAD played the game since he was a child and had studied its nuances like a student pours over a textbook. But like many others, he was not prepared for the impact of the three-point play. George Mikan was commissioner of the American Basketball Association—a league formed a decade later. It copied many ABL rule changes, and the legendary big man compared the three-pointer to the excitement generated by the home run in baseball.

Because of scheduling problems, the San Francisco Saints and Los Angeles Jets opened the ABL season on October 27, 1961, a day earlier than the rest of the league. History was made in the Saints' 99–96 victory for six three-point baskets: three by Larry Farmer, two by George Yardley, and one by Larry Friend. It is believed Farmer hit the first one, but no one is sure. What is clear is that teams were viewing the shot as a weapon, not a novelty.

With his eye for the basket, Roger became known for his long-range proficiency. In 1961, he hit 72 of 238 from beyond the line. Roger was the team's second-highest scorer with 1,556 points and a 19.4 average per game. He was the fifth best scorer in the ABL behind Connie Hawkins, Bill Spivey, teammate Dan Swartz, and Bill Bridges. He also hit 89 percent of his free throws, second in the league behind Swartz at 90.5 percent.

Roger's high game came at Schofield Barracks in Hawaii. "It had a sunken floor and a half roof and maybe 3,000 seats. I got 51 points that night," he says. He was one of only four players to score fifty or more points in the short history of the league.

Though individual franchises were mired in debt, the ABL kept up a happy face as team officials looked ahead to a second season. Cohen hoped the move to New York would help the Tapers, but after attendance continued to flounder, he relocated the team to Philadelphia, hoping to take advantage of the Warriors' recent move to San Francisco.

Roger and Beverly rented a house in Dale during the off-season where their daughter Jill was born. His time was spent as a substitute mailer carrier under his father. When camp opened, their growing family moved in with relatives in New Jersey, and Roger commuted to Philadelphia for practices and games.

Late in December, the Tapers were in Cleveland to play the Pipers, and Roger was unable to suit up because of severe abdominal distress. When the pain worsened, he was rushed to a local hospital. Doctors wanted to operate but he said no.

"My car was in Philadelphia, my wife was in New Jersey, and my home was in Indiana. I took a plane back to Philadelphia, where I was diagnosed with an ulcer. While in the hospital, my family visited, and my cousin, Sonny Cooper, said I didn't have a job anymore since the ABL had folded. That's how I heard that I was finished as a pro basketball player," Roger says.

The ABL officially went out of business on December 31, 1962. Roger's gear was still in his bag, so he left with his Philadelphia Tapers uniform and a game ball he had ended up with after an earlier finishing with memories and a few collectibles.

During that abbreviated season, he averaged 17.3 points a game—second on the team to Sylvester Blye and ninth in the league. His 44.6 percent in three-point shooting was tops in the league. He averaged 18.9 points a night for his two-year career, recorded 97 three-pointers in 107 games, and was good on 88.2 percent of his free throws. Roger finished as the ABL's fifth leading scorer all-time behind Connie Hawkins, Bill Bridges, Bill Spivey, and Larry Staverman.

As soon as the ABL's demise was reported, NBA teams began to scoop up talent. Some former players returned to the league, and younger players were able to find work. Some veterans retired and others went back to the Eastern League, the industrial leagues, and AAU ball. Roger found himself in limbo, labeled by some insiders as a three-point specialist who was too small for the NBA, which would not employ the three-pointer until the 1979–1980 season.

Most ABL players were unemployed and in search of a paycheck. Roger was not among that group at least. Owner Paul Cohen offered Sylvester Blye, Gene Conley, Roger, and some other players positions with Tuck Technical Tape Corporation. He even told Roger he could work out of Atlanta.

Then the Chicago Zephyrs called. The floundering Packers that had released him less than three years before had changed their nickname but not their fortunes. They soon would be reincarnated as the Baltimore Bullets. The club still held NBA rights to Roger and General Manager Frank Lane called to see if he would be interested in joining the team for the remainder of the season.

"I know you. You're Trader Lane," Roger said.

"How do you know me?" the GM said, chuckling quietly.

"I'm a baseball fan so I know all about you."

It was Trader Lane, a member of the front office of several Major League Baseball teams, including the Chicago White Sox, St. Louis Cardinals, and Cleveland Indians. He had also been general manager of the Kansas City Athletics, working for volatile owner Charley Finley. That did not work out well, and they abruptly parted company with Lane filing a lawsuit against Charley O.

Because of the pending lawsuit, Lane was not allowed to work for another baseball team, so he joined the NBA Zephyrs. He assured Roger that he was not planning to make a deal. "I'm not going to trade you," he said. "I want to sign you. Some of our people think you can help us."

After observing the inner workings of the ABL and realizing that players were pawns on a rich guy's chessboard, Roger did not answer immediately. Two years with the Tapers had shown him that he was a homebody who did not enjoy the pull and tug of travel. "Pro basketball, unless you're really getting paid for it, is a real grind and a bad life. At least it was for me," he says.

Those things were on his mind as he talked with Lane and the Zephyrs. Though the money was tempting, his ABL experience showed him that he loved the game but not the business. "If I come, I want a no-cut contract," he told the Chicago general manager.

Lane said that was not possible, that the club had a policy against no-cut deals. He told Roger to call him if he changed his mind. When he hung up, Roger figured his career in professional basketball was over. Before long, he and Beverly were on the road to Atlanta, a city that would become their permanent home.

He left a hero and came back as a salesman.

14
The Slow Road to Coaching

"Teaching is a profession that teaches all other professions."

Roger Kaiser never intended to be a basketball coach. He had seen too much and he knew too much. He watched his hometown run off four high school coaches whose only visible flaw was an inability to win the last game of the season. He looked into the tired faces of coaches in the Southeastern Conference, men he respected, who had to teach physical education classes so they could pay the bills. He watched professional coaches come and go and played for a team that had three head coaches at the same time. He knew these things, but when Whack Hyder called, he could not say no.

His road into coaching was not a fast track, though. The ABL folded on the last day of 1962, and two weeks later, Roger and his family collected their belongings from New Jersey and Indiana and traveled south. Tuck Technical Tape Corporation handled the move, and they arrived in Atlanta on January 13, two days before Carl Sanders was inaugurated as Georgia's seventy-fourth governor. Every motel in town was filled that weekend, and the Kaisers had to go all the way to Marietta to find a place to stay.

Finding an apartment in Atlanta that included a washer and dryer would be almost as difficult, but before the movers arrived, they found a comfortable apartment near the intersection of Buford Highway and Clairmont Road. This would be their address until they could afford a home of their own.

Representing Cohen's company, Roger made regular sales calls all over the state. With a wife and two baby girls, he wanted to be home every night, and that was not always easy. Beverly took a job at the

First National Bank of Atlanta that first year, at a time the company wanted to expand Roger's sales territory into two other Southeastern states. When he asked about a raise, he was told that he started off being paid like a basketball player and that he was already making more than his colleagues.

He had lived in Atlanta before, but life was different now. He was not a college student anymore, and afternoons were spent calling on customers, not practicing basketball. He and Beverly were pushing two babies around in strollers, and they spent their free time stocking up on diapers and baby food instead of playing Bridge or going to movies with friends.

Though Roger was not making headlines, he was still a celebrity. He received invitations to speak to civic clubs and church groups and even modeled and promoted Lee Jeans in clothing stores all over town. They paid him in denim, not cash. He also appeared at sporting goods stores, and an outlet in Decatur bought a large ad that invited customers to meet Roger Kaiser in person—rain or shine.

When Teeter Umstead heard Roger was back, the former Tech basketball captain invited him to play ball for Morningside Presbyterian Church. Dave Denton was on the team, along with former Yellow Jacket football player Henry Hair and Jay Hanlon of Virginia Tech. With Roger pouring in points, Morningside began to dominate local leagues and amateur tournaments all over the state.

One out-of-town trip was to the Bibb Invitational Tournament, an annual event played in a tiny mill village within the city limits of Columbus, where the recreation director was Fred Hyder, one of Coach Hyder's younger brothers. While he was there, Roger made a business call for Tuck Tape at a nearby cotton mill. Basketball opened that door. His appearance had been ballyhooed in both local newspapers, so the textile official knew why Roger was in Columbus.

"We thought you were here to play basketball," the mill manager said, "but this is really your lucky day. We've been talking about changing vendors and we're ready to do business right now."

The order was so expansive that Roger had to call in support. By the time he headed back to Atlanta, Tuck Tape had an important new customer, and he had led the Morningside quintet to the championship of a tournament that attracted players from Auburn University and Columbus College, along with colorful unknowns from textile leagues in Georgia and Alabama.

Roger became a fixture in tournaments such as the Bibb Invitational. He became friends with Columbus Roberts, the Coca-Cola bottler in Columbus, and several times he played for the Coke team, earning first place trophies for the local company. Young fans looked forward to Roger's appearances at Comer Auditorium and his epic scoring duels with mill league stars.

Bobby Howard the baseball coach at Central High School in Phenix City, was just kid then and that tournament gave him an opportunity to see big-time basketball. At Columbus High, he won fourteen Georgia state titles, but he remembers the thrills of seeing Roger and friends at Comer.

"I was outside in the lobby getting a hot dog when I noticed a commotion at the front door. I asked somebody what was going on, and they said Kaiser and Denton were arriving. People were all around them getting autographs and stuff. They were like rock stars," Howard says.

On the court, Roger was often unstoppable, but one wily opponent figured out a way to slow him down. Roger and his teammates had entered the Gold Medal Tournament in Hapeville, a suburb near the Atlanta Airport. Like the Bibb Invitational, it drew a bevy of top teams from around the state. Morningside won their first two outings, but before their next game, Fred Edmondson—a former University of Georgia basketball captain and the director of the Hapeville Recreation Department—approached Umstead and Roger. He informed them that a formal protest had been filed about Roger's participation.

"He said I couldn't play, that I was a pro. I was upset and I pointed out that Dave Denton had played in the same professional league, and nobody was questioning his eligibility. I dropped out but the rest of the guys kept playing," he recalls.

As he was leaving the recreation center, Roger met Don Bryant for the first time. A former prep basketball player at Clarkston High School, he was a busy local homebuilder and realtor who sponsored many basketball and softball teams. Bryant assured Roger that he did not file the protest and added that if the opportunity ever came, he would like Roger to play for his team.

Roger did join Bryant's team, and through the years, their families took vacations together and the two men traveled to a number of Final Fours. They also played a lot of basketball, and whether they laced up their sneakers as Key Realty Company, the Southeastern Conference All-Stars, the Atlanta All-Stars, or the Roger Kaiser All-Stars, they drew fans and raised money for charities and good causes all over Georgia.

Kaiser put up points and Bryant handled logistics. Though the roster was mainly composed of former stars from Tech and small college power Oglethorpe University, the lineup was tweaked every night, depending on which players were able to make it. Bryant was a player-coach. He put up the entry fees so he got his minutes.

The nucleus of the team included Roger, Denton, Josh Powell, Alan Nass, Jim Caldwell, Mike Tomasovich, and Pres Judy of Tech, along with Tommy Norwood, Bobby Nance, Bobby Sexton, Morris Mitchell, Roger Couch, Mike Dahl, and Billy Carter of Oglethorpe.

The team played all over the area and it is clear by looking at old newspaper articles, that Roger was the hottest draw and hottest shooter. But an experience in the hills of Alabama taught Bryant that he had better check with Beverly Kaiser if he wanted Roger in his backcourt — a lesson learned in Arab, Alabama.

"It's not far from Marietta, just over the state line," they were advised. But when they got into Alabama and kept driving and driving, they knew something was wrong. They made it to Arab and won the opener with ease. Some of the guys stayed over, but Roger had told Beverly he would be home that night, so Roger, Bryant, and Denton started the long drive home. It was in the wee hours of the morning when Roger put the key in the lock at home. Beverly, with two toddlers in tow, was part frantic and part livid.

"I hope you lost because you're not going back," she announced.

Hoping she would change her mind, Bryant did not immediately call the players who stayed behind in Arab. The next day, he checked in with Roger who said Beverly was still upset and that he would be staying home.

By the time Bryant tried to reach Norwood, Nance, and the others in Alabama, they had already checked out of the motel. There were no cell phones then, and nobody answered the house phone at the gym. They were on their own. The fellows put on their uniforms and started warming up, assuming their teammates would show up any minute. Fans noticed their absence and grew restless. They had bought tickets to see Roger and Denton play. Now where were they?

When it was announced that the game had been forfeited, Roger's teammates bore the brunt of boos and catcalls, so they grabbed their street clothes and rushed straight to their cars. And, as you might imagine, they never went back to Arab.

MARQUES HAYNES NEVER considered himself a clown. Maybe not. But in a sports-entertainment career spanning more than five decades, he dribbled his way through thousands of basketball games and rode thousands of miles in dilapidated buses—and because he did, millions of people went to bed with smiles on their faces.

Various names were stitched on his jersey, but he was always a Globetrotter. In 1947, after graduating from Langston University, he joined the Kansas City Stars, a farm club of the barnstorming basketball team, and a year later, he was a member of the world famous Harlem Globetrotters. He was billed as "the world's greatest dribbler," a guy who could dribble the ball six times a second. His costar was Reece "Goose" Tatum, basketball's original Clown Prince.

Haynes and Tatum were the headliners at a time the club could play as well as clown. They left the Globetrotters in 1953 after a serious pay dispute with owner Abe Saperstein, and the legendary duo formed the Harlem Magicians, taking with them the laugh-provoking antics that Tatum had made famous.

With the Stars in his rookie year, Haynes traveled to Mexico City, one of six players on the international trip. When they arrived, they discovered that their opponent, Chihuahua State Teachers College, had pulled in the area's twenty best players. Chihuahua's coach substituted a fresh unit every few minutes, and, coupled with the severe altitude, the Globetrotters were gasping for air.

At the start of the fourth quarter, foul troubles left the Globetrotters with four players and a one-point lead. Teammates wanted to call a time-out, but Haynes told them to give him the ball. He dribbled the ball until the buzzer sounded and no one could catch him. His antics were described in a 1985 profile of Haynes that Frank Deford wrote in *Sports Illustrated.*

> While the players and fans watched in amazement, Marques went into his dribbling routine. The Chihuahua players gave chase, but no one could catch him. He dribbled half-circles around the key, slid down on one knee, actually sat on the floor, and the ball never stopped. He bounced it so low (only two or three inches off the floor) and so fast that the ball sounded like a machine gun. And whether he was running, standing still, kneeling, or lying flat, no one could take the ball. It wasn't just how fast he was dribbling that made it so remarkable, it was how fast he was moving. He would start and stop, change directions, fake one way and go the other, as if his knee joints were made of rubber, instead of tendon and cartilage. Then, he raced in for a layup just as time expired, giving the Stars a three-point victory.

Haynes was still dribbling in 1964. Tatum was gone, but the ball-handling whiz was headlining another traveling show that was part Vaudeville, part basketball. There were discussions about Bryant and Roger playing the Magicians at Sewanee University on the Cumberland Plateau between Chattanooga and Nashville. When they contacted Lon Varnell of the Magicians, he suggested they think bigger and play in Atlanta.

In the wintertime, Varnell was the colorful head coach at Sewanee, sometimes known as the University of the South. It was his Tigers that upset Georgia Tech in 1955, a week before the Yellow Jackets ended top-ranked Kentucky's home winning streak.

A Methodist minister and a shrewd entrepreneur, Varnell was the advance man for the Globetrotters and a concert promoter that represented acts such as Lawrence Welk, Peter, Paul and Mary, Bob

Hope, Liberace, and Kate Smith. His promotional firm in Nashville continued after his death in 1991, and it organized George Strait's retirement tour and Garth Brooks's long-awaited return to the stage in 2014.

Varnell understood the Atlanta market. He brought the Globetrotters there in 1955 where they played before the city's first integrated audience at the Municipal Auditorium. From their discussions came a game in 1964 at that same venue between what newspaper ads called the Fabulous Harlem Magicians and the Atlanta All-Stars. It was billed as a matchup of Haynes, the world's greatest dribbler, and set-shot artist Josh Grider competing against Roger Kaiser, Alan Nass, Tommy Norwood, Bobby Nance, Dave Denton, and Josh Powell. Tickets ranged from $1.50 to $3.00.

Discussions were frank.

"We are not the Washington Generals," Roger said, referring to the long-suffering team that traveled with the Globetrotters.

"That's fine. We're here to play ball. We're not just showmen," Haynes said.

Talks continued and at the last minute, Haynes—the club's owner-manager—wanted to adapt the rules to fit their script, leaving more time for their familiar gimmicks. Roger and Bryant refused to turn it into a sideshow, and the argument grew so heated that the game itself was in jeopardy.

Bryant put an end to that. "We live here," he said. "You guys get paid to travel, and if we don't play, you'll be out the money, not us,"

Haynes's lineup was composed of Grider, Robert "Trick" Woods (who replaced Tatum as the resident clown), Bernard Wilson, Hawk Gipson, Jim Dew, Paul Martin, and Sweetwater Clifton, a former New York Knickerbocker whom Roger knew very well.

"I played against Sweetwater in the ABL, and he has the greatest hands I've ever seen. He was their rebounder. Didn't do much shooting, but he can sure shoot. He's a grand guy, a great player. He could still be with an NBA team, I guess. He'd just rather play with a bunch like the Magicians so he can get some fun out of life," Roger said in a pregame interview.

In an unusual decision, the *Journal-Constitution* sent a sportswriter to cover the game. Such events were considered entertainment rather than sports, but veteran reporter Ed Miles had a courtside seat. In his article in the Sunday sports section, Miles noted that Grider scored a basket off the opening tip, but after that, the game belonged to the locals who led at every break en route to an 85–79 victory. It was the Magicians' first defeat in 823 games or, put another way, three turns of the calendar. In that year alone, the Magicians had won 123 straight games.

Roger scored 31 points and Norwood, a former captain of the Stormy Petrels, was right behind with 29. Denton added 18, including a seventy-five-foot basket from the opposite free throw line at the end of the third quarter. Haynes led the Magicians with 24, trailed by Wilson with 21 and Clifton with 14.

Haynes told Miles that the Atlanta team was the best they had played that season and the best shooting club they had seen in five years. "Roger should be in the League," he said, meaning the NBA. "Yes, sir, that Kaiser is one of the best shots I've ever seen and one of the best floor men, and I have to say that Norwood and Denton are right up there with him. I congratulate the Atlanta team. They're really great, and they're great sports, too."

The teams left the court as friends but not before some testy moments. Competing on a concrete playing surface made falls more painful, and the action was rough-and-tumble. Playing from behind, the Magicians started fouling very early, hoping to exchange one point for two. Bryant noticed that the clock-operator, an employee of the Magicians, was not restarting the clock on time, so he sat someone next to the timekeeper to be sure the clock was ticking when it should. Afterward, hard feelings were put aside, and there was talk of a rematch the following year.

Things were different in 1965. Haynes prepared for a ball game, not a stage show. On the way, he stopped the team bus all along the Eastern Seaboard, picking up fresh talent. By the time he arrived in Georgia, his bus was full. Roger also did some recruiting, adding Don Keiser, a former Georgia Bulldog; Jim Caldwell, an all-SEC player from Tech; Jerry Shipp, the leading scorer on the 1964 United States

Olympic team; and Tommy Mahaffey, the oldest of the four Mahaffey brothers to play at Clemson.

That Sunday afternoon, the old outplayed the young. Haynes was on the court thirty-eight of the forty minutes, and the forty-three-year-old showman led the Magicians to a 96–82 victory. He scored 22 and got ample support from former St. Louis Hawks draft pick Willie Murrell with 21. Murrell, a former all-American at Kansas State, was one of the players Haynes recruited especially for that game.

Norwood paced the locals with 23, two more than Roger. Shipp added 19 but the newcomers hindered rather than helped. "We had too many players that needed the ball," Roger says. "Our chemistry was way off, and Marques added some really good guys. They beat us pretty good."

AN OLD KENTUCKY backcourt star planted the seed, but carrying out Vern Hatton's idea was not easy. Hatton, remembered for scoring 30 points and sparking the Wildcats to an NCAA championship in 1958, came to the Chicago Packers in a trade with the Philadelphia Warriors. He and Roger Kaiser competed for a job with the fledgling expansion club but neither was hired.

Training camp was crazy, with players coming and going regularly. There was plenty of time to talk, and in a conversation after practice Hatton gave Roger the idea of starting a summer basketball camp. After rolling the concept around his head for several years, Roger began to act on Hatton's suggestion.

Beverly and Roger were living ordinary lives. She worked at a bank. He worked for Cohen's tape company, though he planned a move into insurance in partnership with Reinhart, his childhood pal who also wanted to be involved with the camp.

The thought of a summer camp for young people appealed to Roger and Bob more and more. "We incorporated ourselves, and at the ripe old age of twenty-three, I was the president of a full-fledged corporation and Bob was the vice president," he says.

The structure was in place. Now all they needed was land and facilities. Roger was playing for a summer baseball team with Bob.

Hyder set up an appointment for them to look at property in North Georgia the day after a Sunday afternoon game in Holland.

"With that long drive back to Georgia ahead of us, and with our car packed and our wives in the stands, the game went into extra innings. The best part was that I hit a home run to win the game. Bob looked at me and said, 'What took you so long?'"

Hyder put them in touch with Norris Dean, the former track coach at Georgia Tech. Dean owned an old campsite near Batesville, Georgia, and Lake Rabun that had been dormant for several years. The place needed work but the price was right.

"Just fix it up and run it," Dean said.

An adventure that would last for nearly fifteen years began, and so did their labors. There were no phone lines and level ground was at a premium, but they climbed on borrowed tractors and built a basketball court. An old deer field was transformed into a softball field, and a run-down dormitory and mess hall needed to be refurbished. After months of work, the Roger Kaiser Sports Camp began to take shape.

One major roadblock stood in the way of the camp, and that roadblock was Sam Burke, the dictatorial head of the Georgia High School Association. He ruled high school sports in Georgia with an iron hand, and Burke told Roger and Bob that the youth who came to their camp would run the risk of being ineligible to play.

What Burke said was law, and no high school or college coach in Georgia was brave enough to challenge him. Lawyers were another matter. Attorneys Arthur Howell and Jim Harper voluntarily informed Roger that Burke did not have the law on his side. With their support, Roger was able to launch the camp with a full slate of participatory sports. Over the next few years, Harper's sons—Steve, Tom and Jimbo—spent their summers with Roger and Bob.

Howell and Harper were not their only early supporters. A.J. "Duck" Swann was the 1948 SEC golf champion and the captain of Tech's 1949 SEC title winners. In 1983, he became the first foreign golfer to win the British Senior Open Amateur Tournament, and he was inducted into the Georgia Golf of Fame in 2013. But in 1964, the Macon native was looking for a place to send his sons for the summer.

Swann had known Hyder for years, so he called and asked him to recommend a camp. Hyder offered his blessing to one that was not even open yet. Solely based on Hyder's word, Swann showed up at the camp and signed up his son Albert while little brother Brad went fishing. A year later, Duck Swann returned with a bus loaded with young people from Middle Georgia.

Roger and Bob were known for basketball, but their camp had something for everyone. There was a lake for fishing and swimming, a range for archery, and a range for skeet shooting. Campers played flag football and softball, and there was always time for Ping-Pong. Campers and counselors also competed at the annual talent show.

"We offer a boy more than just the fundamentals of team sports, such as football, basketball and baseball," Roger once told a reporter. "We endeavor to instill among our campers, the dedication ... the responsibility that is necessary to succeed, not only in athletics but in life."

Brad Swann was only seven that first year so he had to go back home with his father, but he attended every camp after that, enjoying summers at all three locations. He was a regular camper, junior counselor, and counselor. He even worked in the kitchen.

"The charm of the camp was that Coach Kaiser let boys do what they wanted to do—with supervision," Swann says. "That's why you loved it. I enjoyed the variety of competition. If you weren't good at basketball, maybe you were good at Ping-Pong. There were always random forms of competition, even a talent show that you could win. At night they might have the boys from Macon play the boys from Atlanta in basketball. But whatever you did was all right. There was a general structure, but it was never rigid."

Structure or not, there was fun.

On nights he was pulling duty in the kitchen, Swann had to go to bed at a reasonable hour since he got up early to set the tables for breakfast. One particular night, he was sleeping soundly when Coach Reinhart awakened him.

"You're late," he screamed. "Get up! Get up! It's time to set the tables."

Swann managed to get up and pull on his clothes. Still in a haze, he wandered through the campground on his way to the kitchen. Dragging his feet on the gravel, he woke up Coach Kaiser, who came outside to see what was going on.

"Brad, what in the world are you doing out here?"

"I'm on my way to the kitchen, Coach," he said.

"But it's only one in the morning."

David Jones never fell for one of Bob's jokes, but he did spend time in the kitchen. He was one of the Macon boys Duck Swann rounded up that second year, and Jones remembers Miss Lavinia in the kitchen teaching him to make lemon pies. He returned every year, and to him, the camp was special because of Roger and Bob.

"Roger was clearly the lead dog," he says. "Roger was always Roger and Bob was a genuine character. They knew each other so well. They didn't have to think about things because they were always in lockstep."

Jones's memories could fill a scrapbook. There was the night campers and counselors got together and watched Neil Armstrong walk on the moon. There were snipe hunts where the boys used golf clubs to hit the snipes. There were hikes through the woods, with Roger marking the trail with an axe. There was the time a camper arrived by helicopter and the night an all-star basketball team from Dahlonega came down to play Roger, Bob, and the counselors.

"Coach took them to the woodshed," Jones recalls. "He was always so nice. Then you played him on the basketball court and realized how tough he was. He would just wear you out."

Campers learned more than basketball. They learned to survive away from home, Mama, and television. They learned new activities and made new friends. They learned how to pull in a big bass and how to clean a table after you finished your meal.

"It wasn't highbrow, just fun," Jones says.

The Roger Kaiser Sports Camp operated at two different sites north of Atlanta before being relocated to Carrollton when Roger became head basketball coach at West Georgia College. It was never the same in a campus setting, and it closed in 1972.

"Moving it to West Georgia was my biggest mistake," Roger says.

THE KAISER FAMILY drew close to many of the regular campers. Beverly came up most weekends and brought the children. It became a summer ritual, and having Jenny, Jill, and Chip around added to the family atmosphere. They became particularly close to David Jones and his parents. "My daddy loved them and I loved them, too. My daddy knew then how much Roger was investing in us, and he appreciated that."

Roger was his hero. Jones wanted to play basketball like his mentor but flatly says he was terrible. But even terrible players grow up. He went from being a six-foot tall, one-hundred-sixty-pound kid to a six-foot-nine, two-hundred-pound teenager. By then, Roger was at West Georgia, and David Jones was on his list of recruits. It came down to the wire, and Roger tested speed limits on his way to Macon to sign his former summer camper to a four-year scholarship.

When he got to their front door, Roger found David and his mother in tears. "He always says I went to Mercer because of my mama and my grandpa, that they wanted me to stay at home," Jones says. "Really, I just didn't think I could play for him. We were too close. How would he have ever been able to discipline me?"

Playing in his hometown, Jones was a four-year letterman and two-time captain. Coached by former Georgia Tech assistant Dwane Morrison, he was at Mercer University when the school made the transition from Division II to Division I. For his career, he averaged 4.7 points per game and 4.4 rebounds.

He graduated cum laude from Mercer. After graduating from the Medical College of Georgia, Doctor David Jones set up practice in Atlanta. He is board certified in pediatric cardiology. His close relationship with the Kaisers has continued, and when one of their grandchildren had a cardiac need, they called on him for a medical opinion.

In 1999, Jones was on the NCAA Silver Anniversary team that was introduced at the Final Four in St. Petersburg, Florida. Bill Walton and Jamaal Wilkes of UCLA, Len Elmore of Maryland, and Lon Krueger of Kansas State joined Jones on the mythical squad—an honor that Roger has also received.

"They averaged twenty-five points a game and I averaged four," he says. "I won this award because of what Roger Kaiser taught me long ago. I had leadership qualities, and I always played the best player on the floor."

CHANGE CAME RAPIDLY after Roger and Beverly put down roots in Georgia. He sold technical tape for Paul Cohen and life insurance with Bob Reinhart. He played basketball with Don Bryant and opened a sports camp with his old high school teammate. As the camp grew, he found he needed a job that would give him time off in the summer and enough income to feed his family.

Pro basketball still had his number, and there were feelers from the American Basketball Association and the NBA. The Pittsburgh Condors claimed his rights in the ABA, and a team executive came to the Atlanta airport to meet with Roger. The Condors, with ABL standout Connie Hawkins leading the way, won the league's first title, and they were aware of Roger's ability to hit the three-point shot.

Nearer home, the Atlanta Hawks also contacted him. Assistant Coach Gene Tormohlen knew him from high school in Indiana and also played against him in the SEC and the ABL. He introduced him to head coach Richie Guerin, and Roger still remembers the phone call he received from Hawks general manager Marty Blake, one of the NBA's most astute talent scouts. He thought it was a prank.

"This is Marty Blake," the voice on the phone said.

"No, it's not. Who is this?"

"Well, who do you want it to be?" Blake said.

Roger quietly worked out with the Hawks, which saw in him an ability to sell tickets and the ability to hit the open jumper. But memories of travel and turmoil were fresh in his mind, and he was not interested in either league.

Reinhart had coached two seasons at Oakland High School back home, until he was fired after kicking one guy off the team and calling another player a sissy. He spent summers at the youth camp in Georgia, and now he was moving his family there, planning to find a coaching job in Atlanta

Coaching was not on Roger's radar screen and never had been. Past experiences soured him on that profession, though he certainly admired coaches like Whack Hyder. But at the age of twenty-five, offers started to come his way.

The first one came from the city of Decatur, though it was not a typical coaching job. The Atlanta suburb wanted Roger to become director of recreation. City Manager John Markland made an attractive offer, and Roger accepted, figuring it would give him time for the camp in the summer.

Then an unexpected call came from Georgia State College, a school with more potential than history. Classes were held in a converted parking garage near Five Points in Atlanta, and its low-budget basketball team practiced at the YWCA, though the urban college intended to expand. They planned to join the NCAA and in 1963 welcomed their first group of players on scholarship.

Recruited from area high schools, they played that season under Stoney Burgess, an easygoing fellow who had nursed Georgia State teams for years. Athletic Director Francis Bridges approached Roger about being coach of the Panthers. Bridges promised an on-campus arena within three years. Several important issues had to be decided, and nothing was final when their meetings made headlines in the Atlanta newspapers.

"I have talked to them but haven't made the decision if I want to coach there or not. A story that said I had been offered the job was premature," Roger told one writer. Another report said Decatur had agreed to let Roger continue as recreation director and to allow the Panthers to play their home games in the 1,300-seat rec center until the university's facility was ready.

Markland said Roger had not resigned and that the city would let him keep his position when he took over at Georgia State. "He has done an excellent job, and we feel he can easily make up any time he may miss while coaching. We also agreed to let Georgia State play in our recreation center, and we think the setup will be ideal for both parties," the city manager said.

Negotiations continued on the sports pages. Roger was uncomfortable with what his role would be on campus at Georgia State, and soon the offer was off the table. Richard Wehr, a short-term performer in the NBA with advanced degrees in physical education and an old friend of Bridges, got the job. Burgess was 1–21 and Wehr went 2–20 in 1965. And Georgia State's arena was not built for more than a decade.

Roger stayed with the city of Decatur and continued to operate his summer camp. Then Whack Hyder called. He needed a freshman coach. It was a part-time position but an important one since Tech—for the first time competing as an independent—had a large, talented class reporting in the fall.

It became his entry into a profession he would never leave.

FOR THE SECOND time, Roger Kaiser came to Georgia Tech because Whack Hyder asked. The former player was honest with a man that he considered to be his second father. He reminded Hyder that he had never coached.

"If you have any questions, come see me," Hyder said.

But there was more.

"Oh, by the way, you will have twelve scholarship players."

Twelve fellows expecting playing time added to the challenge, though Roger laughs about never having a shortage of players or subs. To make matters worse, they were all about the same size.

The roster included Phil Wagner, Ted Tomasovich, Pete Thorne, Bob Brizendine, Terry Akins, Ray Ridenhour, Rick Tyler, Tom Bowling, and Ken Krueger, along with three Hoosiers—Stan Guth of Dale, Dave Clark of Tell City, and John Partin of Columbus.

It was a special time for Guth, who grew up watching Roger break all the records as a member of the Golden Aces. Guth chose Tech because of Roger, but he signed before he was hired. Having his childhood hero on the bench was a bonus.

During practices, Roger worked with Guth as a shooter, advising him to find his own system and to do it the same way every time he shot. "He was intense all right and always stressed the fundamentals," Guth remembers.

He could be tough, too.

"The first time the freshmen went down to the coliseum floor to scrimmage the varsity, it was intimidating to look across and see (R.C.) Craddock, (Jim) Caldwell, and (Ron) Scharf. Time was running out, and I had the ball in the middle of the court. The clock was ticking, and I just held the ball. I was completely frozen. Roger started screaming: 'Shoot the ball, Stan. Shoot the damn ball.' I didn't move a muscle. I just stood there holding the ball."

The varsity coach offered Roger advice only once.

"Who you gonna start?" Hyder asked on the eve of the freshman team's opening game against Auburn at Alexander Memorial Coliseum. Roger ran down his lineup, and it did not include Wagner, who had missed several practices because of an injury.

"Start Wagner," Hyder said. "He's homesick and he's talking about going home to Kentucky."

Remembering his own situation Roger penciled in Wagner's name.

His team lost their opener—their only defeat in fifteen games. It came on a last-second shot after a costly turnover. It was a promising group that with one exception stayed together for the next three years. Wagner and Thorne eventually were voted into Tech's basketball Hall of Fame and Tomasovich was inducted for baseball.

"They could have whined, but only one ever complained about not getting enough playing time. They were a good group that had a lot of fun. Of course, it helped that we only lost one game," he says.

Roger Kaiser had been playing organized basketball most of his life, and he never had any desire to coach. Most of the time, he openly resisted any such talk. The enjoyment of that season with Stan Guth and his teammates helped open that door.

"We got him off on the right foot, didn't we?"

15

A Yellow Jacket Becomes a Bulldog

"When the bus goes over the cliff, it does not matter whether you are in the front seat or the backseat."

His oldest friend was in need of a coaching job, and Roger Kaiser wanted to help. Only his appointment with the superintendent of schools did not go as planned. Decatur High hired Bob Reinhart, all right, but the job he got was not the one that was advertised.

Reinhart had been fired at a high school in Oakland, Indiana, after two years even though his players took to the streets in protest. He and Jane moved their family to Georgia near Roger and Beverly. He helped with the Roger Kaiser Sports Camp, sold life insurance and was a substitute teacher at Briarcliff High. But he needed a full-time job.

The volatile Roger Couch left Decatur High in 1965 to become head coach at Gulf Coast Junior College in Panama City, Florida, leaving behind a 92–29 record and some promising players in the cupboard. Knowing these things, Kaiser, whose office was only a block away, arranged a meeting with Doctor Carl Renfroe, intending to recommend his friend.

"I've got your coach for you," he told the superintendent.

"Yeah, it's you," Renfroe said.

"No, you don't understand. I'm here to recommend my best friend."

"What does he teach?"

"Biology."

Roger gave Renfroe a summary of Reinhart's resume, including the fact that he had a four-year degree from Indiana University and that he had been captain of the Hoosier baseball team. That is when Roger learned that Decatur High also needed a baseball coach.

Renfroe set up another conference. When they reconvened, the superintendent presented Roger a totally new proposal: "You be the basketball coach, and he'll be your assistant. In the spring, he will be the head baseball coach, and you can be his assistant."

Roger reminded the educator that he did not have a Georgia teaching certificate and said he did not think the school could afford him. That did not faze Renfroe. "Congratulations, you're a math teacher," he announced, advising Roger that he could teach with a provisional certificate until he completed the prescribed education courses. Money would not be a problem.

In a matter of moments, a Yellow Jacket became a Bulldog.

Roger and Bob were a team again. They installed the pick-and-roll, just like Hurst Livengood taught them. They guided Decatur High to the state tournament and—overcoming the strain of desegregation—built a program that other schools envied.

It was a time of immense change. Roger was teaching physical education in nine elementary schools, so he saw the social changes firsthand. Overnight, it seemed twenty-two "For Sale" signs went up on homes near the school. Changes in the community were evident on the basketball court, for Roger's first Decatur team had one African American player. By his final season, the racial makeup of the roster had totally reversed.

Home games were played at the Decatur Recreation Center, which provided unusual home court advantages. Promises were made that an on-campus gymnasium was on the way, but the Rec Center stayed around until 2009—which was all right with Roger and Bob. Lighting was so poor that they considered darkness their sixth man, and it was so cozy that fans often walked through their huddles during timeouts, sometimes offering free advice. Late in games, the student body made opposing teams cringe by chanting: *"Crank up the bus! Crank up the bus!"*

The best part was a constant flow of exceptional talent. Decatur was the only high school in the city system, and local middle schools provided the Bulldogs a natural feeder system. Roger's first team was supposed to include two of the best players in the state—Bob Marley and Herb White—but in a rude welcome to high school coaching, he lost one of his stars on a Friday night during football season.

Marley, a graceful six-foot-five senior, was ready for a breakout season in the frisky wide-open offense Roger and Bob were implementing. Practice had not even begun when the star player went to a high school football game with some friends. They were on their way home when the driver of the car in which he was riding swerved in front of a school bus loaded with Decatur fans.

That was when the moon came up.

People in the bus were shocked when someone in the car in front of them dropped his pants and mooned them out the back window. When school officials determined it was Marley's backside on display, he was summarily kicked off the basketball team.

Roger intervened.

"I pleaded his case with members of the school board, and they began to listen. They called a special meeting to decide whether he should be reinstated. I did what I could, reminding them he was just a kid and that kids do stupid things. Most of them were sympathetic, and they were about to let him back on the team when someone asked Marley what he had to say. Basically, he said he wasn't sorry for what he did. Right then, I heard the books slam shut," Roger says.

Roger felt it was his job to break the news to Marley's parents, so he went straight to their house and told them what happened at the board meeting. "Bob got home while we were talking, and he walked over to the bookcase and—with a sweep of his hands—knocked every basketball trophy off the shelf. And his parents didn't say a word."

With Marley gone, the Bulldog team effectively belonged to White, who, though only six-foot-two, is remembered as the greatest leaper in Georgia's high school history. Joining the team that season was Jack Williams, the quarterback on the Bulldog football team, who had chosen not to play under Couch.

White did not have to be introduced to his new coach. When he was younger, he listened to Tech games on the radio. Al Ciraldo, the voice of the Yellow Jackets, was a neighbor and a family friend, so White had heard all the Roger Kaiser stories. "I knew Al from childhood. He would come over to our house to eat spaghetti, and we would talk basketball."

White remembers the transition from Couch to Kaiser.

"For three years, we ran the wheel. On a good night, we might score 40 points as a team," he says. "The offense changed overnight when Coach Kaiser got there, and he changed my approach, too. Under Couch's system, you waited on the offense to get to you. All of a sudden, they wanted me to shoot. 'Give it to Herbie and get out of the way,' Roger said. That was hard for me."

Roger and Bob had seen enough of his shooting shyness.

"Just take it, Herbie!" Roger screamed.

When Herbie did not react, they sat their star player down in the middle of practice. That also happened to be the day that University of Georgia coach Ken Rosemond came there to see White in action. Despite his reticence about shooting, the Bulldog coach must have liked what he saw, for he offered him a scholarship.

Most days after practice, White went one-on-one with his coach. Reinhart was on the sideline, teasing them. The high school senior respected Roger and wanted to impress him. While doing that, his own game was being polished. These daily matchups prepared White for college where he had to guard LSU's Pete Maravich.

"I held him to fifty-seven one night," he says.

Going against his coach was a workout. Until he faced Maravich, he thought Roger was the best he had ever seen. Though Maravich had the sizzle and was given the freedom to score in so many ways, White said Roger was the pure shooter. "He could hit from seventeen, eighteen, or twenty feet, and that kick of his was always so distinctive."

His one season with Roger was a good one. With Williams—a future Georgia Tech quarterback—delivering the ball, White sparked the team to the Georgia AAA State Tournament—the first of three postseason visits in Roger's four years at Decatur.

White went to the University of Georgia with a sterling reputation and was dubbed "The Elevator from Decatur." He struggled through an up-and-down career that saw him become a full-time starter only in his senior year. He averaged 9.8 points and 6.4 rebounds a game in

1970. But despite his mediocre numbers, the Atlanta Hawks drafted him in the eighth round, mainly based on his unusual jumping ability.

One season made White a leaping legend, as noted in a 1983 article by Scott Ostler in the *Los Angeles Times*. Ostler interviewed Wilt Chamberlain, who singled him out when asked whether there were ever any great leapers whose skin was white.

> Wilt mentioned a few names, then said, "You know, there was a white boy who played for Atlanta around 1970. Never got off the bench, but in warm-ups he could dunk better than anyone I've ever seen."
>
> Chamberlain couldn't remember the player's name, but Rod Thorn did. The mystery leaper was—and is—Herb White, 6-foot-2, eyes of blue, from Decatur, Ga.
>
> As with most leaping legends, Herb's aerial reputation often preceded him … Before his senior year, White happened to work out with some Atlanta Hawks players and they went to Coach Richie Guerin with tales of this amazing leaper. Herb made the 1970–71 team as a point-guard backup and the road roommate of another rookie, Pete Maravich. White started five games, but was mostly a mop-up guy, then was injured and finished his career in a pro league in Mexico.
>
> White made the NBA all-time all-warm-up team that one season. Pregame warm-ups were his showtime. He would perform a reverse dunk-dunk with two balls. He would toss the ball off the backboard and then slam it home. In Madison Square Garden, he got a standing ovation for his warm-up dunks.
>
> "I won the unofficial NBA slam dunk title that season," said White. "In warm-ups, we would always check out the other team and get into little contests with their guys. All the teams did that. By word of mouth, you would get to know who the best dunkers were, and by the end of the season it was pretty much agreed the best two were a Portland guy named Claude English and me.

> "We played Portland in the last game of the season. Before the game, English and I went back and forth. Finally he did a 360, one handed. So I did a 360, two handed, and he conceded."

White enjoyed a long career with Georgia Public Television, raising money to bring high school sports to the statewide network. His friendships with Roger and Bob never stopped. Every year he plays in Lexi's Game, the Kaiser family's annual celebrity golf tournament. In 2014, friends gathered for a getaway dinner organized after White and his wife shocked everyone with an announcement that they were moving to a gated golf community in Mexico.

Success continued after White graduated, and some of Decatur's most memorable outings came against a familiar foe. Couch left Gulf Coast after recording a 21–6 record and returned to high school coaching at Druid Hills, one of Decatur's fiercest rivals. For several years, the neighboring schools were among the most powerful programs in the state. "We were in the same region," Roger says, "and over the years, we had some great games with Druid Hills."

The longer he was around the profession, the more it was apparent that coaching was always in his blood. He enjoyed working with young people, and he discovered the intrinsic rewards of teaching and sharing what he knew about basketball and about life.

His calm demeanor helped guide Decatur through some tough times in the community. On the court, he led the Bulldogs to a region title and three postseason tournaments in four seasons, including one trip to the State AAA finals. His 77–26 record spoke for itself.

And people began to notice.

WEST GEORGIA WAS a fast-growing institution located in Carrollton, about fifty miles from Atlanta. It was founded in 1907 as a two-year school with the prescribed mission of educating rural youth. Fifty years later, West Georgia A&M became a four-year institution. By 1969, its enrollment had grown to more than 6,000 students.

Intercollegiate basketball began in 1958, but the program did not prosper. Three coaches in twelve years produced two winning seasons.

Officials determined they needed a leader who would help the entire athletic program grow—one who would "expand, reorganize and dramatize the scope of athletics."

Steve McCutcheon, who played freshman basketball at Auburn University, had become the assistant to Doctor James Boyd, the president of the college. He had recently earned his doctorate at Indiana University and when he arrived in Carrolton in 1968 he became a regular at West Georgia basketball games. He was not impressed. Coach Jan Bennett's team was slow and cumbersome and not very entertaining. More importantly, only a few students or local people bothered to come to the games.

"We can do better than this," he told Boyd.

With Boyd's blessing, McCutcheon assembled a plan to improve and restructure the athletic program. The college was totally desegregating in the fall of 1969, and he determined that an improved basketball team could help in that uneasy time and might also help smooth out the rocky relationship between the community and the campus—commonly known as town and gown. More than anything, McCutcheon wanted someone who would instill pride.

Boyd also accepted that—unlike in the past—a new athletic director should operate independently from the physical education department. He first thought that McCutcheon ought to assume the expanded role himself but the newly minted Ph.D. believed the school needed someone more experienced in athletics.

As his search began, McCutcheon thought of Ken Ringer. They were classmates at Auburn and their wives were sorority sisters so they had remained friends. He lived in Atlanta and was immersed in the local sports community so McCutcheon shared his plans and asked if a candidate came to mind. Ringer brought up the familiar name of Roger Kaiser. They played church softball together so McCutcheon asked Ringer if he would gauge whether he might be interested. Ringer threw out the idea during a softball game and a formal meeting was arranged.

"The three of us met at the Hyatt Regency Hotel in Atlanta, where I interviewed Roger for the very first time. Only then did I mention his name to the president. Doctor Boyd was a graduate of Georgia Tech.

He was a professor there when Roger was playing, and years later he served as Tech's acting president. His eyes lit up when I told him Roger was interested. Looking back, that was a pivotal moment in West Georgia history," McCutcheon says.

West Georgia already had an athletic director in Tom Leaming, the head of the physical education department, who agreed to give up the AD job when a successor was found. They also had a basketball coach in Bennett, but McCutcheon candidly told Roger that he did not think the former Ole Miss freshman coach would succeed. West Georgia offered Roger a nondescript administrative position with several assignments that included the athletic directorship.

Everything seemed to fit, though Roger and Beverly shared private laughs over roadside signs they saw on their first drive to Carroll County. One said: "We Sale Gulf Gas." The other advertised: "We fix lawn mores."

The community was vastly different then. Interstate 20 took you out of Atlanta but ended around Douglasville. You came into town on a two-lane highway, which was all right with two people who cherished memories of growing up in a small town. They relished the prospect of rearing their children in a town like Carrollton, where folks cheered the high school football team on Friday nights and bowed their heads in prayer on Sunday mornings.

Mulling over McCutcheon's offer for more than a month, Roger accepted. After the final session at his sports camp that summer, he packed for his move. He reported at the beginning of the fall term, but Beverly and the kids stayed behind in Atlanta until their new house was finished in Carrollton.

While they were still in DeKalb County, they had a call from the Reverend Don Harp, a United Methodist minister in Carrollton. His was not a downtown congregation. It was small, near the college campus, with a membership of young and active folks. "I know you but you don't know me. I'm the pastor of St. Andrews Methodist Church," he said. "I know you're a Methodist. And when you get here, you are going to be a member of my church."

Harp became a lifelong friend. His friendly gesture encouraged Roger and Beverly that Carrollton was right for them and Jenny, Jill, and Chip. “When you’re told you are wanted, you feel wanted,” Beverly says.

Leaving Decatur High was not easy, though. “It certainly has been a wonderful four years,” he told an Atlanta reporter. “You just can’t realize how I hate to give it up. But I think things will go real well at West Georgia.”

Things did go well. As a PR man, Roger was an overnight success. He spent the 1969 school year telling the story of West Georgia athletics to anyone who would listen. He was visible on and off campus, meeting with student organizations, speaking to civic groups, calling on business leaders, and selling tickets at every stop.

Carrollton, he discovered, also had a lively sense of humor. Soon after they moved to town, the McCutcheons invited Roger and Beverly to a backyard barbecue. Among the guests was Fred Hutchins, the president of the People’s Bank, known to one and all as “Friendly Fred.” Hutchins asked Beverly about her job at the First National Bank of Atlanta.

“Are you interested in a banking job here in Carrolton?”

“I am, but with young children at home, I can’t work Saturdays. And I need Wednesdays off.”

“We’ve got that job,” the banker said.

“You do?”

With that, Hutchins dropped down to one knee.

“Yes, but PLEASE, Mrs. Kaiser, don’t take my job.”

16

“They’ll Get You, Too”

“They know you care when you are there.”

Changing coaches is usually difficult, and the firing and hiring of a basketball coach at West Georgia College in 1970 was left to Steve McCutcheon. It was a complicated proposition that transformed athletic director Roger Kaiser into the school’s head coach and turned former headman Jan Bennett into his assistant.

Roger insists that was not the plan when he went there, but McCutcheon says a change was inevitable. The situation became more delicate when it was determined that the assistant to the president would have to deal with Bennett’s firing, since he would still be under contract as an instructor in the physical education department.

When McCutcheon asked him if he wanted the coaching job, Roger was in no hurry to reply. He was enjoying small-town life with a schedule that allowed him to be at home for dinner and gave him time to play with his children, play softball, or go fishing.

“It doesn’t feel right,” he said.

“Well, we’re going to hire someone,” McCutcheon pointed out.

Once Roger accepted the job, McCutcheon informed Bennett, and it was a tedious conversation. The University of Tennessee-Chattanooga graduate had coached the Braves for three years. He broke in with a 12–10 record, the school’s first winning season since 1964 followed by disappointing records of 11–13 and 8–15.

“Roger has all the qualifications necessary for the position, and I am delighted that he has agreed to accept the challenge,” McCutcheon told *The West Georgian*, the college newspaper.

Though awkward for both of them, Bennett became his assistant, and he handled the situation like a professional. Roger praises his performance during a problematical basketball season. "Jan did everything I asked. He scouted our opponents, and his scouting reports were amazing," Roger says.

Bennett left West Georgia after the 1971 season and returned to high school basketball in Florida. He retired in 2000 after coaching in five decades and racking up 563 victories.

ROGER KAISER BECAME the fifth basketball coach in West Georgia history. Kenneth Johnson was the first, followed by Richard Ottinger, Howard Corder, and Bennett. In thirteen seasons, the school had two winning seasons. Corder went 15–7 in 1964 and Bennett was 12–10 in 1968. Their composite record was 91–175, and not one of the departed coaches left behind a winning record. This was the unenviable situation thirty-one-year-old Roger found himself in 1970.

One of the first things he did was take a trip home. A friend in Dale told him about an impressive junior college coach, and then he got a phone call from him. They had never met, but the fellow said he wanted to work for him. Roger mostly listened. After one conversation, he knew Jerry Reynolds could talk. But could he coach? They set up a meeting at Paul "Wop" Fritch's bar in Jasper, and the two Indiana boys sized each other up over a plate of the owner's world-famous chicken livers.

Reynolds was a boyish twenty-seven. He hailed from Hillham, a postage stamp suburb of French Lick—home of Hurst Livengood and Larry Bird. He was an undersized guard at Spring Valley High, where he scored more than 1,200 points and averaged 18 points a game. He attended Vincennes University, where he put up 10 points a game, and Oakland City College, where he coached the 1966 freshman team to a 10–3 record.

He was an assistant coach at Vincennes—the oldest junior college in America—during a time the Trailblazers ranked first in national polls four times and compiled a 153–28 record. He signed twelve high school all-Americans and twenty all-state performers

"I knew the legend of Roger Kaiser when we met, but I had to look up Carrollton on a map. It was close to Atlanta, and I may not be too smart, but I told my wife … it might have been snowing when I told her … that it had to be warmer than French Lick. When I met Roger, I was amazed at how humble he was. I remember that during our first practice game at West Georgia, I looked at that wild guy next to me, and I knew he meant business," Reynolds says.

Teaming a shy, reserved guy like Roger with a wunderkind like Reynolds was genius. One was dignified and looked like he was about to usher at church, and the other was a standup comedian without a stage. Reynolds even made recruiting fun, announcing they needed players who were more than LGA—his term for *Looks Good in Airports*.

A partnership forged over chicken livers changed their lives and made history in the state of Georgia. Even before they discussed his paltry salary, Reynolds poured out names of players they could sign, and he was not exaggerating. "The way I recruited, I pointed out the positives. I think I was good at that. And when we got them to campus, Roger understood that not everyone had the ability to be a star, but he let the guys who were good be good."

Reynolds had one shaky moment. His unimpressive office included a state-owned desk that survived longer than the people who used it. Reynolds made himself at home. When Reynolds unloaded his things, he found a hidden message taped into a desk drawer. He went looking for Roger to show him what it said.

The message listed three names: former coaches West, Corder, and Bennett. It also contained a stern warning to all who used that desk in the future: *"And they'll get you, too."*

Reynolds was shaken.

"Get me another desk," he begged. "I don't want this one."

Reynolds has spent more than thirty years in the NBA, including two stints as head coach of the Sacramento Kings. He is currently a colorful member of the club's broadcasting team. It is hard to imagine that he took a cut in pay to come South, but something pushed him toward a school that had never won games and never drew fans.

Roger and his comical sidekick were neither blind nor naive. As they surveyed the talent they were assembling, they knew something special was about to happen. "We made an immediate turnaround. We knew we would be good. Roger was a natural competitor, and it started seeping through to the team. He just had a special knack at utilizing talent."

And they were right. Something good was about to happen.

IN A ROOM with Charlie Grisham you were in the presence of Carroll County royalty. But Roger Kaiser did not go see him so he could kiss his ring. He was new in town, and he wanted the legendary football coach to share his wisdom.

Roger wanted his team to be relevant, like the Trojans of Carrollton High School. People in town had never been interested in Braves' basketball, but they would pile into school buses and follow Grisham's teams to the hills of Habersham or the valleys of Hall.

Grisham had coached the Trojans since 1958. He stayed twenty-nine years and retired with a 261–69–13 record, five state championships, sixteen region titles, and eight North Georgia championships. His favorite team was his 1961 edition, and it was not because they were unbeaten and number one in the state. "We had four doctors and three pharmacists on that team, and all but one of the guys graduated from college."

What the local legend told Roger was important.

"You have to win or tie," he said.

"I can't tie."

"Then win, Roger."

When Roger complained about the size of his crowds, Grisham pointed out that key folks in town were starting to show up at his basketball games.

"Coach, you got 'em," Grisham said.

"How's that?"

"You heard Old Ray standing up and yelling at you the other night? That means he cares. He's been helping me coach for twelve years."

Grisham offered one negative observation.

"You won too quick," he said. "Now they'll expect that every year."

Fans were filling the seats, but they came because of more than victories. When Roger and Beverly moved to town, Chip had not started to school and Jenny and Jill were assigned to two different elementary schools. The Kaisers joined both PTA and were constantly in and out of the schools meeting kids and becoming friends with their parents.

These new friends started coming to ball games—first to support the parents of their children's friends, and then to watch a team that breathed excitement and flair. The town got behind the team before the students, and when students joined the party, it was a circus. Games became family events. Youngsters begged their parents to get there early so they could grab seats on the front row. They cried when there was no room.

Tim Criswell was one of them. He was in elementary school, a classmate of Roger's daughter Jill. The noise and atmosphere was fascinating to a ten-year-old. Attraction to basketball came later, bringing him to that same court as a high-scoring guard. Much later, he became head basketball coach at Carrollton High.

"West Georgia College games were the place to be in Carrollton, even for kids," he says. "There was a guy in the stands who always rang a cowbell, and I knew every player by name. My first favorite was Charlie Hamilton. We would sit on the front row of the bleachers. And if there wasn't a seat, I remember sitting Indian style on the floor. I didn't want to miss a thing."

CHARLIE HAMILTON STOOD in the middle of the magic. A native of Kentucky, the junior college transfer was among Roger's early signees. He came knowing that he and Stan Horton would be among the few African American students on an overwhelmingly white campus and the focal point of a basketball program that had never thrived. Hamilton, six-foot-five and a chiseled two-hundred-forty-pounds, was man enough to face either challenge.

McCutcheon credits Hamilton's personality and presence for making desegregation work smoothly at West Georgia. "Charlie fit in. People liked him as a person, and they liked the way he carried himself on the basketball court."

Hamilton led Roger's first edition by averaging 18 points and 14.1 rebounds a game. He was joined by teammates who came from every direction: Auburn transfer Bobby York, University of Georgia transfer Skeet Crigler, ABAC transfer Harley Stewart, Anderson Junior College transfer Stan Horton, and Indiana native Glenn Andrew. They helped the 1971 Braves to a 14–11 record.

With the victories came fans.

"It just took off," says McCutcheon, the radio play-by-play man for the Braves. "Later on, we started renting buses and taking opinion-makers to games in Valdosta and Columbus. This helped us smooth out the integration issue and overcome a touchy situation where some psychology professors set up a commune out in the county that upset a lot of people in town."

More new faces arrived, beginning with a talented trio from Vincennes: five-foot-eight Greg Allen, six-foot-six Alan Gustavel, and six-foot-five Tom Turner. After them came six-foot-one Barry Allen from Truett-McConnell Junior College, five-foot-eleven Whit Matthews from Marion Junior College, six-foot-four Willie Joe Lewis from Anderson Junior College, and six-foot-five Max Pfeifer from Bluffton, Indiana.

Coaches set down "Seven Success Steps," and after the 1972 season, six of them were met. The goals were to win the Chattanooga Tip-Off Tournament; win the Hubbard Classic; win more games than any Braves' team in history; win the school's first GIAC title and first NAIA District 25 championship; earn a trip to the NAIA national tournament; and be a credit to themselves, the college, and the community. The GIAC title was the only goal left unmet.

Things seemed bleak in the finals of the conference tournament when perennial nemesis Valdosta State romped past Roger's club 122–84, a stinging 38-point margin. To make matters worse, West Georgia had to play Armstrong State at home in the NAIA district tournament forty-eight hours later. They were in control with two minutes to play when it was announced that Albany State had upset Valdosta 80–78. If the Braves won that game, the District 25 finals would be in Carrollton one night later.

Despite a break in concentration, the Braves defeated the Pirates 81–75, with Hamilton pulling down 25 rebounds to go with 14 points. Stewart, York, and Turner—only recently eligible—led the scoring.

In the finals, West Georgia made up a six-point deficit in the closing minutes to defeat Albany State 72–69. Hamilton—pestered by seven-foot-one Caldwell Jones—scored 20. Gustavel came off the bench for 13, and York, Allen, and Stewart had 10 apiece.

Pandemonium ruled. Coaches rode on the shoulders of players. Nets were cut down. Supporters took turns dunking each other in an adjacent indoor pool. Time seemed to freeze as a campus and a town celebrated a moment they never thought would come. "This is a dream come true," Roger said, knowing his club was on its way to Kansas City for the first time.

A small contingent of West Georgia fans headed west in March 1972. In a crusty downtown auditorium, they found an event that had been a fixture there since 1937. For serious fans, the NAIA Tournament was a smorgasbord of college basketball. Games began in the morning and went late into the night. To take home the trophy, a team had to survive five games in six days. With the team were reporters from both Atlanta newspapers, signaling that the Braves were suddenly front-page news.

Roger wanted the Braves to show they belonged, and they did, hitting basket after basket in the early going against Northwestern of Iowa. But the Red Raiders stormed back. The Braves overcame a sloppy performance and won 73–69, in overtime. Hamilton scored 24 points and grabbed 23 rebounds. Stewart chipped in 23 points.

That earned them the right to meet the team everyone came to see. Kentucky State had won the tournament the previous two years and featured six-foot-seven Travis Grant. They called him "The Machine" for good reason. He scored 60 against Minot State in the opener and finished his college career with 4,045 points—more than any player in history. (Yes, that included Pete Maravich.)

West Georgia hung around for fifteen minutes until strength and experience took its toll. Grant scored 43 points in Kentucky State's 112–83 win. A few nights later, Grant led KSU to their third national title. In a strange twist, after a short career in pro basketball, Grant earned a master's degree at West Georgia. He retired as a high school principal in Atlanta.

Roger talked to reporters after the loss: "I was tremendously proud of the way our kids stayed right in there the entire game. In fact, I am prouder of our play and hustle in this loss than I was in our win over Northwestern the night before."

Stepping from behind Hamilton's shadow, Stewart led West Georgia with 24 points and 12 rebounds. "It wasn't so much the statistics that made Harley look good. It was the competition he got them against," his coach said.

Hamilton was plagued by fouls in a game that capped his sparkling career. He was the team's first all-American, earning third-team honors. He averaged 19 points and a school record 20 rebounds a game. The Atlanta Tip-Off Club named him the state's college player of the year, and for the first time, tabbed Roger as college coach of the year for his surprising 28–6 record.

That team meant more to Carrollton than the players ever imagined. They proved they could win, and they proved basketball could draw fans. West Georgia College finally felt the pride that McCutcheon hoped for when he originally hired Roger. An editorial in *The Carrollton Times-Free Press* put that pride into print:

> West Georgia Coach Roger Kaiser, in the few short years he has lived here, has become one of Carrollton's most beloved citizens. He wasted little time in bridging the gap between "town and gown" through his participation in civic or community endeavors. Coach Kaiser's enthusiasm, determination and dedication are reflected through the attitude and performance of those young men who carried the Braves' banner to the national tournament. West Georgia College and this area could not have asked for better ambassadors to the national sporting circle. This newspaper issues a hearty "thank you" to Coach Kaiser and his Braves for a job well done.

They did not win the national title they sought, but senior Bobby York described that eventful season better than anyone. "We got beat, sure, but it took the best team in the United States to do it."

17
The Feats of Foots

"Be happy with what you have while working for what you want."

Foots Walker sounds like an old blues musician, but he made beautiful music on a basketball court, not in a smoke-filled dive. As a swirling point guard, he was an artist between the lines … improvising, harmonizing, and expressing … and leaving in his wake a legacy of championship trophies, thunderstruck fans, and incredulous opponents.

A native of New York City, he glided into Carrollton in the spring of 1972 more accustomed to sidewalks than pine trees. He arrived after a rewarding journey to the cornfields of Kansas, where he engineered Vincennes University's rise to the National Junior College championship. He was most valuable player on the 34–0 Trailblazers and scored 21 points against Ferrum College in the title game. Then, with a cavalcade of big time basketball coaches nipping at his heels, he visited unheralded West Georgia College.

Walker knew nothing about the town, the campus, or even the head coach's name. He came because of Jerry Reynolds, a motor-mouthed junior college assistant coach whom he met when he was a skinny high school kid on Long Island. He put his trust in Reynolds, and if his mentor said West Georgia was a good place, it must have been where he was supposed to be.

Walker and Reynolds met before other coaches began to call. "My high school coach was six-foot-four, and he weighed more than three hundred pounds. When Coach Reynolds came around he looked down at him and said he was putting me in his hands. He told him if he didn't treat me right, that he would have to answer to him," Walker says.

Reynolds picked up Walker at the airport in Atlanta and drove him to Carrollton, talking nonstop all the way. He told him about the school, the people in town, and he told him about Roger Kaiser—how he was an all-American at Georgia Tech and how Oscar Robertson and Jerry West beat him out for the Olympic team. He said Roger was a good man who would treat him right.

Walker is still impressed at what he saw at West Georgia.

"I was a long way from home, but when I hit the campus, there were signs all over the place welcoming me. They were all over the gym and all over town. Friends and students of Coach Kais made them, and they were everywhere. Coach Reynolds took me to stores in town, and everything felt warm and real. People were all the same. They made me feel welcome and at home. It didn't cross my mind to be afraid, because I knew I was the type of person that could get along with anybody. Then I met Coach Kais, and he was genuine, just a special guy. He introduced me to his wife, his girls, and to Chip. The atmosphere was wonderful."

Walker was a two-time high school all-American. He led Southampton High to an unbelievable seventy-three straight victories. He averaged 12.5, 20.2, 29.0, and 29.6, with a high of 59 points in one game, second in school history to baseball Hall of Famer Carl Yastremski of the Boston Red Sox.

Following Reynolds to Vincennes, he averaged 11.2 points a game as a freshman and 18 points and 8.9 rebounds as a sophomore on a team that only lost four games in two years and included future Hall of Famer Bob McAdoo, his friend and roommate. His was the exalted resume of a player that normally would not end up at a school like West Georgia, and Reynolds was the magnet that drew him to Georgia. "I knew how good he was, and there was no doubt in our minds that he could make us better and take us to the championship level," Reynolds says.

Several of Walker's junior college teammates were already enrolled at West Georgia, but major college programs such as Louisville, St. Johns, and North Carolina State had watched him dazzle everyone at the junior college tournament and were in hot pursuit. Walker remained fiercely loyal to Reynolds. Those warm feelings quickly extended to the man who became his new head coach.

"I can't imagine someone who couldn't play for Coach Kais," Walker says. "He gave respect and he got respect. He was a player's coach. He was easygoing, but if you stepped out of line, he could put his foot down. I could have played for him forever."

His new teammates were drawn to Walker immediately and elected him team captain. An example of the faith the school had in Walker is found on the cover of the Braves' 1972–1973 media guide. On the right of the picture is a youthful Roger Kaiser wearing the dark suit of a banker or a minister. On the left is Jerry Reynolds, hair flopping in the breeze, wearing stylish black-and-white shoes. Between them is Foots Walker wearing a West Georgia warm-up suit and clutching a basketball in his hands.

And he had yet to play a game.

MUSCULAR CHARLES HAMILTON'S departure left a gaping hole in the West Georgia lineup. In two short seasons, he ravaged the school record book and led the Braves to their first national tournament. His physical play inspired Roger to push the ball inside, but Walker's magical ball handling and Tom Turner's emerging jump shot changed that strategy overnight.

Returning was all-GIAC guard Greg Allen, Barry Allen, super sub Alan Gustavel, Willie Joe Lewis, Sandy Lee, and Max Pfeifer. Three promising transfers joined them: high-flying Jerry Faulkner, the only five-foot-eleven center in college basketball; six-foot-eight Randy Rountree; and six-foot-seven Pat Magley.

Turner played part of a season with the team that went to Kansas City in 1972, and the route he took to West Georgia would amaze a travel agent. He was on two Indiana state championship teams at Vincennes High, then stayed home to play on a national junior college championship squad at Vincennes University. He signed with the University of Southwest Louisiana. But feeling uncomfortable, he joined a high school teammate at Keene University in New Hampshire.

"That was all in ten months," Turner says. "Lafayette was too big and Keene was too small. I called Coach Reynolds and headed for West Georgia. I put some miles on the road, boy."

He had never met Roger and knew nothing about him, so he had no idea that their hometowns in Indiana were only fifty-five miles apart. But he had the head coach's home address in Carrollton, so Turner and his wife showed up at his front door. "Everything just clicked," he says. "I met some good town people, and they took up with me. They were good country people like I had grown up with."

Turner felt at home.

"This is the biggest part of the whole story," Turner says. "We were good, but so were a lot of teams we played against. We were like a family. We looked after one another from top to bottom. Some of the guys had a little more money than the rest of us, but that didn't matter. We were always there for each other."

What could have been a rebuilding year turned into another impressive season. Roger especially enjoyed a trip to Bowling Green where his squad met Western Kentucky University, two years after the Hilltoppers earned a berth in the Final Four.

With 10,000 disbelieving fans looking on, West Georgia shocked the home team 89–88. The star of the game was Magley, a surprise starter who scored 30 points. Mostly remembered for sporting the largest Afro of any white player in the country, his two free throws with fifty-six seconds remaining sealed the win.

It was a partisan crowd, but a few fans were cheering for the Braves. The proudest supporters in the arena drove all the way from Indiana. Louanna and Elmer Kaiser were proud of their oldest son, and that night they were also proud of his basketball team. They enjoyed the game so much that when they went back to their hotel room, they watched a replay on a local cable station.

The Braves won their first ten games and topped the 100-point plateau four times. Their first loss was to perennial nemesis Valdosta State,—one of three losses to the Blazers that season. The last one came in the NAIA District 25 tournament and closed a 23–5 season on a disappointing note. That victory meant the Blazers went to Kansas City, not the Braves.

Over three short seasons, a program that had struggled for so long recorded an impressive 65–22 record, went to the district finals twice, and made the nationals in Kansas City. Fans began to believe the Braves could go even higher.

Roger and Reynolds began to search for the missing piece to their puzzle, the one that would take them over the top. As usual, Reynolds found that player at Vincennes. His name was Dave Edmonds, like Walker a product of New York City. By the 1973–1974 season, Roger had honed his rotation to five players—Walker, Turner, Edmonds, Faulkner, and Rountree. As a group, they understood there would be no shortcuts to Kansas City.

SMALL COLLEGE BASKETBALL in Georgia was at its highest plateau. Rivalries were intense, and the level of play had never been better. The founding of the South Atlantic Conference added to that atmosphere. It replaced the old Georgia Intercollegiate Athletic Conference and featured some of the fastest growing campuses in the university system: West Georgia, Valdosta State, Armstrong Atlantic, Augusta State, Southern Tech, Columbus State, North Georgia College, and Georgia Southwestern. Roger continued to schedule longtime rivals LaGrange College, Jacksonville State, and Albany State, so every game was a headliner. The Braves captured the first SAC title that season with a 96–71 victory over Valdosta State. Turner scored 30 points and was the tournament MVP.

These things created a flurry of excitement, and the level of enthusiasm grew with every game. The campus had been wrapped up in the spirit of the 1960s. Students were edgy. They created a scene when rocker Johnny Rivers was late for a concert and walked out on Al Capp—the creator of comic strip character Li'l Abner—when they did not agree with his politics. When streakers were flashing college campuses all over the country, a naked skydiver tumbled out of an airplane and landed on the intramural field.

Those antics were forgotten. Attention was focused on a basketball team that was once ignored. Fans started traveling with the team, but it was at home where West Georgia's reputation blossomed. An article in *The Chieftain*, the school yearbook, offered a jovial but somewhat accurate description of a typical fan:

> Once again at West Georgia College, basketball reigned supreme during winter quarter. All of the students' activities in one way or another were related to basketball. Studying was performed at such strange times as 2:00 a.m. or 3:30 p.m. or disregarded completely. On nights of a scheduled basketball game, Curt's and all of the other Carroll County beer stores did a booming business. A few of the more dedicated even hoarded their spare change in an effort to obtain gasoline, in the face of a fuel crisis, to attend out-of-town games. This rabid student support has gained the college field house a reputation around the state as a terrifying place for opposing coaches and players … The Braves basketball fan is a strange creature, indeed. Invariably dressed in sneakers, blue jeans, and a Disneyland tee shirt, he sits in the east stands of the gym for two hours in a drunken stupor, proclaiming the Braves an equal match with any basketball team created by God, man, or John Wooden. When the game ends, unless he is restrained, he will run out onto the court, madly screaming. There is, of course, no particular reason for doing this. It is just the thing to do.

The stands were filled with colorful characters that made things fun and kept folks coming back. Professor Tommy Davidson clanged his cowbell. Jimmy "Saffo" White made noise with his air horn, garbage can lids, or hubcaps. On road games, his Volkswagen bus was usually filled with cheerleaders. Orin Whitman had a favorite seat, and so did Newt Gingrich, a West Georgia history professor who would one day be the Speaker of the House in Washington. And before every game, the Reverend Don Harp offered special prayers for the team.

After the games came late-night parties that usually had a victory to celebrate. Players partied with the townspeople and Noc-A-Homa frequently showed up in full Native American gear. His legal name was Levi Walker, and he was a full-blooded Ottawa Indian. He lived near Carrollton, and longtime fans of the Atlanta Braves remember his war dances on the pitcher's mound at Atlanta-Fulton County Stadium.

Walker was introduced to West Georgia fans in 1974 after Roger hired him to be grand marshal of the school's annual homecoming parade. He came cheap, too. "Our grand marshal didn't ask for cash. He wanted to know if I could get him some rope he needed for a project he was working on," Roger says.

That night, Walker cheered West Georgia to a homecoming victory. "The basketball team set four school records and the crowd was fantastic," he recalls. "At one time during the game, the referee asked me to sit down, and the crowd booed. I think it fired up the team."

The maestro of this madness was Roger Kaiser, who usually appeared to be the calmest guy in the house. Beverly, Jenny, and Jill were constantly cheering. Chip, enjoying the fruits of being the coach's kid, was the ball boy, sitting at the other end of the bench from his dad and occasionally going on road trips with the team. Sometimes Elmer and Louanna came in from Indiana.

Players who had been stars in the past accepted lesser roles. They came to believe that if they did what they were expected to do, good things would happen. Players genuinely liked each other and had fun together, but on the court, they took no prisoners.

Foots Walker sees a game at Albany State as a turning point. Albany was a tough place to play and a challenging place to win. Calls seldom went for the visitors and for eighteen seasons one of the Jones brothers stood guard in the middle. Wilbert, Melvin, Major, Caldwell, Oliver, and Charles came out of Arkansas, and four of the six went on to play in the NBA. Major, the president of the NBA Retired Players Association, was the force behind the 1974 Golden Rams and Walker wondered how his teammates would deal with his six-foot-nine presence.

"They didn't see me flinch so they didn't flinch," Walker says. "They followed my lead and nobody was fazed. Games like that helped me realize what a great bond we had. This came from the bench and from the court."

Turner was one of the few married players on the team. When Brenda, his pregnant wife, was about to deliver her first baby at the hospital in Carrollton, it turned into a team event. Players celebrated all over the maternity ward, and when they got too rowdy, several of them were asked to leave.

With a family to feed, Turner struggled to survive, which concerned small business owner Orin Whitman. He was not an alum or a wealthy booster, but when he saw holes in Turner's shoes and blue jeans, he offered to help. Whitman had a farm across the Alabama state line and owned a glass company in Carrollton. He became a surrogate grandfather to the Turners. A country boy at heart, Turner enjoyed walking in the woods on Whitman's farm, and the World War II veteran often cooked breakfast for the ball player's family. When no one was looking, he and Turner shared sips from a jar of moonshine liquor that he kept on a shelf in the kitchen.

White lightning was not Turner's drink of choice, though. He freely admits that he has been a daily beer drinker since he was a teenager, and that serious habit continued at West Georgia. "I don't know to this day why referees never smelled beer on my breath, because I had a couple before every game," says Turner, now a retired police officer in Vincennes.

Turner became a dilemma for his coach. Along the way, Roger learned that his player was a habitual drinker. But Turner was older, married with a new baby, and living on his own off campus. He caused no trouble. He went to class. He was on time, and people close to him claimed pregame beers helped him stay calm and focused. Turner kept his drinking relatively private, but that was hard to do on the road.

"I packed light and filled most of the suitcase up with cans of beer. They were heavy, and one time Coach Kais offered to carry my bag for me. When he picked it up, he noticed how heavy it was. I told him I had packed several pairs of extra shoes."

After the team checked into the hotel, Turner went straight to his room, filled up the washbasin with cans of beer, and headed to the ice machine. Once the beers were iced, he popped one open and flopped down on his bed with a cold one in his hand.

"There was a knock on the door, and it was Coach. I stuck the beer under the covers, and he sat down to talk. He stayed and stayed, and we both knew what he was doing. I finally reached under the cover, got my beer, and took a big sip."

"What are you doing?" he asked.

"I figured you weren't going to quit talking, and my beer was getting warm."

Turner faced a dilemma of his own in Kansas City in 1974. West Georgia drew the 9:30 a.m. game on opening day, and the sun was still sleeping when the team departed its hotel. Turner prided himself on not drinking in the morning, so he played without a beer.

Only a few thousand people were in the auditorium when the game began, but twenty-three pro scouts got up early to check out Foots Walker. He did not disappoint, dishing out the ball to Turner who led all scorers with 30 points. That should have shown Turner that not having a beer did not affect his play, but he never acknowledged that. As time passed, his drinking crossed the line, and former coaches and teammates began to worry about him, even considering an intervention. Contacted for this book, Turner sent a message to Roger.

"Tell him I still like my beer."

PLAYERS AND FANS were hardly settled into their hotels when Roger, after watching his team demolish third-seeded Gardner-Webb and future Atlanta Hawk John Drew, broke a cardinal rule of coaching in a conversation with his wife. "He told me I ought to call the folks back home and tell them to hurry out to Kansas City. We just might win this thing," Beverly says. "He had never done anything like that before."

By the end of the week, more than 200 excited supporters from back home had assembled. Ken Thompson, one of the team's loyal fans, had called Delta Airlines and secured as many seats as were available. People gobbled them up right away.

Mitt Conerly, a real estate man and a slow-pitch softball teammate of Roger's, says the problem in Kansas City was transportation. "Dan McBrayer, a former West Georgia basketball player, went out there in an old station wagon. Saffo White had his VW van, and the two of them ran constant shuttles carrying folks from the airport to the hotels."

Orin Whitman and Roger first met at the Carrollton Tastee Grill. Whitman soon became a close family friend. The Kaiser kids looked at him as their Georgia grandfather. Whitman promised Beverly that he would come if the team won a few games, and he lived up to his promise. He still marvels at the size of a dinner check he picked up one night in Kansas City. "I was at a table full of Carrollton folks, and I was about half drunk. I grabbed the check and handed the waiter my American Express card. When I got my bill, I couldn't believe how big it was."

Conerly was reminded of the warm relationships between local people and members of the basketball team. His five-year-old son Chuck was too small to reach the buttons on the elevator, and in the rush at their hotel, he got on one of the lifts without his dad. "We looked up and he was gone. I didn't know what to do, but we got on another elevator, and, in the lobby, there was Jerry Faulkner holding Chuck in his arms."

Not everything on the home front went well, however. Chip was pouting because he was told he had to stay home, a decision he has never let his parents forget. He had been the official team ball boy all season, and the seven-year-old could not understand why all of a sudden he had to listen to the games on radio.

Chip's sisters were not in Kansas City either. Jenny and Jill were in Savannah with the eleven-and-twelve-year-old girls' basketball team from the Carrollton Recreation Department. The girls won the state championship on the same weekend of the NAIA Finals.

Beverly and Roger had mixed emotions when they received a telegram at their hotel from Coach Dennis Phagan that said Jenny and Jill's team had won the state title. "Win the big one," Phagan wrote.

And so they did. In Kansas City, they defeated Huron 102–71, Indiana (Pa.) State 103–69, Gardner-Webb 116–101, and Kentucky State 79–75 en route to the finals against Alcorn State, a team from Mississippi that was deep with talent. With its pressing defense in high gear, West Georgia had spurts before and after halftime, and early in the second half, the outcome was evident.

Sitting in the stands, Conerly and his friend Gene Beckham sensed that on their own. Looking ahead to a postgame celebration, Conerly wondered if anyone had a knife that the team could use to cut down the nets.

"We gotta get something," he said.

Beckham, a Carrollton lawyer with a classic Southern accent, accepted the assignment. He asked people around them if they had a knife he could buy or borrow, and when they did not have one, he moved to other rows. A few minutes later, he was back in his seat with a small penknife in his hand.

"Where'd you get that?" Conerly said.

"From that fellow up there," he said, pointing to a man several rows behind them.

Conerly noticed the fellow's big smile.

"How much did you pay him?"

"A hundred dollars."

"What?"

"I didn't have any change," Beckham explained.

That blade came in handy, for the Braves did cut down the nets after disposing of Alcorn State 97–79, with Roger's starters being on the court for thirty-five of the forty minutes. It was a team effort, but that team also featured one of the tournament's most fascinating performers, as noted by *Sports Illustrated*'s Ron Reid:

> The towns they hail from are not yet on the Dairy Queen expansion list, much less the NBA's, and again they were all seeded with the clairvoyance of a Farmer's Almanac, but if the teams were overshadowed by the players in the nation's oldest and longest collegiate basketball tournament, there were some obvious reasons. One player, for instance, was 10 years older and six inches shorter than his replacement. Another was a super frosh. Overshadowing everything, however, were the feats of Foots.
>
> Foots is the nickname of Clarence Walker—Foots Walker, heh, heh—of West Georgia College, which won the 37th NAIA championship by bopping Alcorn State 97–79 in an All-Southern, All-Braves final. Walker, a six-foot-one 172-pound guard with dazzling body control, coil-spring legs and internal

radar when it comes to hitting either the bucket or the open man, surpassed his small college all-America reputation. He also delighted the six-day crowd of 72,082, the student body back in Carrollton, Ga. and the pro scouts who saw his magic.

En route to the tournament's Most Valuable Player award, which was a shoo-in, Foots scored 111 points and had 44 assists, playing virtually every minute. The title game was Walker's fifth of the week, but he scored 24 points, got 11 assists and said afterward, "I usually play all 40 minutes, so I wasn't worried about getting tired. I never come out. Right now I feel like I could go again in another one." …

Kaiser, albeit biased, thinks Walker is a cinch for the NBA. "He wouldn't have to score a point for us to be a very valuable man," he said, "and I think he's an excellent prospect. Anyone who needs a guy to get the ball to the shooters will take him in a minute." Indeed, Foots should be some helping hand.

What that team did was important to a school, a town, and a state. The Braves were the first college basketball team from Georgia to win a national title. At the helm was a man who, as a player, was the state's first basketball celebrity. Now he was a coach, and he was back on the big stage. Roger Kaiser assembled, encouraged, and directed an unusual array of personalities, and he did so without gyrations or histrionics.

"We're brothers, man," Turner says. "We played as a unit, and that's how we were able to beat teams with perhaps more physical ability. Kais allowed us a lot of personal freedoms. He treated us with a lot more respect than most coaches do. If he had been a dictator, we never would have gone to Kansas City."

Roger talked about satisfaction more than trophies or awards. "There's no question this is the most satisfying thing that has happened to me in basketball. Oh boy, I get so much more excited as a coach than I did as a player."

THE CELEBRATION BEGAN in Kansas City. It continued on the flight to Georgia and really erupted at the Atlanta airport, where 500 fans greeted the team Sunday morning. Festivities culminated in Carrollton after a police escort delivered the team to campus. This was a party like the quiet little town had never seen before. Players and coaches were the guests of honor, including Turner's toddler, who was passed from shoulder to shoulder.

West Georgia president Ward Pafford and his wife hooked up with the motorcade coming into town, and they were among the partiers. Going to the podium, Pafford proclaimed: "We're number one," after shaking every player's hand. "This is one of the greatest moments in the history of West Georgia College," he said.

Congratulatory telegrams arrived from United States senator Sam Nunn and Georgia governor Jimmy Carter, both citing past experiences on the basketball court. Roger showed the same humility he exhibited as a player. He accepted the glory but did not demand it. Mostly, he shared the attention with an assistant coach who was now part of three national championships—two at Vincennes and one at West Georgia.

"I'd resign as head coach to keep Reynolds," he said.

The Times-Georgian devoted its entire front page to the championship and included an editorial that noted that this was the most national publicity the school had ever received.

> "Those of us who have watched the college and community grow from a rural status to a leader in the state in many areas know that the college and community are important to each other. They are inseparable. The so-called town-gown gap has been something created by a small group of headline seekers in both communities, and if for no other reason, the national championship has shown that the two entities are very much a part of each other ... It is with pride that we devote our entire front page to the West Georgia Braves. Good news is the best news and we can't think of any other single event that will, in the long run, be so beneficial to our college and community."

Steve McCutcheon's body was weary, and his voice was raspy after being behind the microphone for five games in Kansas City.

McCutcheon brought Roger Kaiser to the school to do more than win championships. The national title was a bonus when compared to the bridges he built between academics and athletics and between the college and downtown Carrollton.

What happened in 1974 is still important. Roger Kaiser and West Georgia fielded one of the finest teams in the history of college basketball in Georgia and the NAIA. And in Foots Walker, they produced the state's most honored individual performer since the time of his head coach. At that moment, the small college Braves could have competed with any major college basketball program in Georgia and many in the SEC.

"I'll tell you one thing," Reynolds said. "When we played Kentucky State, there were no small college players on the floor. There were just major college players playing with small college jerseys on. When the University of Georgia played Auburn, there were a lot of small college players on the floor with major college jerseys on."

18

Making New Friends

"If you want to be rich, count your blessings!"

These were moments to savor. Though, in the excitement, no one stopped to consider that this group of people would never come together as part of such a joyous celebration again. The breakup began almost immediately.

Assistant Jerry Reynolds stayed around West Georgia College for one more year before becoming head coach at Rockhurst College, on his way to a long career in the NBA as a coach and executive with the Sacramento Kings. Four starters from that championship team—Foots Walker, Tom Turner, Jerry Faulkner, and Randy Rountree—were seniors, and were not around the following season. Walker, Turner, Faulkner, and Dave Edmonds were chosen in the NBA draft, and Foots enjoyed a ten-year career with the Cleveland Cavaliers and New Jersey Nets. Turner left behind a library of records and departed as the school's all-time leading scorer with 1,696 points. His 47 points against Berry College set an individual single-game standard.

A year later, teammates and friends sadly reunited to mourn the death of Jerry Faulkner. The star rebounder from the championship team was the victim of a tragic shooting. Roger vividly remembers the wave of helpless emotions he felt as he sat through the trial of Faulkner's killer in a Carroll County courthouse. His daughter Jenny still carries sad memories of the popular player's funeral in Munfordsville, Kentucky. The next time the team gathered was for a reunion on campus in 2004—the thirtieth anniversary of their championship run.

Internal changes were also on the horizon. The year after the national title, Doctor Ward Pafford retired as president. Doctor Maurice Townsend, a political scientist, succeeded him and served until his death in 1993. Three years after that, the school achieved university status and was renamed the University of West Georgia.

The Braves gave up their membership in the NAIA to compete solely in NCAA Division II after carrying a dual membership in 1974. When the South Atlantic Conference dissolved less than a decade later, the Braves joined the Gulf South Conference, completing the cycle of change.

Without Walker, Turner, and friends, Roger rebuilt the roster and guided the 1975 team to an 18–8 record, the semifinals of the SAC Tournament, and a berth in the NCAA Southern Regionals. He enjoyed seven more twenty-win seasons at West Georgia, but the Braves have never made it to the national finals.

COMPETING IN THE GIAC and the SAC was personally rewarding because of the intense rivalries between the schools and the deep friendships that were shared among the coaches. Road trips began with bitter competition but ended with warm conversations among close friends.

The list of colleagues was long: Doctor Marinus Kregel at Georgia Southwestern; Sonny Clements and Herbert Greene at Columbus College; James Dominey at Valdosta State; Bill Alexander at Armstrong State; Marvin Vanover at Augusta State; Al Marriotti at LaGrange College; Arthur McAfee at Morehouse College; Bill Jones at Jacksonville State; Bill Ensley at North Georgia College; Bill Jones at North Alabama; and Don Maestri at Troy.

Kregel was flamboyant, eccentric, and controversial, and he was also a dear friend. He had a Ph.D. from Indiana University, and the subject of his thesis was *The Part Versus the Whole Method in Teaching Free Throw Shooting in Basketball.* That topic said a lot about the way he treated life and basketball. "He would get mad and go to the scorer's table in the middle of a game and hit the buzzer," Roger says. "But I remember being on the golf course with him in Americus and he stopped play so Chip could meet Dan Reaves."

Beverly remembers the affection that developed between Doc Kregel and the entire Kaiser family. She was sitting behind the West Georgia bench for a game at Georgia Southwestern when she noticed Kregel get up, whisper something to his assistant, and shakily slip out of the gym.

"I was worried about him, and when I found out he had gone home, I managed to find his house. When I got there he was gravely ill. He said he wasn't going to call 911, but I insisted. It turned out he had suffered a heart attack right on the bench. Several years later, on a Sunday afternoon, we were all together at home when he called on the phone. He talked to me, to Roger, Chip, Jill, and Jenny, and he said he loved us. He died that same week."

McAfee could always make Roger laugh. He remembers when the Morehouse coach realized Chip was playing for his dad. "I thought white guys were smart," he said. "You should send your sons to me so they get a minority scholarship."

From Greene, he learned a lesson about pregame meals. "We were in Albany at a tournament, and I was concerned about getting my players together for a pregame meal. Herbert said he had quit doing that. 'I just buy them hamburgers. That's what the guys like to eat anyway.'"

CARROLLTON WAS HOME. As the coach of the local college team, Roger was the toast of the town, but his love of the community went deeper than basketball. He and Beverly enjoyed being members of Don Harp's congregation on Sundays and spending evenings with their family. Beverly began a successful career in real estate and enjoyed a weekly bridge game that has never ended. Jenny and Jill were active in school, and—like their mother—they were cheerleaders.

Chip does not remember when basketball was not part of their lives. He knew that his father had been a player, and, for as long as Chip could remember, he was a coach. He figured out he was special when he went to Alexander Memorial Coliseum and saw his dad's jersey hanging from the rafters.

"Coach Whack Hyder gave me a scholarship when I was born, and he said I could cash it in later. It hung on my wall as a kid, and it still hangs in the basement at my house," he says.

Through elementary school, Chip was a fixture on the bench at home games. To him, it was awesome to be a coach's kid. He learned good things and bad things. Most of the players were like big brothers. But there was also the time he got into a water-bottle battle on the bench with Pat Magley, a reserve on the national championship team.

"And I was the one who got banned from the bench," Chip says.

Instead of running from comparisons with his father, Chip celebrated Roger's legendary status. But for Chip, Jenny, and Jill, there were also dinners he had to miss and important events from which he was absent or late. Mostly, they cherish times they spent together. "I remember one-on-one games in our driveway, which I never won," Chip says. "I also played against Jill. But the first time I ever beat her, she quit."

When Chip began to play organized basketball, he chose number 21. He was a natural gym rat, and when someone saw him shooting around, that person would ask Chip a question he would often be asked.

"You going to be as good as your father?"

"No, way. He was one of the five best players in the country."

Chip became team captain of the Carrollton High Trojans, averaged 15.3 points a game, was twice voted offensive MVP, and was honorable mention all-state in 1986. His dad did not get to see him play as often as he would have liked. When he did, Chip was nervous but proud.

"We were on the court for a game across the county, and it was almost time for tip-off. This player on the other team who didn't know me said, 'Hey, the coach from West Georgia is here.'"

CARROLLTON PEOPLE GRABBED their hearts and never turned them loose, which was perfectly all right to a couple that puts such value on friendship. Friends came from every direction. Roger played in a regular card game that included the heads of the English Department, the Computer Center, Financial Aide, Campus Housing, and the Drama Department. He played in men's basketball leagues where he could still put on a show. He played softball in several local leagues with people like Mitt Conerly, a diehard Auburn fan who overlooked Roger's strong allegiance to Georgia Tech.

Conerly remembers their first meeting.

"I had heard we hired a guy who was supposed to be a hotshot player, and one day he walked into the gym where I was shooting around. I asked if he wanted to play a game of twenty-one, and he said, 'Why don't you shoot first?' I missed and I bounced the ball to Roger. He hit 21 in a row and asked if I wanted to play again."

He calls Roger an unflappable perfectionist.

"If you want someone to make a basket or get a big hit, you want him up. There was this softball game we were playing in Peachtree City. Roger had a sprained ankle, and he couldn't even stand up. Late in the game, the score was tied, and the other players wanted me to let Roger hit. I gave him a bat and he fell down. Later in the game, I did put him up there. Know what he did? He hit a walk-off home run, and it must have taken him five minutes to get around the bases."

When Tim Criswell was growing up in Carrollton, slow-pitch softball was a popular activity, and Roger was always in the lineup. "I watched him play all my life. I grew up chasing balls at the field. He was as good a hitter as there was," he says.

Criswell came in contact with him as a coach when he was a ninth grader playing varsity basketball at Carrollton High. "I scored a lot of points against one of our rivals one night, and I went to my left all the time. He came up to me after the game and told me that he knew I was more comfortable doing that, but that if I learned to go to my right, I could be a good ball player. I had never heard that before," he says.

He was recruited by a number of Division I programs and when he signed to play basketball at Furman University, Roger made him a promise. "You have bigger and better things going on, but if you ever want to come back home and play, there will be a spot for you," Roger told him.

Criswell returned to be a three-point shooting star on West Georgia's Gulf South co-championship team in 1986. He finished as the school's second leading scorer and set a school record by hitting 87.2 of his free throws in 1984. He was later a student coach.

One of Roger's most beloved friends never saw him play. The late Orin Whitman had already met Beverly when he dropped by the Tastee Grill for lunch. There was one vacant seat, and it was at

Roger's table. Whitman had heard people talk about the new basketball coach. Fact is he had grown tired of it. But over lunch, a deep friendship began. "He's a real good fellow," Whitman says, "and he's better than that at coaching."

Whitman bases life on a homespun philosophy that has rubbed off on Roger and Beverly. They call him the smartest man they have ever known with a seventh grade education. Roger often talks about the World War II veteran's definition of friendship: "If you were in Marietta and ran out of gas, if I did not have a way to get there, I would start walking with my gas can." He also says that you "don't know who your friend is until you ask him for his time when he is busy and his money when he does not have a lot."

He always has time for Roger, Beverly, and their children who were just "lap young'uns" when they first met. Jill would sit on one knee, and Jenny on the other. He taught them to fish but admits they did not get much fishing done. "The girls would get their hooks caught in their hair, and I would have to get it untangled."

Whitman loves bluegrass music, knows everything there is to know about the Civil War, and has never forgotten the horrible things he saw in the South Pacific during World War II. He worked hard when he was a young boy and has never shied away from work. Roger learned that soon after they met. He was headed to Dahlonega to get his sports camp ready for a summer season, and Whitman offered to go with him.

"I need somebody to work."

"I'll work," the older man said.

He outworked Roger and set up a tripod. When it was time to eat, he cooked pinto beans over an open fire. It was an experience Roger still remembers. They always enjoyed his company, and the Kaisers made sure that Whitman was in Washington, D.C., for the dedication of the World War II Memorial and that he got to visit George Washington's Masonic Lodge in Alexandria, Virginia.

"I sat in his chair and held his Bible," he says.

When he became unable to travel, Beverly and Roger dropped by his simple house in Carrollton. Technology frightens many senior citizens. Not Whitman. He was equipped with the latest model iPad and iPhone and said that if he spent as much time reading the Bible as he did on those two gadgets, he could teach Sunday school. A chance meeting at lunch turned into so much more. They came to love him and he loved the Kaisers.

They also love Don Harp. He was their pastor and friend, and he has always been there in times of need. When Harp retired from the ministry in 2008, Roger wrote him a letter that recalled their years together in Carrollton.

> *For all practical purposes you have been our minister since November 1969. You have been so many things besides all the things that a preacher is to everyone. You have been my friend and my counselor. Don, when you were my teammate in softball—what a blast! You had a problem of wanting to run over every catcher in the league. What a competitor. You also helped recruit players for our West Georgia teams. How well I remember our trip to Indiana, how foul-mouthed Jack Butcher was—by the way, he is the winningest high school coach in the state of Indiana ...*
>
> *The New Year's Eves we spent with you and Mary Ellen will forever be special times for us. What fun we had. We enjoyed the many meals out of your kitchen but for me, the shrimp will always be at the top of the list. We didn't need too much excitement on New Year's Eve. We had it most of the other days of the year ...*
>
> *I feel that listening to your sermons has made me a better person. Don, you have always been a special friend and I will have a tough time calling anyone else my PREACHER.*

Another one of his friends almost did not make it to town. Rick Camp made the fatal mistake of asking Roger how to get to Carrollton. If he had asked, people who know the coach would have warned him that this fellow whose jump shot was as accurate as radar is cursed with a horrible sense of direction.

It started with a random phone call from Camp. Everyone in the athletic office had gone home, so Roger answered. The caller identified himself and announced that he wanted to pitch for the West Georgia baseball team. He was coming to Carrollton for a game, and Coach Archie White was going to watch him throw.

Roger offered convoluted directions that got Camp to the baseball field just as the ball game was ending. White was about to leave, but he agreed to stay around and let the young man throw. An assistant coach said he would catch him. In a matter of minutes, White realized that this young man was special. West Georgia was about to sign its greatest baseball star, and Roger Kaiser was about to begin a lifelong friendship.

Camp originally left Trion, Georgia, to play quarterback at Tennessee Tech. He had a cannon for an arm, but after a year of football, he wanted to concentrate on baseball. That led him to West Georgia, where his two-year record was an impeccable 21–3. Twelve of the victories came in 1974, with five of them coming in seven days. Impressed by his workhorse attitude and strong right arm, the Atlanta Braves drafted him in the seventh round and signed him that spring.

By then Camp and Roger were fishing together and hunting birds together and the basketball coach frequently lent him his old blue pickup truck. Camp was a regular at basketball games, and when the 1974 championship team landed at the Atlanta airport, Camp was waiting on them.

"How did you do today?" Roger asked.

"We had a doubleheader, and I pitched in both of them."

Camp was with the Atlanta Braves nine years. His lifetime record was 56–49, and his best year was 1982 when he was 9–3 with a 1.78 earned run average. His most memorable moment came at 4 a.m., on the Fourth of July in 1985, in the eighteenth inning of a game against the New York Mets. The scene was set by former Braves announcer John Sterling, who was talking to the legendary Ernie Johnson: "Ernie, if he hits a home run to tie this game up, this game will be certified as absolutely the nuttiest in the history of baseball."

It was nutty all right. The club was out of pinch-hitters, so the weak-hitting Camp was forced to hit for himself. He slammed it out of the park to tie the game and earned a mention in the Braves' history book. Few people remember that in the nineteenth inning, Camp fell apart and let the Mets go ahead. He struck out to end the marathon.

The family had gathered to celebrate Independence Day and that night Beverly could not sleep. She got up in the wee hours and turned on the TV. She was shocked to see the Braves were still playing and even more shocked to see Rick Camp coming up to bat. "When he hit that home run, I screamed so much that I woke up the whole house," she says.

Roger and Beverly were often his guests in spring training. At the peak of his success, Camp donated two athletic scholarships to West Georgia and got owner Ted Turner to match them. The Braves released him in 1986, and Camp became a registered lobbyist and frequently visited Carrollton when he was calling on Speaker of the House Tom Murphy in Bremen.

Beset by personal and financial problems, Camp and three other people were convicted in 2005 of conspiring to steal more than $2 million from a community health center in Augusta. He served three years in a minimum-security lockup at Maxwell Air Force Base in Montgomery, Alabama. "We visited him several times and continued to love him through the hard times," Roger says.

By 2013 his health was failing rapidly. He was fifty-nine years old but looked older. Despite his setbacks, he was still loudly cheered when he appeared at old-timers games in Atlanta. His friendship with Roger ended just as it began: on the telephone.

"We talked about how he was feeling, and then he told me he would call me tomorrow, that his cell phone was running down. The next day, I got a call from a police officer in Rydal, Georgia, that said they were trying to locate the family of Rick Camp. I told him I had talked to him the night before. He knew that already and said I was the last call on his cell phone."

THE SMALL-TOWN atmosphere first attracted them, but as time passed, the people of Carrollton made Roger and Beverly stay. Their children were born in other places, but Carrollton was home. If Roger did not know that before, he understood that in 1977, when he came home from an unpublished trip to Indiana with an offer to become head basketball coach at the University of Evansville—an offer he will never forget.

The selling points were many. He would be in Indiana. He and Beverly would be near family and old friends, and the salary would be double what he was making at Division II West Georgia. He liked what he heard at the school and was sorely tempted until he heard from his kids.

Jenny was sixteen. Jill was fifteen. Chip was ten. Carrollton was all they knew and all they remembered. He spelled out what was being offered and waited for their reaction. "They didn't say much," Roger said. "Mostly they cried. They were upset at the possibility of leaving. It made me realize that I had come to love the town as they had. We decided there were a lot of intangible things there that were important and meaningful to all of us."

A close friend from Indiana was a vice president at the University of Evansville. It was difficult to turn him down, but family came first. Six months later, a DC-3 carrying the Purple Aces basketball team crashed on takeoff on its way to a game in Tennessee. Twenty-nine lives were lost, including players, coaches, support personnel, and the three-person crew. One player had stayed home, and, in a peculiar twist of fate, a drunk driver killed him two weeks after the crash.

"The first feeling I had when I heard about the plane crash was that sick feeling in my throat, in my stomach. I wondered who was on the plane that I knew. I never thought that it could have been me. That never crossed my mind," Roger told a reporter in 1977.

Days after the crash, Roger and his team went to a holiday tournament in Owensboro, Kentucky, only forty miles from Evansville. News of the tragedy was everywhere. Even Roger's players were affected. No one complained about aching muscles or long workouts. No one knew the players who went down in that plane, but in their own way, they mourned their deaths.

It could have been Roger. But years later he still refuses to think that way. He does realize he was fortunate and blessed. "I've always been lucky," he says. "At least that's what people have always said."

19

Football Meets Cancer

"It is what you learn after you know it all that counts."

Blame it on Erk—a drainage ditch that assumed mythical powers—and a bellicose college president who refused to listen to his faculty and student body and resuscitated a Georgia Southern football program that had been left for dead forty years before the administrator arrived.

The president's name was Dale Lick. He came to Statesboro in 1976. Within two years, he drummed up support for a football team that nobody seemed to want but him. He surprised the football world by hiring Erk Russell, an assistant coach at the University of Georgia with a head as hard and bare as Stone Mountain. He was the architect of Vince Dooley's Junkyard Dog defense and the darling of sportswriters all over the state. It was Russell who convinced his players there was magic in the waters of a gnat-infested stream he called Eagles Creek.

What is magic is the story of a football program that school officials call the front-porch of the university. They believe that once people sit a spell on the porch and look inside and see what they offer, they will send their kids there. Since 1982, the era of Lick and Russell, football at Georgia Southern has grown into a Division I program, and enrollment has more than tripled.

Other schools in Georgia followed what was happening in Statesboro, and even before Russell inspired Georgia Southern to its first of six national championships, sister institutions were looking into football. Today, following their lead, football is played at Berry College, Mercer University, Reinhardt College, Shorter College,

LaGrange College, Georgia State University, Kennesaw University, Point University, and Valdosta State University.

West Georgia College was one of the first, and the success of Roger Kaiser's basketball team helped fuel that fire. Supporters of football figured that if a sport like basketball could boost enrollment, invigorate alumni, and excite the town, imagine what football could do.

President Maurice Townsend had reservations. He had never been a fan of athletics. He liked to tell people that he graduated from the University of Chicago, where they abolished their football program. Since his inauguration in 1975, Townsend had tolerated the West Georgia athletic program more than he had supported it.

Everyone knew that Roger was a basketball man through and through. But more than his love of the round ball, he feared the cost of starting a football program and wondered if there was a fan base for the college game outside of Georgia, Georgia Tech, Auburn, and other established Division I programs.

In a town like Carrollton, which loved its high school team, and a state like Georgia, which treated football with religious reverence, the idea of restarting football was not a hard sell. As athletic director, Roger found himself in the middle of a conversation that he did not instigate, one that began in town and spread to the campus.

Bruce Lyon, the vice president of student affairs, was a member of a committee formed by Townsend to gauge the demand for football. He said that from the beginning Roger tried to maintain an objective view. "He was a basketball guy, and he wanted to protect the basketball program, but he was also a realist. He knew football was coming, that it was almost inevitable."

WEST GEORGIA WAS restoring an old tradition. As a junior college, it competed against other two-year schools in the area. When it became a four-year college in 1957, football was considered a vital part of the athletic program, though the won-loss record hardly reflected that. After going 0–8 and 0–6 in successive seasons, the administration elected to get out of the football business. Twenty-three years later, those memories had faded, and the slate was clean.

Students voted in favor of a student activity fee to help fund a team, though some people privately doubted the veracity of the poll. Discussions grew more serious. But the path they followed was different than the one taken in Statesboro. Lyon said the committee believed a non-scholarship program was the most appropriate way to go.

Roger began to build a foundation for a Division III football program. He called Ed Murphy, the basketball coach at West Alabama. His school had recently added football, so he figured Murphy could tell him what to expect. Murphy's colorful response did not make Roger sleep any better, though. "He said starting a football team was like digging a big hole and pouring your money into it."

Neither of them imagined that within ten years, Murphy would be the head coach and athletic director at West Georgia, trying to balance the support between basketball and football.

Roger's first order of business was finding a head football coach. He wanted one in place early in the process so that person could be involved in every decision. When he began that search, Roger's phone was constantly busy, and many were from pranksters.

"I even heard from someone claiming to be Woody Hayes saying he would be interested in the job." So naturally, Roger was skeptical when he was told Vince Dooley was on the line. "I picked up the phone ready to have a laugh, but it was really Vince calling to recommend Danny Cronic, one of his former players. We hired him as an assistant coach, and today he's head coach at Reinhardt College."

Roger selected Bobby Pate, an assistant coach at Western Carolina University. He previously had a 72–13–2 record in eight years as a head coach at three Georgia high schools. Pate played under former Florida State University coach Bobby Bowden at South Georgia Junior College and was a star halfback at Presbyterian College

West Georgia's first team in twenty-three years took the field in 1981 and shocked even their most fervent fans by going 9–1. Their only setback was a 10–3 decision to Widener College, which went on to win the national title. This was football in its purest state. No scholarships were offered. No network TV contracts were on the table. Players strapped on helmets because they loved the game, not because they dreamed of playing on Sundays. For one shining moment, West

Georgia sampled a brand of magic that major college football had long since forgotten.

Sports Illustrated previewed Pate's second season this way:

> It didn't take long for mania to build in Carrollton, Ga. (pop. 14,078). The prefab program at West Georgia College, which was undefeated in its inaugural Division III regular season—the first for the school since it dropped the sport in 1958—has all 22 starters back. The Braves started from scratch in '81. After students voted to allow the program to be funded by activity fees, tryouts were scheduled, 300 players showed up, and Coach Bobby Pate said "O.K. you made it" to 115 of them. Uniforms were ordered, home games were played at the local high school stadium and a nearby McDonald's catered press-box meals. Quarterback David Archer, who transferred from Georgia where he was a defensive back, completed 54 of 129 passes for 958 yards and nine TDs and rushed for eight more and will lead the Braves again.

That 1982 campaign was one Pate and Roger would never forget, though their reasons for remembering are vastly different. For the football coach, it was a season that brought victories, and honors, For the athletic director, it was a frightening time, during which Roger faced a diagnosis of cancer for the very first time.

Pate romped through another unbeaten regular season. In December, the NCAA championship bracket called for a second meeting with Widener College, a longtime Division III powerhouse.

"I'll never forget when our buses arrived at Grisham Stadium the morning of the game," says Pate, retired from coaching and living at Lake Hartwell. "The stadium was packed, and it was two hours until kickoff. That was a special time."

Even the press box was full. It was the annual off-week between the Georgia Tech and Georgia game, so Atlanta sports editors Furman Bisher and Jesse Outlar applied for press credentials. Outlar would one day include that game among his favorite events in a forty-one-year career at the *Atlanta Constitution*.

Four quarters of sparring and the teams were tied. The first overtime was scoreless, though fans almost stopped breathing until Widener missed a twenty-four-yard field goal. The Pioneers from Chester, Pennsylvania, took the lead in the second overtime period, but the Braves pulled even when David Archer threw a twelve-yard scoring pass to Rusty Whaley on fourth down. In the third extra stanza, Harold Long scored on a five-yard run to give West Georgia a 31–24 lead. Four Widener passes fell incomplete, and fans poured out of their seats and covered the field with humanity.

Two weeks later, West Georgia went to Phenix City, Alabama, for the Amos Alonzo Stagg Bowl with the NCAA Division III championship on the line. The Braves defeated Augustana 14–0, just two years after the school's return to college football. They defeated a team that would win four straight national titles between 1983 and 1986.

The school's athletic director was unable to attend either playoff game. Roger was in Tanner Memorial Hospital recovering from colon cancer surgery. His concerns had begun with a call from Doctor John Ware. Physicians seldom call patients with good news, so Roger sensed something was wrong. Beverly was at a real estate closing, so the coach went to the doctor's office alone.

"Roger, you've got cancer," Ware said with little fanfare.

"You're kidding me."

"I wouldn't kid you about something so serious."

Roger was stunned. He felt perfectly healthy. How could he have cancer? He asked his doctor if he would mind if he got a second opinion. He said, "Of course not," and Roger, feeling numb, headed home to meet Beverly.

"When I walked into the house, Roger was lying on the sofa and staring at the ceiling. I knew something was wrong because he had had some tests run earlier, and I had gotten the word the day before. I just couldn't bear to tell him," Beverly says.

Before they told their children about the cancer diagnosis, they set out for Emory University in Atlanta for a second opinion. As they made the familiar trip, Roger kept thinking how he was an athlete—and athletes do not get sick. But the specialists at Emory agreed with Ware. They referred him to Doctor Tom Reeve, a Carrollton surgeon.

This was in November. That evening his basketball team had a major scrimmage. He put his assistant coach in charge, not knowing if the change would be temporary or permanent.

"I was scared to death, and I'm a guy who has never been afraid of anything. I don't think I was afraid I was going to die, but the thought that I might just scared the heck out of me," he says.

The surgeon offered reassuring words. Reeve said they had caught it early before it had spread and that cancer of the colon was a common but serious disease. He believed he could get it all.

Reeve was right. For the next eighteen years, Roger was cancer free, though he was left with only nine inches of his colon and a noticeable scar. He missed fourteen games that season and was back on the court in January 1983.

"That experience made me slow down and take a long look at things. I had a lot of time to think, especially when I was in the hospital. We tend to take for granted how nice we have it. Lying in that hospital room, I appreciated my family, my friends, and my doctors. Thank God for the early detection," he says.

On the day of the rematch with Widener, Mitt Conerly stayed with his friend at the hospital so Beverly could go to the football game at Grisham Stadium. But she did not risk leaving her husband for the ninety-five-minute trip to the championship game in Alabama. They watched it on television at home.

The celebration that followed the NCAA football championship in 1982 rivaled the one for the NAIA basketball championship in 1974. But in the afterglow of being on top, overzealous supporters pushed through a decision that did not seem prudent to Roger or Bruce Lyon.

"Football was big in the community. People were thinking we would soon be at the Ohio State level. On the practical side, the school was too large for Division III. We also knew that with our early success, we would find it difficult to find Division III schools that would play us and that we would have to travel great distances to find games. That propelled us into Division II," Lyon says.

Pate went back to high school coaching in 1985, just three years after creating a college team that performed on national television. He returned to Hart County, the school where he started his coaching career in 1961. In an interview with Carrollton newspaper columnist Joe Garrett in 2014, Pate described the spirit that was lost when the Braves began to play for pay:

"The following Monday after we won the national title game, I was coming back from lunch and looked out on the practice field, and our players were out there playing a touch football game. I just smiled because that's the way our players were. They couldn't get enough. Since we were Division III, none of them had a scholarship. They just loved the game of football."

20

Weathering an Unexpected Storm

"Anger is only one letter away from danger."

Roger Kaiser survived cancer. But he would not survive the feelings that surfaced in his final years on a campus that he served so well and a community that he loved so deeply.

There had always been reasons to cheer his basketball teams, but behind the scenes, envy sometimes festered. Those opinions began right after he arrived as some campus officials questioned the fact that unlike his predecessors or his colleagues, Roger never had to teach. And those feelings never really went away.

Charlie Grisham warned him not to win so quickly, but he did. And from the moment he moved to town, Roger was a Carroll County icon. As a person, he was shy and reserved, but his reputation as an all-American basketball player and his string of winning seasons caused some people to put him on pedestals he never intended to climb. He was a superstar, and people who could not pick the president of the college out of a police lineup recognized the name and face of Roger Kaiser. His celebrity status did not set well with some academicians.

He also made mistakes—out of naivety more than anything else. Early in his tenure, Roger was a partner in a small mobile home park on the edge of town that rented house trailers to West Georgia students and athletes. In the eyes of his critics, this was a conflict of interest. Steve McCutcheon fielded those complaints and determined that operating the trailer park did not violate NAIA rules or policies.

"When people came to me, my question to them was: what is he doing wrong? He's charging them rent? What is wrong with that? They're living off campus. When I talked with Roger, I told him that what he did was not illegal but that it probably wasn't the smartest thing for him to do, even though all he was trying to do was provide for his family," McCutcheon says.

Between 1972 and 1981, Roger was the most successful college basketball coach in the state, winning 213 games and losing just 75. During that impressive span, the Braves made three appearances in NCAA regional play. They went 15–11 in 1982, and then bounced back with four twenty-win seasons over the next five years.

The 1987 squad was 26–5, won the Gulf South Conference title for the second straight year, and made it to the finals of the NCAA South Regionals in Lakeland, where they fell to home-standing Florida Southern. It was the school's best finish since joining Division II. The late Anthony Barge averaged 28.7 points a game to set a new season record, and his 23.8 points a game established a new career standard. And for the venerable head coach, there was a bonus on the bench wearing number 21.

CHIP KAISER WANTED to play basketball for his dad. He was a deadly outside shooter, just like his father. He could have played somewhere else, but that would not have been the same, for he had grown up around that team and that court. When he graduated from high school, he announced he was going to West Georgia College. "Bobby Cremins would have let me sit at the end of his bench, but I knew I wasn't good enough to play at Georgia Tech," he says.

Roger understood that coaching his son would be challenging. "I told Chip that I wished he was really great or really bad. That would have made it easier, but he was neither one. But I would take nothing for the years we spent together as player and coach."

During Chip's sophomore year, whispers circulated around campus that problems were brewing in the basketball program. At the core of the allegations was financial assistance that Roger helped secure for a former player to pay off a student loan. The administration reported the allegations to the Gulf South Conference, and quietly began its own inquiry. The outside investigation reported no findings and did not issue sanctions.

Despite those findings the administration determined that Roger would continue as head coach but not as athletic director. People in town tried to intercede. They found there was nothing they could do but console their old friends. Roger and Beverly remember neighbors and allies unexpectedly dropping by their house just to offer their support. These caring gestures reminded them why they loved that community.

In the middle of this furor was Chip Kaiser, who wondered if his presence on his father's basketball team was keeping the coach from making decisions he might want to make. "I sometimes wondered if my dad was staying at West Georgia because I was there."

Roger intended to weather the storm, though some mornings it was difficult to go to work. Those feelings have mellowed today. He was the person in charge and he accepts total responsibility for what transpired. "I helped a player get a loan, and I wasn't supposed to do that," he says.

Roger has moved on in every way. Despite what happened, he is not bitter at the institution. "People make up West Georgia, not the buildings. That is why I love West Georgia. During that difficult time, so many people on campus and in the community reached out to Beverly and me and reminded us that they loved us. That meant so much then and still does. Friendships are much more important than any title," he says.

Until then, a 13–13 record in 1979 was his worst season as a college coach. He plunged to 4–22 in 1989 and only rebounded to 11–17 the next year, though that group of players flirted with the conference lead early in the year.

Despite the disappointments, he was not really shopping for another job in 1990. Carrollton had become home, and he would have been happy to stay right there. That attitude began to change after he was introduced to a flamboyant figure that was best known as a star of late night television.

And meeting Sid Williams would be a blessing in disguise.

21

The Unforgettable Doctor Sid

"Take a minute to find a special friend—an hour to fully appreciate them—a day to love them—and an entire lifetime to forget them."

People called him Doctor Sid, and Sidney Earl Williams was a force of nature that steam-rolled through life without fearing what was at the end of the dark tunnels that constantly got in his way. He was the visionary founder and president of Life College, a school of chiropractic science near Atlanta. With the swept-back hair, overpowering eyebrows, and sunken cheeks of a Cherokee Indian chief, he became its public face and voice, appearing in a series of television spots that made him a cult hero among late-night viewers of Ted Turner's Superstation.

Those unforgettable commercials on Channel 17 were about all that Roger Kaiser knew about Doctor Sid when he got back to Carrollton after a visit to Indiana in the summer of 1999 and found a lengthy message on his answering machine from Joe Kelly, a man he had never met. The message said that the president of Life College wanted Roger to come to Marietta for an important meeting.

Kelly called several more times, and Roger always avoided making a commitment. He did not know Kelly, and he did not know his boss. When the fifty-one-year-old coach finally gave in and made an appointment to visit Life College, he was left waiting in a room outside the president's office. When Doctor Sid finally opened the door, he discovered that Roger had given up and was on his way back to Carroll County.

Doc was intrigued. Not many people in his world would walk out on him, but Roger did. That made the power-driven administrator more eager than ever to know about this small-town boy, whose college basketball jersey hung high above Doctor Sid's front-row seats at Alexander Memorial Coliseum. Roger was also curious. The more he learned about the unconventional college president, the more he wanted to know why this former Georgia Tech football player was so interested in him.

One thing they had in common was Georgia Tech. His time on North Avenue was important to Doctor Sid, who wore a 1952 Orange Bowl ring on his right hand and his Tech Athletic Hall of Fame ring on the left. As a child, he had gone to Grant Field with his parents who had season tickets in the West Stands near the fifty-yard line. When he was a teenager, he donned his Boy Scout uniform and served as an usher at Rambling Wreck home games.

Doctor Sid was born in Rome, Georgia, but he grew up as an only child in Oakland City, a comfortable neighborhood on Atlanta's west side that was a short trolley ride from downtown. He was an Eagle Scout and an overachiever who excelled at everything he tried. He attended Tech High School, where, against his doting mother's wishes, he joined the football team.

He graduated second in the class of 1946 with a sparkling collection of superlatives ranging from ROTC to track. He was even voted the most handsome boy in school. Williams had scholarship offers from around twenty schools, including Army and Navy, but remembering his childhood, he chose Georgia Tech, which by then was coached by Bobby Dodd.

Southwest Atlanta was a melting pot for athletes, and many of them went to Tech. In addition to Doctor Sid, it produced Franklin "Pepper" Rodgers, Johnny Hunsinger, Cecil Trainer, Charlie Brannon, Norman "Pig" Campbell, Ed "Bulldog" Carrithers, Stan Cochran and Rausey Mason. Years down the road Kim King — a left-handed quarterback who became a fixture in the radio booth — followed them to North Avenue.

Starting far down the depth chart, the undersized end with the do-or-die style caught Dodd's eye. He was elevated to the varsity the week of the first game in 1949, played in every game that year, and for the next two seasons, was a starter at defensive end despite his 167-

pound frame. Teasing teammates called him "The Dead Man" after a Tech lineman looked down on him on the turf after a reckless tackle in a game with Vanderbilt and proclaimed, "That man's dead."

Williams ignored his injuries, even a jolting hit in the 1951 Florida game that severely injured his back. He played through the pain until X-rays later revealed hairline fractures in three vertebrae in the mid-thoracic region. Doctors advised Dodd that he could play because the fractures had already healed, but he would be in pain.

"If you'd keep on playing, Sid, that would please me real good," Dodd said.

"That's the way he talked," Williams said. "It was painful for me to walk or run, but I continued to play football. Like most of the players, I would have walked through fire for him."

The 1951 Yellow Jackets finished 11–0–1, and is considered one of Dodd's greatest teams. Dodd reserved special praise for Sid Williams: "For his size, he is the best end in America. Sid is very clever, can move well, and hits as hard as any defensive end I have ever seen. There is something else about Sid and his preparation for the games; he is UP for everybody. There is no way to overestimate his defensive value to our team."

HIS FOOTBALL CAREER was over, but Doctor Sid's pain did not go away, especially the chronic headaches. His childhood friend Durie D. Humber's brother was a chiropractor in West End. He went to see Doctor T.O. Humber, who performed a series of spinal adjustments that put him on the road to recovery. Doctor Sid was so inspired by the treatments that he and his new bride, the former Nell Kimbrough, honeymooned in Davenport, Iowa. While there, they enrolled at the Palmer Chiropractic College.

Four years later, diplomas in hand, they moved back to Georgia and opened a chiropractic practice in suburban Austell. Within a few years, they had successfully set up thirty-three clinics around Atlanta that served more than 1,500 patients, many in low-income areas.

Doctor Sid emerged as a controversial leader in the teaching of chiropractic science, and in 1974, he founded Life College in Marietta. Twenty-two students attended those early classes in modular buildings near Dobbins Air Force Base whose walls were so thin they could hear workers typing in the offices next door. By 1990, more than 4,500 students were enrolled, making it the largest chiropractic school in the world.

Doctor Sid first got involved with Ted Turner in 1986 when he was a primary backer of the Goodwill Games in Russia. In return, Turner added chiropractors to the medical staff in St. Petersburg. Life College became a regular advertiser on the Superstation. These unusual spots made Doctor Sid a late-night celebrity. They ended with him peering into the camera and imploring viewers to call Life College today. *"We can provide you—YOU!—each of you, a high quality education that will be the foundation of your success."*

The colorful Doctor Sid became such a regular in the Turner Broadcasting community that several times, he participated in the Turner Trumpet Awards telecast as a presenter, introducing luminaries such as Ray Charles and Tyra Banks. Left unsaid was the fact that Doctor Sid and Life University were major sponsors of the award show.

He was a relentless promoter—of himself, his profession, and his school. New ideas constantly danced around in his head. People who had not been around him long would hear Doctor Sid talking about a grandiose idea and never realize that constant chatter was his way of planning something big.

This way of thinking began when he and Doctor Nell were students at Palmer College. He sold cookware and his wife worked in a restaurant to pay their way through school. Things were not going well for him until he had what he called "a mystical experience" while selling Wear Ever cooking utensils. During a presentation, an intense feeling of love for the cookware came over him. There was no thought, just feeling. This oneness with the cookware was an epiphany that spread to his study of chiropractic.

Such unorthodox descriptions of Doctor Sid created a bizarre image that outsiders never understood, but his allies believed he enjoyed being mysterious. A Life University historian called him "a mystic that got messages from the other side"—an assessment he never disputed.

"I had an experience with the idea of chiropractic and I understood it for the first time after I'd been there for two years. I was elated … this was a total, revolutionary new idea that was bigger than religion, law or medicine. That was when I fell in love with chiropractic. I loved it as intimately as anything I ever did. Now I've got my wife, my family, my friends, chiropractic. Everything that I do is in that love capsule."

Doctor Sid came to rely on such moments.

"Every benchmark that I do I don't think of it with my conscious mind. It is revealed to me from within."

Including basketball.

"He didn't want just a basketball team. He wanted a championship team," says D.D. Humber, who grew up with Doctor Sid in Oakland City and never left his side. "If he was going to do something, second place was never a consideration."

Humber remembers him mentioning basketball, but he assumed he was referring to an intramural program. Instead, Doctor Sid wanted a team like colleges around him were putting on the court, and he was willing to do whatever it took to accomplish that dream. He envisioned Life College being to chiropractic what Notre Dame is to Catholicism, and he believed a basketball team could help him reach that goal.

No one questioned him. No one ever did.

"If anyone had tried to talk him out of it, he wouldn't have listened," Humber says. Once those plans came together in his mind, he was not going to let anything get in his way—not even the lack of a place to play.

ROGER KAISER WAS not in the market for another job. What he wanted was an administration that would stand behind him. In Sid Williams, he found the college administrator every coach dreams of finding, though, at first Roger was not sure what to believe about the dynamo that was Doctor Sid.

He left Roger cooling his heels the first time they had an appointment and he did the same thing when the coach came back for a second visit. Both times, Roger gave up and left.

Kelly begged Roger to give Williams another chance and they finally met for dinner at the Georgian Club near the Cobb Galleria. They did not talk about basketball; they talked about life with a small "L."

Doctor Sid spent the evening practicing the skills he had learned selling pots and pans, confident he could sell Roger on coaching a basketball team that did not exist. Roger, meanwhile, tried to size up the audacious Doctor Sid, wondering if he would truly give a basketball program the support it deserved.

Talk was more serious when they met again. Roger finally heard the words he needed to hear when Doctor Sid promised total support—financially and emotionally. "I'm one hundred percent in a lot of things," Doc said. "I am not going to have a basketball team if I don't intend to support it."

Roger found him serious about his basketball coach being a Tech man. Doc did not realize how few Yellow Jackets were in the profession, so he went to Whack Hyder for advice. He invited the retired coach to go to the national tournament to ask others who might be available. Out of the clear blue sky, he recommended Roger Kaiser.

Doctor Sid had found his Tech man. As a bonus, that prospective coach also had a proven resume. "You can talk to people that don't have a lot left, but Coach Kaiser has a lot left. He has a vision," he said.

Doctor Sid wanted Roger, and what Doctor Sid wanted he usually got. There were many questions left unanswered, though. Roger kept asking and Doctor Sid kept answering. Finally, he invited Roger to join him on a stroll around the campus.

"Where's the gymnasium?" Roger asked.

"It's going over there," Doc said, pointing at the site of an old restaurant.

"What will the players study?"

"We'll start an undergraduate program."

"How many scholarships will we have?"

"How many do you need?"

The most probing question came from Doctor Sid. He could see these astonishing things in his mind, and he wondered why Roger could not see them. His primary vision had to do with wanting his team to be not only a winner but a champion.

"Can you win a national championship?"

"I don't know."

"Well, you don't act excited."

"Let me tell you something. I'll act excited when we're playing for one."

Recent experiences weighed heavily on a veteran coach who should have been proud and confident. And though Sid Williams was saying everything he wanted to hear, Roger searched for faith that the fast-talking huckster would deliver. Carrollton was familiar and comfortable. Life College did not even have a team or a place to play.

What Doctor Sid offered Roger was a license to dream. Roger could build a basketball program in his own image just like Doctor Sid had built Life College in his. He would be working for a college president who virtually owned the place and one who wanted to win as badly as he did. It was a match made in basketball heaven, and Roger began to yield to the charisma and vision of an individual who recruited him like he was a high school basketball star looking for a place to play.

Late that summer, Roger Kaiser told Doctor Sid that he had himself a basketball coach. There were several loose ends to sew up, though, and Roger thought his decision would be kept under wraps until those things were finalized. Their meetings had been amazingly private, so no one in Carrollton or at West Georgia knew that their basketball coach of nearly twenty years was even being courted.

Doctor Sid could not keep such exciting news locked inside. Before Roger formally contacted the administration at West Georgia, the Life College president—in one of his weekly campus assemblies—joyfully announced to his staff, faculty, and students that the school would soon have a basketball team and that Roger Kaiser would be the coach.

Hearing the announcement had been made Roger hurried down Interstate 20 to resign as head basketball coach at West Georgia College. He turned in a formal letter of resignation, and then visited the appropriate people on campus and in town to deliver the news face-to-face. He was excited but soon discovered that leaving friends and memories would not be entirely painless. He departed with a record of 381–186 and a cabinet full of trophies, but as he prepared to go, there was so much more to remember.

He remembered the humor and savvy of Jerry Reynolds and the national championship the colorful assistant helped deliver. He remembered Corky Umstead and Lamar Frady being Academic All-Americans. He remembered Stanley Brewer and Dave Edmonds returning to campus to earn their degrees. He remembered Foots Walker becoming a star in the NBA and Tom Turner becoming a lawman in his hometown. He remembered Ken Ross, who never played that much, becoming a high school coach. He remembered Tim Criswell cheering for his hometown Braves as a kid and coming home to be second on the school's all-time scoring list. He remembered how high Jerry Faulkner could leap and how he died. He remembered Daron Richardson's hard work and the inside and outside player that he was. He remembered the firepower of the late Anthony Barge. He remembered the pride that he felt coaching his son and former ball boy Chip Kaiser.

Good times outweighed the bad in the hearts of most people Roger and Beverly left behind. Friends knew how much the Kaiser family had invested in that community, and they appreciated them. They were also excited that Roger was being presented a blank canvas on which he could create a college basketball program in the same city where he was an all-American guard.

Steve McCutcheon, now an investment counselor in Carrollton, says most people never deserted Roger despite the controversy that developed late in his tenure. "He and Beverly fit in so well. They were loved and they are still loved. When people talk about the halcyon days of West Georgia College, they talk with affection for both of them. What they did for the school cannot be measured."

Retired administrator Bruce Lyon says Roger was a friend to many people. "He was an extraordinary basketball coach, and I believe that was always his priority. It is difficult to be a coach and an administrator at the same time. He felt that pressure. And when football came, it intensified. A lot of us hated to see him leave. He's a good man."

Roger and Beverly were excited about the prospect of starting over. At the same time, they were gratified at the way people of Carrollton responded to the news that they were leaving the community.

Roger felt their affection in many ways — such as the day he returned his courtesy car to Dwight Ezell, the owner of Bremen Ford. The car dealer could not understand why Roger was turning in his keys. Jimmy Bone, a local lawyer, helped make that deal for him after Roger was deposed as athletic director. In the years that followed that arrangement Roger and Ezell became friends and the small town car dealer reminded the basketball coach that he was providing the car to him, not the school.

"But I won't be here anymore. I'll be in Marietta," Roger explained.

"That doesn't matter to me. Sell some cars for me over there."

Before long, Life College would be buying cars from Bremen Ford.

A busy year was ahead. Without a team to coach, Roger spent the next twelve months hiring assistant coaches and searching for ball players. One of the assistants he brought on board was Chip Kaiser. His son joined John Barrett and Bill Firnback on that inaugural staff.

Doctor Sid was also hard at work, organizing the school's first undergraduate program in business administration and pushing for completion of an attractive 2,500-seat arena that came to be known as the Eagle's Nest. He also kept recruiting Roger Kaiser.

"He thought everyone should be a chiropractor," Roger says. "I told him I was too old, but he did convince my daughter Jenny to enroll at Life. And he always wanted to recruit my son Chip. Doc really just wanted to see people become better people. And for him, the way to do that was to become a chiropractor."

22

Life Becomes an Adventure

"Life is a not a race—do take it slower; hear the music before the song is over."

Roger Kaiser lived the whole story. But people who could not see what had gone on behind the curtains wondered why a basketball coach would leave an established program at a state school and take a job at an unknown college that did not have a team or a gymnasium and whose unconventional president was a chiropractor best known for his bombastic television commercials.

His colleagues in coaching had other questions, and so did his close friends who earnestly believed that Roger would eventually end up at a Division I school, not a college that turned out graduates who made their living manipulating the spine. Sportswriters joined that chorus, talking the same brand of smack that opposing teams would use. They ignored the fact that he would have a chance to create a program from scratch and recruit athletes who would see Life College as an opportunity to make amends for past transgressions and a chance to make a future.

I was one of those typewriter skeptics. I had known about Roger since I was a teenager in Atlanta. He played in the first college basketball game I saw in person and one season later, I watched on television as the Yellow Jackets ventured into NCAA tournament play for the very first time.

When I became assistant sports information director at Georgia Tech, I was assigned to the basketball team, and I watched every game the fellows Roger had coached as freshmen played on the varsity.

Later, after a short stint with the Atlanta Hawks, I joined the *Atlanta Constitution* where I covered college basketball.

Watching every level of the game, I concluded that the quality of play among smaller colleges in the state was often stronger than the teams on display in the larger arenas and that games between LaGrange College and West Georgia could be more interesting and entertaining than ones between Georgia and Georgia Tech. That assignment took me to Kansas City for the 1972 NAIA Tournament where Roger's Braves fell to Kentucky State, the eventual national champions. Along the way I became friends with Roger and Beverly, though I saw them infrequently after I left Atlanta to become sports editor of the *Enquirer*, the morning newspaper in Columbus, Georgia.

I left sports for the news department in Columbus before returning to what people laughingly referred to as the Toy Shop. In August 1990, I was executive sports editor of the *Ledger-Enquirer*. Four days a week, I wrote a six hundred word column about people and events that interested me. That led to a whimsical piece about Roger Kaiser leaving West Georgia for Life College.

The headline said it all: *"Has Kaiser Slipped a Disc?"* You did not have to read the entire column to understand that I could not believe my old friend was making this move. Here is what I said that morning:

> You might say Roger Kaiser is in for some spine-tingling basketball.
>
> You might say it and many will, for the longtime West Georgia College coach has accepted a new job at Life College, a school that specializes in turning out chiropractors.
>
> It will be an adjustment for Kaiser, the former Georgia Tech all-American and the only basketball coach in the state to ever have a team win a national championship.
>
> Dr. Sid Williams, the chief chiropractor and founder of the 16-year-old school located in Marietta, Ga., made the announcement Tuesday. A former Tech football player himself, Dr. Sid founded the school in 1974 and since then has turned loose 4,500 chiropractors on an unsuspecting world.

Sorry, Roger. It's just hard for me to take seriously a place that teaches students to manipulate a spine so that he can cure everything from psoriasis to piles.

Well, maybe cure isn't exactly the right word. But if you will come in for an adjustment once a week for the next 17 or 18 years they might keep your problem under control. Oh, and do you have insurance?

My first thought was that Kaiser would have trouble finding guys six-foot-seven or six-foot-eight who could play whose lifelong dream has been to help mankind by being a chiropractor.

"That was the first question I asked," Kaiser said. "But they're adding a new field of study."

Not that Life isn't accredited. It has the seal of approval of the Council on Chiropractic Education and the Southern Association of Colleges and Schools. That sure impresses me. What about you?

Kaiser has been at West Georgia 20 years. He's a big boy. But I hope he knows what he's getting into.

He'll be starting an athletic program from the first vertebra on. He'll hear snickers from his colleagues who will try to hold back their laughs when they're recruiting against him. He'll have parents ask him what a chiropractic degree will mean for their tall little darlin'. He'll hear the taunts of frolicking fans on the road.

For openers, what will their nickname be? The Bone Crushers?

What will their mascot be? A dancing spine?

Will they need a trainer, or will Dr. Sid just give them an adjustment and tell them that knee injury will be all right?

What will the school song be? "Touch Me, Heal Me?"

It's a lot like when Oral Roberts got a message from above to open a university and to start a basketball program that would compete in Division I and let his son Richard sing the National Anthem.

Fortunately, The Man Upstairs never told Oral that he would bring him home if the school got on probation for ORU was known to break the NCAA commandments.

Dr. Sid has similar ideas.

"Our vision is to become a university," he said. He also wants a bona-fide athletic program. Or is that *bone-afide*?

To Kaiser's credit, he played it straight — as straight as his spine. The questioner fished but he never took the bait.

He talked about Life's new field house. About how they could play a schedule within two or three hours drive. And about Dr. Sid's ability to sell.

"I didn't think much about it when he first called. Then it became more attractive."

Is he a regular at a Carrollton chiropractor? Does a doctor play notes on his spine?

"Never been to one," he said. "But I'm learning about it. Why I learned a whole lot just today."

Hope you've got a lot of backbone, Roger, because the learning has just begun.

Doctor Sid was not a fan of my work. A friend of his in Columbus sent along my column and when he read what I wrote, familiar emotions churned inside. He had been going to war on behalf of chiropractic science most of his adult life, but this was probably the first time he had found a critic on the sports page.

He called Roger into his office, and the new coach realized a storm was brewing. Doctor Sid ordered him to prepare for a one-hundred-mile trip to Columbus. He intended to confront the writer of that disparaging piece and demand a retraction. When Roger mentioned we were old friends that really infuriated the college president. How could a friend write such stuff?

Most people who worked for Doctor Sid snapped to attention when he called their name, but from the beginning, Roger's relationship with his volatile boss was different. He was able to bring his emotions down a few notches and the drive to Muscogee County was soon forgotten, though Roger carried around a copy of that article for years.

This would not be the last time that the Life College team was a target of verbal abuse and they soon discovered that the best way to deal with trash talkers was on the basketball court.

THE NEW TEAM was called the Running Eagles, an appropriate nickname since everyone concerned with the embryonic program spent that first year on the run. Opening night was more than a season away, but Roger and his staff were running full speed to buy equipment, schedule games, scout for talent, and set up a game plan for a team that was not yet assembled.

Their search for players led them to Derrick Engram, a former blue-chip prospect, who by then was running from himself. Engram had given up on basketball and his future. He was spending his days sprawled on a couch at his family's home in Cocoa Beach, Florida, wondering where life was going to take him. Nothing had gone right. Now that he was older, he knew it was his fault, not the coaches or the schools that recruited him.

After a brilliant high school career, he attended several different colleges in several different states and tried his hand at both football and basketball. One of the stops he made was West Georgia College, where his path first crossed Roger Kaiser's.

"I was immature and never focused on education. I knew I was good enough to play ball all along, but all I really wanted to do was keep my parents off my back. I was a mess," he admits.

By 1991 he had been out of high school five years, and he had little to show for that journey. He was once a coveted prospect, but no one showed interest now, and he was ready to give up. He was doing nothing with his life, and when the telephone rang, he figured the call was for someone else. Who would be calling him?

The caller was John Barrett, an assistant coach at Life College, a school near Atlanta. They were starting a basketball program, and he was calling to talk to Engram about coming there to play at a time in his life when most coaches had thrown away his phone number.

"I was at a standstill," Engram says. "I was really shocked when he mentioned Coach Kais because I had left West Georgia with only three hours' notice. He could have written me off his list, but he didn't. I didn't know where they got my phone number, but that call changed my life."

Barrett called Brevard to inquire about a five-foot-eleven guard named Tyree McGhee, and Coach Don Smith mentioned his well-traveled post player. When Barrett mentioned Engram, Roger remembered his abilities, and the strange family situation that caused him to leave West Georgia with little warning.

Engram became the first player offered a basketball scholarship to Life College. Lamar Harris, a six-foot-five high school star at nearby Wheeler High would be the first player signed, but Engram was the first recruit.

"They had faith in me, so I had faith in them. We took a visit to the school, and they told us we would be the foundation of something special. I wanted to be part of that. Coach Kaiser said we would come in and compete. He also painted a picture of education and told us we would be part of a new business administration program. We had no idea what to expect. We were following his vision," Engram says.

That first team was a blend of junior college transfers and raw high school talent. Engram is still impressed at how they came together. "It started instantly. We became one. They recruited guys who knew how to become a family. There were no egos. We fought like hell on the basketball court, but we were brothers off the court. We learned quickly that Coach didn't bring us there to go 9-20. He planned for us to be 20-9."

Their first practice was a sideshow. Doctor Sid wanted that moment properly preserved, and so it was. Cameras recorded the team's every move. "They filmed the whole practice and took pictures of everything we did. People like to be part of tradition. That was a big selling point for us," Roger said afterward. "We couldn't tell the kids we won the conference championship the year before. What we did tell them was that they were part of a dream and that they were going to play a key role in that dream."

Preparation ended on November 13, 1991, when DeVry College came to the Eagles Nest for Life College's first venture into college basketball. It was a meeting of two schools that recruited students with late-night television spots, but now they were competing on the basketball court. It was showtime, and on opening night, players and fans alike were shocked at how Life was able to pull together such a spectacle.

The cast of characters was large. There was Doc, a life-sized eagle who wore an eight thousand dollar costume … a slew of energetic cheerleaders waving green and white pompons … a fifteen-piece pep band called the "Spinal Cords" … and a troop of go-go girls named the D.C. Dancers (as in Doctor of Chiropractic).

Camera crews, as usual, preserved the festivities. Josh Powell, a teammate of Roger's at Georgia Tech, took time from his career as a traveling opera singer to sing the "National Anthem." Whack Hyder, their coach when they played for the Yellow Jackets, was among the boisterous standing-room-only crowd of two thousand fans. And the undisputed star of the opening ceremonies was Doctor Sid Williams. He received a standing ovation when he was introduced.

Presiding was Freddie Miller, a pioneer personality on early Atlanta TV stations. He was best known as the loquacious voice of World Championship Wrestling on Ted Turner's Superstation. Wrestling fans still remember his catch phrase: "BEEEE THEEEERE!" Miller used that same over-the-top style after Doctor Sid installed him as the public address announcer. Before the teams took the court, Miller said, "Well, everybody's in a big, happy mood because this is history for us."

Six seconds into the game, Engram insured himself a spot in the college archives. At 7:39 p.m., he scored the Eagles' first-ever point, recording the second free throw of a two-shot opportunity. Utilizing a relentless full-court press sparked by Engram's junior college teammate, Tyree McGee, Roger's team rushed to a 110-78 victory. Bruce White with 23 points and Robert Richburg with 21 led the way. McGee finished with 18.

Fans also contributed.

"The noise was so tremendous that night that you could not hear anything five feet from you," DeVry Coach George Trawick said. That reception came from a bunch of atypical college students that scurried around campus with skeletons in one arm and books in the other.

Engram said the school embraced them well. “We didn’t know what to expect from our student body. They were mostly older graduate students, but they fell in love with us. They made it a fun place to play and helped us hit the scene running.”

The Eagles soared to thirteen victories in their first fifteen starts on their way to a shocking 26-9 record that helped them crack the NAIA Top 25 in their maiden season. This helped absorb the verbal needles the players were receiving at every turn. The most used slam was referring to Life as “Cadaver University.”

“We would hear the slipped disc comment and all that stuff. No one took us for real. They thought they would run all over us. They didn’t see us coming,” Engram believes.

As the leader of the Life defense, McGhee enjoyed every moment. “We were sold on the fact that we were coming to Life College to build a winning tradition, and that is exactly what we are doing.”

Against Berry in the District 25 finals, Life led by three points with forty-nine seconds to play and ended up losing by three. Fans who could not fit into the arena watched on monitors all over campus as the Eagles made some bonehead plays that cost them a spot in the national tournament. The first-year program waited for an invitation from Kansas City but they heard nothing. “The feeling of frustration was big because we had come from nothing,” Roger said.

Life went 30-5 that next season, and Engram recalls the upset victory over Pfeifer University when the Falcons were ranked third in the country. “I was in the hotel lobby when I heard one of their players on the telephone telling somebody they were going to beat those busters from Marietta by twenty points. I called a team meeting and told the others what I had heard. Nobody said a word, and we went out and won by ten points.”

Most of the players in that first group of recruits at Life never made it to Kansas City, though they won two Georgia Intercollegiate Athletic Conference titles. It was 1993 before the Eagles made it to the nationals, and by then Derrick Engram was a college graduate. It was an achievement that he credits to that phone call from John Barrett and the faith that Roger Kaiser showed in him as a player and a person. He was about to fall between the cracks. NCAA schools could no longer recruit him because he had been out of high school too long, and with his uneven track record, many NAIA schools were unwilling to take a chance on him.

As it did with many athletes over the years, Roger's support for Engram extended beyond basketball. Engram told the coach that he wanted to be a college graduate, and Roger was determined to do what he could to help him. What he found was alarming. Engram could read, but his inability to express himself in writing was holding him back.

Roger was discussing Engram with someone familiar with Coach John Thompson at Georgetown. That person said Patrick Ewing had the same basic problem. "He told me Ewing couldn't write a paragraph but that they got permission to have him tested orally and that he was going to graduate. Why couldn't we do that for Derrick, I wondered."

Once tests determined that Engram had a learning disability, the school was able to assign him a tutor who prepared him for every subject. She went along on basketball road trips, and before long, teammates were also offering support.

Engram has never forgotten what Roger did.

"He didn't try to be a father figure, but we always knew he was there. He knew when to back off, and he knew when to get rough and tough. We were there at the right time and the right place. He gave me my last chance. No one else was willing to take a chance on me, but he did."

When Engram accepted his diploma from Life University in 1994, Doctor Sid Williams was waiting at the bottom of the stairs. He offered him a job as a student recruiter, which the grateful athlete accepted on the spot.

Engram is the proud father of two Division I athletes. His son Evan is a tight end at Ole Miss and his daughter Mackenzie is a basketball player at the University of Georgia. He recognizes what his experience as a player under Roger has meant to him and his children.

His children know Engram's story and so do many of the young people he works with as vice president of business development with the Leeward Team, a national consulting firm that markets Crossroads, a software that teaches critical thinking skills to student athletes.

His crossroads came the day he received that unexpected call from Life College. Thus began the final chapter of Derrick Engram's unsettling journey. "I was a grown man when I got there, but I learned how to be a man while I was at Life, and Coach Kaiser was a big part of that growth."

23

Living on Tulsa Time

"What you are is God's gift to you---what you make of it is your gift to God."

Midnight kept coming early, and it began to look as if Roger Kaiser was never going to wear the glass slipper again. He built an overnight powerhouse at Life University but victories in the regular season do not mean as much as ones in March and his teams kept coming up short in the NAIA national tournament.

The Running Eagles received an invitation to the 1993 tournament, were runner-ups in 1994 and were the second seeded team in 1995 and 1996 though they went home early both years. So despite winning 150 games and losing only thirty times in five seasons Doctor Sid's trophy case remained bare.

No one imagined it but a loss at the Eagles Nest during the 1993 campaign would be the last time Roger's team lost at home for nearly six seasons. But as it was at West Georgia College, being successful so soon came back to haunt him. So did his school's nasty label as an institution populated by "quacks and cultists." Building a representative schedule was simple in the beginning but once schools tasted his up-tempo brand of basketball and learned how Life was drubbing all comers, some old colleagues began to avoid him.

"I had one coach tell me he was dropping us because he needed a couple of wins and he had scheduled a couple of teams he thought he could beat. Both those teams beat him that year," Roger noted.

Other coaches continued to schedule him.

"We love playing against them," said Glenn Duhon of Georgia Southwestern. "We hope to play them for now on … We can't beat them either. But if you hope to be the best, you have to play the best, and Life is the best. I tell Roger he should jump to Division I and stop this mess."

With success came insinuations. Some opponents whispered that Life's record was a product of administrative and academic sleight of hand coupled with Doctor Sid Williams' deep pockets. Mason Barfield, the coach at Clayton State, told a reporter that Roger's teams played hard and clean and provided good competition. At the same time, he voiced concerns that the playing field was not always level.

"State institutions have more rigid rules than non-traditional schools like Life. They have some other degrees, but they are really a chiropractic college. I have never accused Life of breaking any rules. They have just created an environment where it would be very difficult for anyone to lose," Barfield said.

Such attitudes led to Life being drummed out of the GIAC in 1993. Other conference members met without informing Life — winners of the first two GIAC titles. At that meeting, their peers dissolved the league then turned around and formed the Georgia Athletic Conference. The GAC included every school in the GIAC but Life and Kennesaw State, which was about to move to NCAA Division II.

North Georgia College's Bill Ensley, the president of the new GAC, tried to explain their reasoning. "Our people, if you want to know the truth, realized they were going to be a powerhouse and were going to put into their program more than could be put into the average program. It boiled down to members not inviting them to be a member for the simple reason they are a good team. We thought the Life program was on the upswing and a higher budget and was attracting a higher caliber athlete. It was a program beyond what any of us could produce."

Roger was disappointed at how the meeting was conducted but said what those schools truly lacked was a Doctor Sid. "We do have more money. That's because I have a college president who values athletics. He sees us spreading the gospel of chiropractic through athletics … We have a narrow curriculum, yes. But our degree program meets every standard. What am I supposed to do about that? … I've even had some coaches complain because we have a chiropractor on our staff and they don't. I'm sure I could help them find one."

Life College was officially transformed into Life University in 1996 but Sid Williams was not through building and he was not about to let critics get in the way of his dreams. "I've gotten used to the criticism," he said. "The idea in basketball was to play for the championship, not just to play … We will play by the rules."

George Perides, head coach at Southern Tech, whose campus almost adjoined Life's, said competing with Roger's teams was like going to war with a water gun when the other side has a Magnum. "What do I do, drown them? … They are a different type institution from most others. And there is not a coach in this league that wouldn't break both legs to get over there if they thought that job was open."

ROGER KAISER RETURNED to Kansas City in 1993, but this trip was not as enjoyable as the one in 1974. With West Georgia he won the NAIA championship but Life College was not so successful on its first visit. The Running Eagles were seeded 13th in spite of their 30-5 record and they hoped a 97-62 victory over Benedict College in the opener would show tournament officials they deserved a higher ranking. It meant little though, for Life lost 94-89 to David Lipscomb in the second round.

They returned a year later and for the first time since 1937 the NAIA tournament had a new home. It was moved to the Mabee Center in Tulsa, Oklahoma — the home court of Oral Roberts University. The unseeded Eagles arrived with a 29-10 record and a crowd of fans led by Doctor Sid and Doctor Nell. They took a tour of the ORU campus and were impressed by a 200-foot prayer tower and a giant pair of praying hands. Doc was so impressed that he commissioned an eighteen-foot piece of art that replicated his own hands, even the Georgia Tech rings he wore. The bronze statuary erected near the Eagles Nest represents a chiropractor's healing hands.

Led by all purpose guard Billy Lewis, Life upset Oklahoma Christian, Westmont, Hawaii Pacific and Midwestern State on its way to the finals against crowd-favorite Oklahoma Baptist. The Eagles ran out of steam and lost the championship game 99-81, but Lewis — a two-time NAIA all-American — was awarded the Charles Stevenson Hustle Award.

Roger made it back in 1995 and 1996 but came home disappointed despite being second seeded both times. They lost in a first round upset to Montana State-Northern in 1995 and the following year fell in the second round to Belmont University — a team they had embarrassed during the regular season.

But 1997 would be another story. The Running Eagles breezed through their schedule with a 37-1 record and Roger was named National Coach of the Year. Arriving as pre-tournament favorites, Life romped past Huston Tillotson 107-68 and defeated Brigham Young-Hawaii 81-65 before squeaking by Birmingham-Southern 66-64.

In the semi-finals, the Eagles downed Cumberland 69-52 and earned the James Naismith Trophy for the first time by upending perennial power Oklahoma Baptist 73-64 in the title game. Bob Hoffman, now the coach of Mercer University, coached the second place team. Roger accepted the championship trophy with a bandage on his chin after being injured in the post-game celebration. Life's James Harris, who scored only six points in the finale, was the tournament MVP.

A team that did not exist until 1990 earned a national reputation overnight and so did their head coach. The former Tech sharpshooter now had two notches on his gun, earned at two different schools, and opponents soon learned he was not through yet.

The Eagles were building a small-college dynasty and they returned to Tulsa in 1998, losing in the second round to surprising Southern Nazarene 94-90 in overtime. But two backcourt magicians were about to perform magic in two different games in two different seasons in two different arenas.

FROM THE BEGINNING, Roger felt at home in the friendly confines of the Eagles Nest. His team won their first game against DeVry and never slowed down, establishing a tradition that was on the minds of every opponent that came to visit. The Running Eagles lost three home games in their inaugural season, two in their second year and one in 1993. Then came the streak, and it seemed to be one that would never end.

"I hope tradition plays a big factor and we talk about pride a lot. You get tradition based on your pride, and every team playing us at home is gunning to stop that streak. You can't go with what's on paper, you have to go with how tough you are," Roger said as the streak made its way into the nineties.

As the 1999 season began, no one knew where that year would lead. They had lost all five starters from the year before and as pre-season workouts began there were injuries and academic question marks.

When they defeated Athens State 69-64 that January the streak reached 99 games, the longest in any level of college basketball at that time. That put them in a tie with St. Bonaventure, which was perfect at home from 1948 to 1961 and moved them past John Wooden's UCLA teams of 1970 to 1976. They were in striking distance of the NAIA record of 106 straight wins set by Marymount of Kansas from 1971 to 1978. However, the NCAA Division I standard of 129 straight set by Kentucky between 1947 and 1955 was only something to dream about.

"It's definitely an elite group. I think it reflects how much pride our guys have in this team. We've got it written on the blackboard here. Nobody comes in here and beats us at home," Roger said, as Talladega College and its 2-14 record prepared for a weekend rematch with the Running Eagles. "We know it's going to end one day. We just don't want it to be on Saturday."

As they usually did, officials at Life planned a big party to mark the milestone. Green placards were prepared with "100" printed on them. Every fan entering the building was given a bag of confetti. No one considered anything but a victory. No one except Talladega College.

Life led by ten points with a fraction over seven minutes to play but the next few minutes belonged to the visitors despite Chummy Johnson's 26 points. "It was a great run, but you hate to see it end like that," Roger said. "We had a 10-point lead and couldn't put them away. They wanted it more than we did."

Once the streak came to an end, Life racked up seven wins in a row at home. Then came an unplanned visit from Larry Chapman. Auburn-Montgomery's veteran coach had grown tired of losing in the Eagles Nest. He lost seven straight games at Life, twice when it appeared his team had the game won. When schedules were put together that season AUM did not chose to schedule a rematch.

"That's no accident," Chapman admitted.

As fate would have it, the NAIA Southeast Regions were held at Life and the home team's opponent would be the Senators of AUM. This time around Chapman came out on top 88-73, and earned an automatic berth in the national tournament. The Eagles' only hope of going back to Tulsa was an at-large bid.

Fate played one more trick. On the day at-large invitations were issued, Roger was rushed to the hospital in Carrollton and kept overnight suffering from an attack of kidney stones. He thought his team and its 23-10 record deserved a spot in the tournament and during the event Roger was to be inducted into the NAIA Hall of Fame. But pain overruled such thoughts.

"I checked into the hospital and went into surgery for two hours but they couldn't get them out. I don't have as much pain as I had before but I still have some pain … I went to see my doctor on Friday and he told me they couldn't do anything right now. So I am going to Oklahoma and I'll see my doctor when I get back," Roger said.

The invitation came and a weakened Roger was somehow on the bench for the opener. Life upset Faulkner University 64-58 with Corey Evans scoring 19 points. During the game, stents that were surgically attached in Georgia pulled loose and Roger was taken to a hospital in Tulsa where two kidney stones were removed. Doctors also located gallstones that would be removed at a later date. That procedure kept him on the sidelines for his team's 87-74 victory over Oklahoma State University leaving assistant coaches John Barrett, Bill Firnbach and Chip Kaiser in charge.

Fighting off the pain, Roger made it to the NAIA Hall of Fame ceremony where in his acceptance speech Roger said, "My career has been better because a lot of people cared. Imagine, having a job coaching the sport you love."

Roger loved it enough to rejoin the team for its 83-67 win over Concordia. Jamal Horton was the leader with 32 points. Foreshadowing what was to come, the Eagles needed a 30-4 run to overcome a 16-point halftime deficit and defeat Azusa Pacific 83-67.

Only Mobile University stood in the way of Life University's second national championship in three years. The Rams started fast and built a huge lead at halftime. In the Life dressing room Roger talked about pride. "I told them if you have individual pride, team pride and pride in your school, a lot of good things can happen."

With 17:09 left in the game Mobile still led by 26 points. Those last minutes turned into a blur. Going on a remarkable 34-8 run they finally drew even with 1:13 left in the game. It came down to one final play with the score tied at 60.

Evans, a six-foot point guard from Cocoa, Fla., brought the ball up court. A spin move got him free around midcourt with about six seconds left, and a crossover at about 25 feet freed him of his last defender. He went up at the three-point arc with three seconds left, but the last defender he juked managed to recover and flew across his path, from right to left. Evans double-clutched, falling forward to avoid touching down before letting go of the ball. He flung the ball toward the basket. A you-had-to-see-it-to-believe-it shot that does not always work on the playground dropped through the net with 2.2 seconds left while Evans skidded on his chest, shooting arm beneath him, watching it the whole way.

The Running Eagles were champions once again.

Capping a season in which he tallied 15.1 points a game, Evans averaged 24.8 during the post-season. Overall, he was second on the team behind Horton who averaged 18.1 points a game. Evans was tournament MVP and Horton and Derrick Shaw joined him on the all-Tournament team. The Atlanta Tip-Off Club later honored Evans as the NAIA Co-Player of the Year in Georgia.

To their coach, this was redemption. "If you were going to write a story or a movie, how could you write one better than that or pick a person who had a better tournament than Corey to get the shot? It was something that people will remember for a long time because of the way it happened."

A cheering crowd greeted the team and the coaches at the Atlanta airport. Fans redecorated Gate B-11 with green, yellow and white balloons. Corey Evans was the undisputed man of the hour as the 1999 basketball season ended, but twelve months later a new hero would emerge — a hero who watched that game on television.

WHEN THE REVEREND Wiley Johnson heard the hungry newborn smacking his lips on the way home from the hospital he laughed and said his grandson sounded like a snapping turtle. Snapping soon turned to "Snap," and the nickname stuck. Even now basketball followers around the world know him as Jimmie "Snap" Hunter.

From the first time he walked on to a court in Memphis he knew playing basketball was second nature. Snap was twelve-years-old and had never shot at a legitimate hoop before, but he was able to do things fellows who played all the time could not do. He became a schoolboy legend in a town known for its basketball. He was a star freshman at the University of Memphis when he was introduced to Corey Evans and Life University.

Watching the NAIA championship on TV at home he focused on Evans and saw he was in a rhythm. He decided that if Evans got a clean look he could make the shot. Less than a year later, Snap and Evans were in the same backcourt on the same team but right then he was not sure where Life University was located.

Snap averaged 16.1 points a game for Memphis and showed promise of good times ahead. But there were storms in the extended forecast. He had never been a serious student. He spent his first year out of high school trying to qualify for college. He was in trouble academically and had other issues that he has never talked about.

He was one test short in summer school and would have to sit out another whole year to be eligible at Memphis. Advisors suggested he needed another year of college basketball to ready himself for the NBA, and NAIA rules would allow him to transfer to another school and play immediately.

A friend going to school in Atlanta told him about Life University and when Roger heard Jimmie Hunter was interested in coming to school there he called NBA super scout Marty Blake. Roger referred to him as Jimmie but Blake knew a lot more about Snap Hunter and he pushed Roger to pursue the talented guard.

Snap enrolled at Life University and in the 2000 season he and Evans became one of the most exciting guard tandems in college basketball. Snap led the team in scoring with a 22.1 average and was second to Evans in assists. But it always comes down to March.

Life opened the tournament with a victory over Southern University setting up an unlikely match with Southern Tech. After taking care of their neighbors, they defeated The Masters and Olivet Nazarene. As it had the season before, it came down to the finals and a game against Georgetown of Kentucky. A colorful article by John Donovan on CNNSI.com brought up an aspect of Life University and its three crowns in four years that others chose to ignore:

> The odds, you have to think, are downright staggering. Two national championship games in two straight seasons. Both tied with less than 10 seconds to play.
>
> Two funky, off-balance shots after two near-disastrous turnovers -- two prayers, when you get right down to it. By two different members of the same team, a year apart.
>
> (These are two guys, by the way, who were both hobbled almost to the point of no return in their respective games and who now, by more happenstance than anything, are roommates.)
>
> Two shots that fall, dead perfect, into the basket.
>
> And, ultimately, two straight national championship trophies.
>
> You can play NCAA tournament games from now until next March -- from now until March 2050, if you'd like -- and you won't get two straight championship games with two endings as mad, as exciting, as far-out unlikely as those two.
>
> But that's just the start of it, really. The back-to-back NAIA national titles for little Life University — an oasis of pine trees and softly rolling hills stuck in the urban sprawl northeast of Atlanta -- are more than simply unlikely.
>
> Something decidedly … different … is going on at Life.

Donovan brought readers up to date on the 1999 title game and all that Evans had done. "I still watch it," Evans said, remembering his miracle play. The writer introduced Snap Hunter and how close he was to Evans, his teammate and roomie. He described Doctor Sid Williams as an Atlanta native with a streak of evangelist in him as wide as an Atlanta freeway: "He's a big smiling, silver-haired preacher of the wonders of chiropractic care, a man who often finds himself in the center of controversy and who always finds himself in the center of something."

That brought him back to Georgetown.

> Life had taken a 13-point halftime lead and seemed ready to coast to its second straight title. But Hunter got twisted up under the basket on a play in the second half and, doubled over in pain, had to leave the game. He was out for more than six minutes. It was Life's fifth game in six days, and it was starting to catch up to the Running Eagles …
>
> By the time Hunter came back in, with somewhere around two minutes left in the game, Georgetown actually had taken a brief one-point lead, at 54-53 with 2:33 left. Hunter made a jumper to get the Running Eagles up by one point with 1:09 remaining, then made two free throws to put them up three with 41 seconds left. But a three-pointer from Georgetown's Mark Williams tied the score at 59 with 26 seconds left.
>
> Life had no timeouts.
>
> "I'm thinking, 'It's coming down to this again,'" Evans said.
>
> "I thought they were going to double me, and I was going to get it to Corey for an open jump shot," Hunter said. "I was looking at the clock, waiting for the double-team to come, and it never came."
>
> Hunter brought the ball up, but lost it in the frontcourt for a split second under heavy pressure from Georgetown's Williams. When Williams lunged for it, Hunter went around his back with the ball, dribbled between Williams and teammate Ricky Ward and got free for a drive to the basket. He planted his left foot at the free throw line, on the left side of the

lane, and floated up for a running one-hander. Williams, trying to recover, dived at Hunter's feet.

On his way down, the ball dropped softly in. Hunter saw it from the seat of his shorts with about four seconds left. "Every time I think about it, that I, like, hit the shot to win a national championship. It's something special," he said.

Hunter was tournament MVP and NAIA Player of the Year — the first time one of Roger's players had been so honored. That was the final game of Hunter's brief but spectacular college career. He became a vagabond traveling around the world playing basketball at every stop. But the big dream was always just out of reach. He was invited to camp with five NBA teams but could never stick. But when he was down, he had the childlike memory of floating through the air and watching his shot win a championship.

MISSING FROM THIS narrative is how John Donovan handled a delicate topic that no one else ever tackled. From the beginning, Doctor John Downes served as Life's team practitioner with Doctor Sid in reserve. Roger tells stories of the miracles he saw performed on that table next to the bench.

First there was Evans. Early in that 1999 title game, Downes pulled him out and stuck him on the table. Evans was having lower back pain, and everyone knew the Eagles would need him down the stretch. "You feel better afterward. I don't know if it's a mental thing or whatever. But it seems to help," Evans noted

A year later came Hunter. He took that spill under the basket and Downes and needed attention. Snap spent six minutes on the table being worked on while his head coach watched the game slipping away. Roger sent Chip to see what was going on.

News from the table was not good. "Doctor Downes said he's not going back in," Chip reported.

"To hell he's not," Roger said.

Before you could snap your fingers, Snap was off the adjusting table. "You can feel it as soon as they adjust you. It helps a lot of things — your balance, your shot," he said. "Who's to say? Adjustment might have made me hit that shot."

Roger never knew what to believe but he appreciated the edge that chiropractic care provided his team. "As a coach I'm looking at any edge I can get," he said. "And I think the rest of them are missing the boat."

Doctor Sid maintained that the contributions of chiropractic science to his school's back-to-back titles were incredible. "It's magical almost, but we experience it every day."

SOCIAL SECURITY WAS several years away and despite two bouts with cancer and other problems that come with age, Roger Kaiser was still young at heart. He had followed Hurst Livengood's lead and parlayed his love of sports into a career others only dream about.

He never planned to coach but when he picked up a whistle, he discovered that God had given him the gift to teach the game as well as play it. After coaching five different decades and more than a thousand basketball games he was just plain tired. He had promised Beverly that someday they would travel and go to places they had never been but there never seemed to be time. He was sixty-two years old, and after a lifetime in basketball it was time for a change.

It was time to put his energy into something else, he said. So after nine years he stepped down as head basketball coach at Life University but announced he would continue as athletic director.

"From what he's accomplished he deserves retirement," Beverly Kaiser said. "We started dating our sophomore year in high school and basketball has been our lives ever since. But no matter what happened Roger never brought it home. He was the same — win, lose or draw. If anything was eating on him, he left it at the office."

Unlike many of his peers, Roger's last game was a victory and that victory came on the national stage. He was on top of his profession and still enjoying the game that he loved. He had a supportive wife who kept the scorebook and pasted clippings in scrapbooks. He had friends at every level, a list of loyal teammates and two grandchildren who loved him.

His career had been magical and distinguished. In thirty-two years as a head coach, he had only two losing seasons. His overall record was 754-280. As a college coach, he retired with 654 lifetime victories, which at the time meant he had won more games than any college basketball coach in the history of the state.

His teams won four national championships, seven conference titles and made it to the NAIA national tournament nine times. Four times he was national Coach of the Year and eleven times he earned Coach of the Year honors in Georgia. He was a member of sports halls of fames from Indiana to Georgia, as well as the NAIA Hall of Fame.

Those championships are what former University of Georgia women's coach Andy Landers graciously mentioned when he broke Roger's record for career victories in 2006. That milestone came against, of all people, Georgia Tech and the game was played at Alexander Memorial Coliseum.

After the win, someone asked Landers about breaking Roger's record. "He has four W's in his total that I don't have," he said, referring to those four national titles. "He is the king. I am just a friend of his."

WHEN THE NEXT season came along, it was the first time in fifty-four years that Roger Kaiser had not been directly connected to a basketball team. John Barrett, his longtime assistant, took over and led the Eagles to a 20-11 record. They earned the right to defend their title but they were back from the NAIA tournament after one game.

There was little time to relax though. For years Roger's doctors gave him glowing reports but in 2001 — twelve months after he quit coaching — he was diagnosed with prostate cancer. His friend and pastor Don Harp was was there when Roger woke up. "Like always, he handled the pain well and he has continued to move along."

Roger commuted from Carrollton to Marietta his first few years at Life. As time passed, he and Beverly bought a condominium near the campus. From the beginning, Doctor Sid begged Beverly to take a job at the university but she always refused. She relented in 1994, and she and Roger spent a lot of time on campus. But despite their closeness they did not sense dangerous undercurrents that were swelling just below the surface.

A growing rift between Doctor Sid and others in his profession exploded when a 2002 report from the Council on Chiropractic Education criticized the curriculum at Life University, specifically inadequacies in teaching students to recognize when patient care could best be provided by a medical doctor. Published reports of his personal income made matters worse. In 1998, it reached over $900,000, which did not include lofty salaries paid to other members of his family.

The council revoked Life University's accreditation, putting the future of the school and its 4,500 students in grave jeopardy. Newspapers pointed fingers directly at Doctor Sid and his family and the *Atlanta Journal-Constitution* called on him to step down:

> In order to save Life University, the school of chiropractic founded by Dr. Sid Williams, the entire family must surrender control. Williams' resignation alone is not enough...If the school is to survive it can no longer be the family business. The founder and his family must separate themselves immediately from the day-to-day operations. Otherwise, the school will die, along with Williams' dream and the careers of thousands of students.

This led to the forced retirement of Doctor Sid along with close relatives that were employees of the school after twenty-eight years on the throne. Before he stepped aside, the university's board of trustees granted Doctor Sid and Doctor Nell a nearly $5 million severance package. If there were any doubts that he was the lightning rod, one year after his ouster accreditation was fully restored.

With enrollment down to around 800 and Doctor Sid out of the picture, the new administration shut down the entire athletic program in 2003, another way for critics to erase the dreams of Sid Williams. Men's basketball did not return to Life until 2007.

The inquisition began in 2002 when the athletic department and its $1.8 million budget became expendable leaving 150 athletes and thirty staff members without a home. Delivering that horrible news was left to the athletic director and for Roger it was not an easy chore. "We've been so successful," he said, his voice cracking as he talked to a reporter. "I think it really helped the university."

Former athletes such as Billy Lewis felt betrayed. He was Roger's first legitimate star, the school's all-time leading scorer with 2,235 points and was twice an NAIA all-American. "All of us who were there in the early stages tried to build a tradition," Lewis said. "To see it fall apart this way is a dark day for everybody."

There was no reason for Roger Kaiser to stay on board, though he did not walk away for good until his 65th birthday in 2003. "I was the last person in the athletic department and I shut off the lights when I went out the door," he said.

Educators saw a side of Roger that went beyond basketball. That view was shared in a letter to the editor of the *Marietta Daily Journal* by Paul Lapides, director of the Michael J. Coles School of Business at Kennesaw State University and a former professor at Life University:

> I had the great pleasure and honor of working with Roger Kaiser many years ago. Yes, pleasure and honor. Kaiser is much more than a former Georgia Tech athletic star, a basketball coach or athletic director. He is a living inspiration to every athlete, student, faculty and staff member that comes in contact with him. Kaiser cares about everyone he meets. He demands a lot from himself and others, yet he cares in a way that is so unique that people are changed — humbled, inspired, at times, almost in awe. I was and still am.
>
> I've watched Kaiser inspire athletes to give more than most thought they had — on the field and in the classroom. And, then develop into leaders, leaders who understand studying, thinking, practicing and teamwork. Individuals who understood that there was a price for success, but that there was also a price for failure.
>
> Kaiser understood, what so many coaches, teachers and soother adults don't know — that the price of failure is always higher. There isn't a college or university that wouldn't be better with Kaiser there. In fact, there isn't a business, non-

profit organization of government agency that wouldn't benefit from Kaiser.

I don't know if a basketball coach has ever been president of a university, but I am certain that if the trustees appointed Kaiser president of Life University last year, Life University would be booming today. He has a following of faculty, students, alumni and staff that is amazing.

The community knows him. People respect him. He's earned their trust. He's not like you and me. In a lifetime, most of us will only get to know a handful of people like Roger Kaiser.

ROGER KAISER CAME to Life when there was nothing. He survived long enough to oversee some of the finest athletic facilities in the small college ranks. His departure removed the final link to the glory days of the university, a time when enrollment and support were highest and when a championship basketball team and Doctor Sid's flamboyancy promoted far more than sports. Roger and Doctor Sid accomplished what no one thought was possible. In nine short years they won three national titles, finished second once and averaged thirty wins a season. They established a dynasty at an unlikely address.

In retirement, Doctor Sid found himself in the shadows, a place where he was never comfortable. His health began to fail. He suffered a stroke in 2011 and died on December 27, 2012 with complications from pneumonia. He was 84 years old and he still wore Georgia Tech rings on both hands.

Some followers deserted him when his power waned and younger people in his profession saw him as a dinosaur. Roger Kaiser saw Sid Williams as a friend who came along when he needed him. The unexpected offer for Roger to join him came at an opportune time. It paved the way for Roger to return to the community where he first became a celebrity and opened many important doors. Doctor Sid saw in Roger someone who would help his dreams come true and believed he could accomplish things even Roger did not believe possible. Together they were magic.

Roger delivered a moving eulogy at Doctor Sid's memorial service and he has never forgotten what their friendship meant to him. Roger laughs at some of his antics, how he wanted to be in every team picture, how he could not understand why ball games had to tip off before he could get there and how he thrived on the spotlight. And he still believes that every college basketball coach in America deserves his own Doctor Sid.

24
The Love of a Teammate

"If you want to go fast, go alone. If you want to go far, go together."

Teammates smile broadly at the mere mention of Julian Falconer Powell, the pride of Stanford, Kentucky. They tell tales about how immovable he was when he posted up down low and how he could devour more than two dozen eggs at a single sitting. They talk about his rich and powerful singing voice and how grown men cried when he belted out "How Great Thou Art" at Coach Bobby Dodd's memorial service.

Mostly, they talk about how much they loved him.

So when some of the surviving members of the 1960 Georgia Tech basketball team reunited on the court at halftime of the Yellow Jackets' game with Florida State University on a Sunday afternoon in 2010, they choked back tears when they looked down the line and saw the indestructible Josh Powell slumping heavily on a wooden walking stick.

Multiple myeloma was taking its toll on this gentle giant as it does with anyone who hears that horrible diagnosis. Cancer sapped his strength but not his will, and Josh had been determined to be there for the fifty-year anniversary reunion of the first Tech basketball team to earn a trip to the NCAA tournament. Only a few of his trusted friends knew how sick he really was until that weekend. They all were overwhelmed when he shuffled to the microphone before the game and in that strong bass-baritone voice of his sang the "National Anthem." "His ovation from the crowd lasted longer than the anthem itself," observed former athletic director Homer Rice.

When they were young, Josh's primary assignment was to grab rebounds and set picks for Roger Kaiser, allowing him to shoot safely behind a screen. "He would always joke that I got the points, and he got the bruises."

A year after that reunion, Josh Powell was dead.

He was not the first teammate Roger had lost. Wayne Richards and Dave Denton, starters on that 1960 team, had already passed away. They had also lost Keith Weekly, another player from that era. Buddy Blemker, the Indiana left-hander who helped recruit Roger to Tech, also died young.

All of them were touched by the loss of their beloved coach in 2003, and the affection those men had for Whack Hyder could not be measured. To many of the fellows he recruited and mentored, he was the father figure they needed away from home. Roger understood that when he was young, and he appreciated Coach Hyder even more as he grew older.

As busy as he was, Bobby Cremins asked Roger and Beverly to escort the aging coach to the Final Four in Denver when Tech made its first appearance in 1990. Then, when Roger left West Georgia for Life College, Hyder wrote him a warm congratulatory note reminiscent of the simple letters he sent to a schoolboy in Indiana decades before.

When they moved back to Atlanta in 1991, Roger and Beverly made a habit of checking on the retired coach whose health was rapidly failing. They visited him at a home for senior citizens a few weeks before his death, and he tried to convince them that he was happy there since it was close to where his daughter Julia lived. They were impressed and relieved that Hyder had been able to close a deal on the home where he and his late wife Vera lived for so long. That transaction was one of the last things on his bucket list.

Not long after that final visit, Roger, two-time Tech captain, Pres Judy, and the coach's only son, Tommy Hyder, delivered heartfelt eulogies at Hyder's memorial. Eight years later, Roger spoke at Powell's service, and he never would have believed that in 2012 he would be a eulogist for Doctor Sid Williams.

Services for Powell celebrated the life of a giant of a man with an even bigger heart. In a 2011 interview with a *Marietta Daily Journal* reporter Roger talked about his dear friend who fit the definition of a true Renaissance man.

"It's almost—where do you start with Josh? He was such an unusual person, just a very talented, rare bird. He could sing opera. He was an auctioneer. He learned to play the guitar and the banjo. Next thing you know, he'd be roasting coffee, then tying flies to go fishing. He had a sock maker where he made his own socks, and he made bow ties. He would work on cars. He'd buy two old cars just for the parts. He could even fly an airplane. I'd just shake my head sometimes and say, 'Why would you want to do that?' and he'd say, 'Well, why not?'"

After finishing his degree at Georgia Tech, Powell graduated from law school at Emory University, and then practiced at a large Atlanta law firm for two years. The law was too confining. He had much more to give to the world, so from the ground up, he built the Josh Powell Day Camp, a rustic summer getaway for children similar to the one Roger operated years before.

Justice Harris Hines of the Georgia Supreme Court went to law school with Powell, and they remained friends. He talked about what an encourager Powell was to people of all ages—especially young people. "He was a big man who wanted big things, liked big open spaces, the big outdoors, loved children, and was just a delightful, genuine person and a true encourager. He had this voice—I don't know what God sounds like when he speaks, but I believe he sounds like Josh Powell."

Roger said Powell was a giver and a reluctant taker.

"When you'd try to do him a favor, he'd say, 'Why? I can do that myself.' He was a very giving person, but he didn't feel good about you doing something for him. You had to demand it, no matter what it was."

More than anything he was fun, Roger told the reporter.

"I'll miss him so much, and the fact that he was so much fun to be around," Kaiser said. "I remembered his prayers when we ate with him, and he'd say, 'And all God's children said Amen.' That's how he always ended it. He has a sign at the camp that says, 'No cry babies allowed.' But his funeral is going to be tough because there are going to be a lot of crybabies. He touched so many lives—I'm just lucky mine was one of them."

EXPLAINING THE BOND between college teammates is difficult, but it lies somewhere between friend and family. When fellows are young and playing together, they watch each other's back and celebrate each other's baskets and steals. They eat together, practice together, go to class together, complain about the coach together, and never consider that these connections will never end.

When Roger was in school, fellows from a variety of homes and backgrounds, started off as strangers with only basketball in common. They competed for playing time, but they bonded as friends. Living like brothers drew them even closer. For Roger and his teammates, those warm relationships continued long after their final college basketball game was played.

It was the same when he became a basketball coach. Roger saw firsthand how, despite their innate differences, individuals morphed into teams. He nursed these young men through problems at home and in the classroom. He saw them grow into men and stood by them through the struggles that went with maturity. He celebrated their successes in the classroom and in life, and more than once, he has mourned at their funerals. But all of these things start with the team.

Team is a collective word. These relationships extend to players who came before and after Roger. If you wore the uniform, you are part of the family. Even football players are included, for they competed under the same flag.

Indiana native Mickey Sermersheim, a recipient of one of Tech's first basketball scholarships, has become close to Roger and Beverly, and so has Ben Register, whose kind soul does not make you think he was ever a United States Army general. Players like Sermersheim, Register, and Teeter Umstead set the stage for the players that followed. Jim Caldwell, another Hoosier, came after Roger, and when his health failied, his Tech family boosted his spirits and pulled him through. They also rallied around three-sport letterman Jerry Priestley when he faced serious health issues.

Some of the younger Tech players have grown to appreciate their heritage, including two backcourt stars who enjoyed successful careers in the NBA. Mark Price's style of play—including his uncanny accuracy at the free throw line—was often compared to Roger's, and they became friends during his time as an all-American guard. Price is now head coach at UNC-Charlotte.

Jarrett Jack is still an NBA point guard, and while he was at Tech, he reached out to Roger, whose jersey dangled from the rafters at Alexander Memorial Coliseum. "He told Bobby Creimins that he wanted to meet that fellow who scored all the points," Roger says. Jack wanted his jersey to be up there so in 2014—ten years after he finished his playing career—he walked across the stage and received his career from Georgia Tech.

HIS TECH TEAMMATES are older now, but the closeness never ends. When their wives and families get together, they lapse into the old routines and bicker like siblings. Roger and John Hoffman argue about which one of them broke down and cried after their parents left them at the dorm for the first time. On the golf course, Mike Tomasovich laughs about how the rest of them have bad knees, shoulders, and backs from setting picks for Roger. When Bobby Dews emerges from the woods of South Georgia, he still complains that Roger never passed him the ball. They remember the games they lost more than the ones they won. They like to tease and tell tales, but when there is a need, teammates always show up.

They rallied around Roger during his two bouts with cancer and his other surgeries, and years ago, teammates also rushed to a hospital in Louisville, Kentucky, where Alan Nass faced a serious operation on his back. The big center was heavily medicated after the surgery, and none of the fellows in the room knew if he was aware they were there.

But he was.

"Connie, my wife, asked if I remembered her being there with me. I said no, but I remember Roger holding my hand and telling me I had to fight. That was the only thing I could remember. He was rough on me. He said I had to get up and fight. So I did."

Several years after that original surgery, Nass faced another delicate operation, this time at the Cleveland Clinic in Cleveland, Ohio. As you might imagine, Roger and Beverly boarded a Delta jet in Atlanta and were at the hospital with Connie on the days following the intricate procedure. That is what teammates do. They kept close tabs on Nass until, after months of rest and rehab, he finally made it home to Indiana.

During one of their frequent phone conversations, Roger told Nass about a T-shirt that he had printed. On the front of it were two words: *NO COMPLAINTS.* This slogan reminded Roger not to complain and ordered others to do likewise. Nass agreed with that sentiment and said he had to have one of those shirts. Roger said he would take care of that.

So, on the busy weekend before Christmas in 2014, Roger got into his car, and, ignoring holiday traffic, he drove from Atlanta to Huntingburg by himself for a quick visit with Alan and Connie. Roger hand-delivered the special T-shirt—for that is what teammates do.

25

Spreading Jill Beams

"First learn to love yourself and then you learn how to give some of it away."

Jill Kaiser Givens handled those painful moments better than her pastor. Don Harp had reconciled himself to the reality that this bubbly mother of two young children was not going to recover from breast cancer and he went to Florida to talk with her about death, heaven and Jesus — subjects a preacher discusses all the time with members of his congregation. It did not take him long to figure out that this conversation was different. He was sitting across from a woman who was like family to him, and she was better prepared for death than he was.

She was seven years old when the Methodist minister first met Jill, her older sister Jenny and her little brother Chip. They had just moved to Carrollton and he was serving Saint Andrews United Methodist Church. He was their pastor, but Harp became much more than that. He watched that little family grow up, and Jill had always made him smile.

Now Jill was desperately ill and she asked Harp to come see her. A friend with a private plane flew the minister to Tallahassee. By then, she was thirty-four years old with a three-year-old son and a two-year-old daughter who could barely remember their beautiful mother when she was well.

Alone with Harp, she turned loose of feelings she had kept tucked away. Jill was worried about her children Bert and Rachel, her sister, her brother and her husband Steve. Most of all she worried about her mother and father and how devastated Beverly and Roger would be when she was gone. She was prepared to go. But were they prepared to stop holding her hand?

Words did not come easy for Harp during that visit. "It was like talking to one of my own. I had to separate myself from being her surrogate uncle and talk to her like a minister of the gospel. If I couldn't do that, I could not be a very good pastor for her. I had to draw a line between being a neutral observer and a friend. I transferred those feelings to myself and I soon found myself in a lonely dark place."

Jill did not want to die, but she was ready to die. As a Christian she knew death was not the end and she reminded Harp of her strong faith in God. Listening to the things she said and the way she said them, he realized she was prepared to deal with what was ahead. He wondered about the people who loved her, the ones who would be left behind. Looking at her, he remembered Jill in happier times, before the cancer. He always said she was a bright sun waiting to shine, spreading little Jill-Beams all around.

But this was a completely different Jill.

CALLING THEM SISTERS does not fully describe the closeness of Jenny and Jill Kaiser. One Mother's Day, Beverly was childless, and by the next May she had two baby girls — and they were not twins. Jill went to Jenny's first birthday party and she was thirty-two days old. This would be the story of their lives.

Their personalities were different but that was never a wedge. Jenny worried about everything. Jill worried about nothing. Jenny never wanted to hurt anybody's feelings. Jill told it like it was. Jenny always had several projects going at once. Jill was happy doing absolutely nothing. Jenny sweated over every exam and every grade. Jill coasted through high school, college and life.

Jill was always Jenny's best friend. "She was one of those naturally pretty girls who didn't know they were pretty. She was funny too, always making people laugh." She was also a free spirit who sometimes made Roger worry.

Such as she did on a night she busted the family curfew. The girls were in high school and Jenny remembers that night well. She was at home but no one knew where Jill was. Roger, in his pajamas, was about to go out and look for her when he heard the front door open. It was Jill.

"Where have you been?" he asked.

"Where are you going?" was her answer.

"To find you."

"I don't think so," Jill said.

The girls played basketball like their father and were cheerleaders like their mother. They learned to shoot on a goal in the driveway and Roger chided Jenny for shooting like a girl. "But I am a girl," she said. They learned their numbers and their colors by playing card games with their father, and he always won.

Even during basketball season, if he was not on the road the five of them ate dinner as a family, waiting until Roger was home from practice. Until they were older the children did not understand why their father was special to so many people. He was just their Dad. They knew people gravitated to him but when they were young they did not know he was considered a celebrity to anyone that followed basketball.

"He is a gentle soul, but he is also very competitive. Our friends were always welcome at our house, and boys our age used to come over on Sunday afternoons. Jill and I figured out that some of them came to shoot hoops with our father, not to see us. They wanted to beat him so badly but they never did. He always strived to be the best and it taught us to work hard," Jenny says.

The girls were always busy. There was church. There was school. And there was Chip — or as his sisters called him — "Chippie." He was six years younger than Jenny and five years younger than Jill and they were his biggest fans. Because of their age, he and Jill played together more than he and Jenny. That also meant he fought more with Jill.

"Did they spoil me? Of course they did. And I loved it," Chip admits.

He does not remember his sisters playing with dolls like the other girls. He does not remember them dressing a Barbie or cuddling a baby doll. He does remember family basketball games in the driveway.

Jill was a natural athlete who never had to work at whatever game she was playing while her sister had to work at everything. They were older, but they were always there for him, even if he needed a paper written for school.

"I had two great sisters," he says.

THEY WERE ONE year apart in age but the sisters started to Auburn University together. Jenny graduated from Carrollton High then attended West Georgia College for a year while her younger sister finished high school. Jenny had pledged Phi Mu Sorority in Carrollton and at Auburn they found a new bond as sorority sisters. But as students, their different approach to life was evident. Jenny pushed hard for good grades. Jill believed it was all right to be average.

"I was always worrying about something but Jill never did. I remember when we were in college and she had a big mid-term coming up in history. She took off on a skiing trip and made a 'C' on the exam. That was something I could have never done, but it didn't bother Jill at all," Jenny says.

They shared a house trailer at Auburn and in the summertime Chip stayed with them while he was attending Auburn coach Sonny Smith's summer basketball camp. He was a promising high school ball player but to Jenny and Jill he was a little brother they cherished and their love for him never faltered. Jenny got a job working for Auburn women's basketball coach Joe Ciampi. She continued to work for the Hall of Fame coach and got her Master's Degree while Jill completed her undergraduate degree.

After college they moved into an apartment together in Atlanta. Jenny first got a job at the John Harland Company. Roger took Jill to the athletic office at Georgia Tech looking for references so she could get a job as a flight attendant at Delta Airlines. They ran into Norman Arey, a former *Atlanta Journal-Constitution* sports writer who was sports information director at Tech. Arey had accompanied Roger's West Georgia team to the NAIA Tournament in 1972 so he had known them for years. When Arey learned Jill had a degree in public relations and journalism, he invited her to come to work for him. It was not long before Jenny joined her at the Edge Building, working for Coach Bill Curry in the football recruiting office.

Arey treated her like a daughter and she felt at home on a campus she knew so well. She became engaged to Steve Givens, a former Florida State University baseball player, a student assistant coach for the Yellow Jackets when they met. One weekend, Jill was going to visit Givens in Florida and Arey invited her to take his "company car."

On her way back from Tallahassee, a semi truck hauling milk literally drove over her car on Interstate 75 near Cordele. Jill escaped serious injury but the athletic department vehicle was demolished. On Monday morning she walked into the SID office at Tech as if nothing had happened. Arey was already at work when she arrived. "Here's your keys," she said to her boss. "But you won't be able to drive your car. It was crushed."

Her beautiful smile made everything all right.

Jill married Steve Givens in 1986 and for the first time in their lives the Kaiser sisters were living separately. Jill moved to Florida and Jenny stayed behind. Her sister never got that job at Delta but Jenny did. She became a flight attendant and later enrolled at Life University where her father coached basketball. She was a loud supporter of the Running Eagles never believing a deficit was too large for them to overcome. Chip was a member of Roger's coaching staff so only Jill was missing from the family circle.

Roger's team had become a small college dynasty but off the court there were setbacks. His mother Louanna died in 1985 at the age of 76 while he was at West Georgia and his father Elmer passed away in 1992 at the age of 88 during his son's first year at Life University. Roger had beat colon cancer but his sister Sharon died of that same disease in 1996.

And cancer was not done with them yet.

ROGER AND BEVERLY'S first grandchild came into the world in 1993. Steven Robert "Bert" Givens arrived first and a year later Susan Rachel Givens was born. Jill and her husband Steve were living a charmed life. The former Atlanta Braves scout was coaching college baseball and working on his Ph.D., and Jill was enjoying every moment with her two adorable babies. She and Jenny talked on the phone almost every day and one day she casually described some discomforts she had been experiencing.

"I told her to go get a mammogram," Jenny says.

Later, when they were together, Jenny felt the nodes in her sister's breast and told her to see her doctor immediately. Everyone thought Jill was too young for this to be serious but when her doctor in Tallahassee delivered the results of her mammogram, the first person Jill called was her big sister. It was breast cancer. She was only thirty-four but cancer did not care how old she was.

Her parents were at the dedication of a sculpture on campus at Life when Jenny found them and shared the terrible news. Their hearts were breaking but before they accepted that diagnosis they wanted her to get a second opinion. They called Doctor David Jones, one of Roger's former summer campers. He said get her to Emory University Hospital as soon as possible that the best cancer doctor in Atlanta would be waiting. Jill was in Atlanta by the next day but the diagnosis was the same.

She was operated on within a week. Her father's cancer in 1982 was discovered in time but an early misdiagnosis allowed Jill's to progress. "Early detection is why Roger's here today," Beverly said. "When Jill was diagnosed they told us that the tumor was aggressive. What they didn't tell us was that word aggressive should be spelled with capital letters."

Eighteen of twenty-one lymph nodes tested positive and Jill's tragic roller coaster ride was underway. Over the next year and a half, there would be a massive mastectomy, chemotherapy, radiation and stem cell replacement therapy. Jenny was at her side every step of the way. They got the news in May of 1996, and when she finished the term at Life University in June, Jenny took a leave of absence from Delta and moved in with Jill — her built-in best friend. She became her caretaker and when she was not looking after Jill she tended to Bert and Rachel.

"I stayed with her at Shand's Hospital on the University of Florida campus in Gainesville for twenty-four days after she had stem cell replacement. We got a chance to talk about everything from when we were kids to her kids. I wouldn't trade those twenty-four days for anything," Jenny said.

Her family searched for answers but found none. Jill never smoked, seldom drank and got more rest than most people her age. She did all the right things but they had to face that bad things happen to good people, which was difficult for such a close-knit family to accept.

Roger, a naturally positive person, felt helpless. "No matter what was happening good in our personal lives, Jill's suffering was always in the back of our minds. We won a national championship in March 1997 but Jill was too sick to make the trip to Tulsa. We left a vacant seat for her at every game. That hurt, because she had always been around for something like that. But what hurt me the most was that she was fighting and fighting and never got any good news. Doctors would think they had the cancer at one place, but it would pop up somewhere else."

Basketball was his only escape and even a game he loved did not come without pain as Life assistant coach John Barrett described. "I've always respected Roger for his courage. But this pain was visible and excruciating. It took all the strength he could muster. There was no way we could shoulder his burden. All we could do was be there and help with the basketball matters."

Watching his sister die and watching his parents deal with the pain was hard on Chip. When he got the news about her diagnosis it was like a punch in the gut. He did not understand how serious it was, but that quickly changed. When Roger had colon cancer, Chip never believed his father would die from it. It was different with Jill. "I knew she was going to die of cancer but you hope it will be ten years instead of ten months."

Jenny shielded the family from her sister's worst days. They only saw the radiant countenance Jill wore if folks came to visit. But when Jill was taking a trip for one of her many treatments, Chip volunteered to drive her. Jenny went along as her nurse. "Jill was in the backseat and I didn't know if she would live through the trip. We pulled out of her driveway in Tallahassee and I watched her tell her kids goodbye and leave them standing there. It was tough."

Jenny watched her sister die a little bit every day as hope turned into acceptance. She did what she could to keep Bert and Rachel from seeing their mother suffer but that became impossible, especially where Bert was concerned. Unlike his baby sister, he remembered his mother when she was vibrant and vital. He could see the changes and Jill learned that in a simple conversation with her little boy.

"Mama, where are we going?" Bert asked his mother.

"Why do you ask?"

"Because you put on your hair."

WHEN HARP CAME to see her, Jill tore away the facades. Roger and Beverly prayed for a cure but Jill knew the end was near. She loved Harp and he loved her so she poured out her heart. She shared detailed plans for her funeral. She wanted him in the pulpit and she said Jenny would speak. A friend in Tallahassee had agreed to host a reception at her home after the service. She did not want people weeping, Jill said, telling Harp she wanted pictures, stories and friends.

They talked about heaven, and Jill told him about her cousin Sarah Graman. She was thirteen and fighting the effects of leukemia. Jill said she wanted to get to heaven so she would be there to take care of Sarah. A few months after Jill's death, the teenager was buried. Jill was not an angry cancer patient but she had one question she intended to ask God. "I'm going to ask Him why He gave me two precious children and then is going to take me away from them."

Roger and Beverly were not ready to surrender. Someone told them about Oasis of Hope, a non-traditional treatment center in Mexico. Doctors there agreed to see Jill if she was able to make the trip. An army of people in Carrollton rallied around them and raised funds to make that journey possible. It was an outpouring of love that the family has never forgotten.

Jenny knew the trip would be hard on Jill.

"Daddy, it's bad," she warned.

As feared, the flight took its toll. At times, they wondered if Jill was going to make it. They flew into San Diego where a hospital van picked them up and drove them to Tijuana and the pristine Mexican treatment center that offered Jill her final ray of hope.

Chip and Steve came on a separate flight and during a layover in Salt Lake City they called to see if Jill was still alive. In her heart, Jenny wondered if they would make it in time but somehow they did.

"Jill waited on them," Jenny believes.

Weak as she was, she opened her eyes, smiled and said, "Hey, Chippie."

Within the hour, her heart started to race and she began to fade in and out of consciousness. Her greatest fear had been that Bert and Rachel would watch her die on her couch at home. That was not God's plan.

The end came on the seventh of November in 1997, and the people who loved her most surrounded her hospital bed. When Jill Kaiser Givens took her final breath, Chip was holding her hand, and it was a long time before he turned it loose.

The return flight was out of San Diego. Authorities helped load Jill's remains on the plane while family members found their seats. As the pilot took a turn over the Pacific Ocean a pelican flew into one of the engines. The smell of burning feathers was overpowering but a flight attendant assured everyone nothing was wrong. Jenny, a veteran of many Delta flights, knew better. Her face turned white. She knew they would have to go back to the airport.

Jenny worked for Delta so the family was using buddy passes which meant their names went back on the list of stand-by passengers. The next flight to Atlanta was full but airline officials bumped five paying customers so the family could board. They did not do it because Roger Kaiser was an all-American basketball player. They did it so Jill could get home.

It was two or three in the morning when they landed in Atlanta. Don Bryant and his friend Hoyt Blalock met them at the gate. Roger, Beverly, Jenny and Chip headed to Marietta. Bryant and Blalock drove Steve Givens to Florida. Their mother was gone, and he wanted the children to hear that from their father.

THE FUNERAL IN Tallahassee was as Jill planned it. The day of the service was emotional and her loved ones have never gotten over it. More than a hundred people from Carroll County filled the pews. So did scores of family members and friends from all over the country. Beverly had a hard time dealing with everything that was going on and the welcome sight of her dear friend Orin Whitman strolling across the yard made her feel things would be all right.

Waiting outside the Presbyterian church before they were guided to their seats, Roger and Beverly felt alone. The sanctuary was filled with people they loved but one important person was missing. Then they looked up. Hovering over their heads were three black and orange butterflies. "They're telling us everything will be okay," Beverly told her husband. And those butterflies did not fly away until Roger and Beverly went inside the church.

In his moving remarks, Don Harp assured everyone that Jill was ready to die even if she did not want to die. "It was one of the hardest days of my life," he says. Jenny Kaiser spoke from the heart just as her sister requested and she did not even cry. "It was like Jill spoke through me. I didn't do that. She did."

A second memorial, organized by Doctor Sid and Doctor Nell, was held later at Life University so friends around Atlanta could tell Jill goodbye. Josh Powell sang. Norman Arey and Don Bryant offered personal remembrances. Family members have tucked away video recordings of that touching service, but no one has ever watched it.

One year before Jill's death, Roger had buried Sharon, his only sister. She also died of cancer. But losing a child was different. He expected to bury his mother and father and his aunts and uncles, but not his daughter. Roger and Beverly were devastated but they have survived with grace. "You're sad. It's terrible. But you can't mourn forever, even though nothing can be as bad as losing your child," he says.

Jenny and Chip lost a sister who never got to meet their children. Jenny looks back at Jill's death with gratitude that she was able to be with her through the months of suffering. Chip says her loss changed his perspective on life. "Today, when one of my kids does something good, I call Jenny. And I wish I could call Jill. It was hard but you don't have a choice. You deal with it. I learned not to sweat the small stuff. Jill's illness and death made me realize what is really important in life."

Roger and Beverly learned to cope. People they do not know continually reach out to them and share poignant stories about losing their children. They never realized how many people had endured similar losses and as time passed Roger and Beverly began to reach out to others, offering their experience, strength and hope.

"We're part of a fraternity that no one wants to belong to," he says.

HER GRANDPARENTS CARRY hearts full of memories but Bert and Rachel Givens only have photographs. Bert was four when Jill died so his recollections are dim. Rachel celebrated her third birthday two weeks after her mother's death so she cannot remember Jill's sweet smile. She only remembers her mother being sick.

The family tells a story about Rachel, when she was a toddler, watching television and asking her grandmother, Edith Givens, who the woman on TV was. Told it was a young mother, Rachel shook her head, "No, she can't be a mother. She's not sick."

After their mother's death Bert and Rachel continued to live with their father in Tallahassee. Their grandparents, Billy and Edith Givens, offered loads of love and support for their son and his children. Steve earned his doctorate degree and is the athletic director at Chipola College. He was married to Jill for thirteen years. Their children grew into outstanding athletes at Lawton Chiles High School.

Bert played football and baseball and as a quarterback he broke his school's single season passing record. He signed a baseball grant-in-aid with Florida State University but was injured and never played for the Seminoles. Transferring to Chipola, he hit .304 as a freshman with nine homers and 42 RBI. He was first-team all-conference. As a sophomore he batted .361 and was the Panhandle Conference Male Scholar of the Year in 2014. His talents earned him a baseball scholarship to Troy University.

Rachel thought she would play soccer, but she developed into a widely recruited long distance runner winning individual state titles in cross-country and the 3200 meters. Even with her success, Bert teased her about running. "He always asked me why would I want to go out and run because he said baseball players have to run for punishment."

When the *Tallahassee Democrat* did a story about breast cancer awareness, they featured seventeen-year-old Rachel and wrote about the value of family photographs. "It's a lot of fun for me to look back and see pictures of her when she was my age. I am older, and better understand everything. I can relate to them now," she said.

A picture of Jill swimming made her laugh. "I can't swim at all. I am like a lead ball that immediately sinks to the bottom of the pool," Rachel said. "And I am pretty sure she disliked running and probably wonders why I do it."

Rachel received a cross country and track scholarship to Auburn, her mother's alma mater, choosing the Tigers over Florida and Alabama. That made a picture of Jill and her sorority sisters taken in front of a campus restaurant very special. When she was being recruited, Rachel stood in that same spot. "Now that was pretty cool," she said.

It did not take Rachel long to make her mark. She had several top five finishes as a freshman and finished 28th at the SEC championships. In the 2014 indoor season she competed in the mile and 300 meter races. In outdoor competitions, she qualified for the NCAA East Preliminaries in the 300-meter Steeplechase and earned spots on the SEC all-Freshman Team in track and cross-country.

Jill and Jenny had different personalities and so do Bert and Rachel. Bert is reserved and reflective. Rachel is curious and shares her feelings. In an interview with a reporter in Tallahassee, Rachel talked about how these things helped them cope with the loss of their mother so long ago.

"We really didn't get into much when we were younger because I just think everyone was trying to rock on, be happy. Now I am old enough to think about it and talk about it. It's not a sad thing, but a happy feeling. We are one of the closest families I know of, and it has helped build me unique and cool relationships with my father and brother. It's really made us depend on each other."

THE LOSS OF Jill left a hole that would never be filled in the lives of her parents, her extended family and her friends. Roger and Beverly never tried to forget, as if they could. When they talk about her there is joy in their voices. On her birthday, friends in Carrollton post playful memories on social media pages. A florist in Tallahassee has a standing order to deliver flowers to her grave. Roger won his first national championship at Life University seven months before she died and even though he celebrated two more titles he always felt someone was missing.

Jenny and Chip were nearby but Bert and Rachel, their only grandchildren, lived two hundred sixty miles away in Florida and they missed them. For a time, they wondered if they would be blessed with other "grands." Chip and Christy Fead married in 1995 and Jenny married Bill Buntin, a pilot at Delta Airlines, in 2000. And in the years that followed, additional blessings would flow into Roger and Beverly's lives.

Like many other veteran employees at the airline Bill was forced to take an early retirement from Delta. The Buntins moved to South Florida and in 2001 the couple happily welcomed William Kaiser "Billy" Buntin into the world. Two years later Elizabeth Jill "Betsy" Buntin was born.

To everyone's delight, Christy Kaiser got pregnant in 2002. Roger had retired as athletic director at Life University and he was living up to an old promise to take Beverly places she had never been before. Joined by Alan and Connie Nass and Josh and Karen Powell, they had signed up for a Georgia Tech Alumni Tour of Europe. Before they left the country, Beverly suggested that Christy Kaiser should check with her doctor one more time.

"Go ahead," the physician said. "You're good for another month."

But the babies had plans of their own.

Nine weeks before the triplets were due, Christy began to have problems. Every day became an issue and a challenge. Chip had learned a lot about dealing with adversity during Jill's illness and he applied those lessons to Christy's worsening condition. "You learn to deal with it," he says. "Are you going to get mad at somebody? No. You can't walk away so you deal with it."

With his parents so far away, Chip called Christy's family. He also contacted Mary Ellen Harp and the minister's wife arrived at the hospital in record time. Doctors and nurses rallied around the frightened couple. When he saw eighteen people crowded into the delivery room, Chip was taken aback. Each of the newborns had a doctor and a nurse assigned to them. Attention was focused on Christy as it should have been but one of the doctors insisted on talking about Georgia Tech basketball.

Chip was nervous and that traffic jam of people wearing hospital gowns did not ease his concerns. He wanted to watch his babies being born, but one physician told him to just sit down behind a curtain with Christy. "See all those people," he said to Chip. "None of them are here for you."

Delivery was quick but a struggle. The babies arrived one minute apart on November 23, 2002. Alexis Ensley "Lexi" Kaiser weighed 2.4 pounds. Kelli Jill Kaiser weighed 2.9 pounds. Roger Allen "Trey" Kaiser III was the most robust at 3.7 pounds. These things did not matter to Chip and Christy. All they wanted to do was hold their three little miracles in their arms, never imagining the roadblocks that lay ahead.

Roger and Beverly were at a hotel in Prague. They were coming home the next day and Beverly called Chip to see what was new in Georgia. "You have three new grandchildren," he informed his mother, offering assurance that everything was fine.

Before they left the Czech Republic, there was an excited phone message from their friend, Doctor David Jones, who had already checked in on the triplets. "I've seen your grandchildren," he said. "Everything is fine, except for one thing: their blood is Bulldog Red."

Only everything was not fine. Each day was a roller coaster ride. Having Doctor Jones come by the hospital every day to check the babies and their charts was a blessing. Everyone was worried about Lexi. Until then all of her vital signs had been good but after her grandparents were home she developed Necrotizing Enterocolitis, which is an inflammation and death of the intestinal tissues.

Chip and Christy were advised by the doctors that she required a delicate operation and that time was of the essence. The intestinal surgery would be followed by medications that carried potentially severe side effects, including cerebral palsy.

"Do you really want to do this?" a surgeon asked.

"Do the surgery," was Chip's adamant response.

Showing amazing resiliency for one so small, Lexi survived the operation but before long there were signs of cerebral palsy. Her brother and sister were released from the hospital and they left her behind at the neo-natal intensive care unit for nearly two months. Christy was back in the hospital during that time, requiring Chip to be at Atlanta's Northside Hospital sixty-two straight days. And before he could get all of them home Chip also had to shop for a larger vehicle.

Over the years, the Kaiser grandchildren showed they were born with some of Roger's athletic skills. It started with Bert and Rachel but they are not alone. Billy Buntin has an innate basketball IQ and in 2014 his youth baseball team played in a tournament in Cooperstown, New York — home of the Baseball Hall of Fame. Trey Kaiser also shows promise in basketball and baseball. Chip is his baseball coach and they went to Cooperstown in 2015 where Trey pitched a complete-game shutout. Meanwhile, Betsy Buntin plays basketball and lacrosse and also runs track. Hallie and Kelli Kaiser are active on the volleyball court.

And do not discount Lexi.

LIFE HAS NOT been easy for Alexis Ensley Kaiser, though you would never know it by her smiling face and unwavering attitude. She describes herself as a happy and loving girl. She has love all around her, coming from Kelli and Trey and from their little sister, Hallie Marie Kaiser. God gave Chip and Christy an extra blessing when she was born in 2005. Her bubbling personality makes her a wonderful sister to the triplets.

Though confined to a wheelchair, Lexi lives life to the fullest. Every Saturday morning during baseball season, she plays in the Sandy Plains Challenger Baseball League and like her teammates she eagerly awaits her times at bat. Her helper Henry Rowling was there to push her around the bases until he enrolled at the University of Georgia. But when he comes home from Athens he is at her side. Her life is filled with obstacles but her face is filled with smiles, some of them coming from her Labrador retrievers, Gus and Woodrow — names the family borrowed from "Lonesome Dove."

To offer love and support for Lexi and other children with special needs, Roger and Beverly formed The Alexis Kaiser Foundation. Its slogan describes its purpose: *Helping Lexi Help Others*. The non-profit foundation benefits Lexi, the Cerebral Palsy Foundation, SafePath, FOCUS, Jacob's Ladder and other organizations that help special needs children.

In 2004, Chip came up with the idea of Lexi's Game, an annual celebrity golf tournament that is the primary fund-raiser for the foundation. Since 2005, it has flourished due to the generosity of friends in sports such as Phil Niekro, Bill Curry, Bobby Cox, Del Harris, Homer Rice, Bob Reinhart, Herb White, Ray Goff, Bobby Cremins, Leo Mazzone, Brian Gregory, Tommy Nobis and many more. The springtime tournament is a labor of love for the entire family They tirelessly work on the event throughout the year.

In college together Chip and Jeff Myers were co-owners of Game in Design, a specialty printing business. Myers was a teammate of Chip's at West Georgia College. Chip also owns Kaiser Marketing, a promotional products sales company.

In 2007, Chip had an appointment to discuss a T-shirt order with Scott Whitlock, the women's softball coach at Kennesaw State University outside of Atlanta. From that meeting grew an important friendship and a fundraiser that Whitlock says is the most rewarding project he has been involved with in more than thirty years of college athletics.

Chip invited Whitlock to play in the golf tournament and during that visit he met Roger and the rest of the family. As the personal relationship grew, Chip became more than his T-shirt guy. When Christy got pregnant, Whitlock did not think that was unusual but it got his attention when he heard she was having triplets. Then came the complications, the surgery, and the Cerebral Palsy that left Lexi in a wheel chair.

At one of the tournaments, someone mentioned she was upset because Kelli and Trey could ride a bicycle and she couldn't. "That hit me like a ton of bricks," Whitlock said. "I grew up in rural Georgia and I couldn't think of life without a bike. That thought gnawed at me for days and I asked Chip what could be done."

Chip explained that there were bicycles available for special needs children but that they cost between $1,500 and $2,000. Whitlock did not flinch. "I thought to myself that though I didn't have a big platform this was a chance for me to help a child right under my nose. I figured if I couldn't help, I wasn't worth very much."

Whitlock promised Chip that his softball team would raise the money for a bike for Lexi. From that emotional moment grew Lexi's Night, an annual women's softball game that benefits the Alexis Kaiser Foundation. Whitlock has moved from the bench to become Kennesaw's Senior Assistant Athletic Director. Assistant coach Wes Holly Jr., succeeded him. But that event is still one of the highlights of the Owls season. Many years, the KSU team is able to schedule Georgia Tech, which adds to the emotions surrounding the game for the Kaiser family.

Lexi and other special needs children are the true stars.

"The players expect to have Lexi's game. When she comes through that gate it's the most humbling experience for those young athletes. Team members sell tickets for the game and spend time with the girls at a meet-and-greet. It's a very positive experience for the ball players and our program. We can't change the world but we can help these beautiful kids who live all around us. I stay involved because the Good Lord game me healthy children and I have to do what I can for the children who aren't so healthy" Whitlock said.

In 2010, Lexi received one of the special tricycles at the game. Since then the foundation has presented bicycles, iPads, scholarships to camp and other items that improve the quality of life for special needs children. Chip still remembers that night. "I'll never forget the smile on her face when she got to ride it around the field," he said.

Whitlock's friendship has extended to Roger, whom he considers a mentor. They get together regularly to talk about college sports and life. "Everybody calls him Coach but if you ask Lexi who her coach is, she says Coach Whitlock. Roger's her grandpa. I'm the coach," he said.

The game was born in Whitlock's heart but it has grown into a campus-wide activity at Kennesaw State University. "It really has become something special," he said. "A lot of times student-athletes don't realize what kind of an impact they can make on someone's life. No matter their age or where they are in their careers, to somebody they are a hero."

26
Keeping Him Young

"A coach is first of all a teacher."

Jim Callis calls Roger Kaiser, "a hero in our midst." He does not describe him that way because of the number of points he scored, the basketball games he won or the number of championships he earned. As the head of Mt. Bethel Christian Academy, Callis has pulled away the curtains and seen a side of the old coach that few have seen.

They met in 2011 the year Callis joined the rapidly growing private school in Cobb County. By then, Roger had been the athletic director and head coach of the middle school basketball team for nine years. His new boss was from Tennessee so he knew little about Georgia Tech and nothing about Roger Kaiser. Only when they went out to lunch and three people Roger did not know interrupted their meal to shake his hand did the administrator realize that his basketball coach was a bona fide celebrity.

"In your life you only meet a few people that qualify as a hero and Roger has the kind of character that deserves all that attention. To have someone as grounded as he is in our students' lives is important. We benefit from that everyday. He doesn't impose himself. You have to invite him in. And he brings the perspective that only history provides," Callis says.

Mt. Bethel Christian Academy serves 572 students, primarily in the eastern portion of Cobb County. It began in 1998 with two kindergarten classes after members of Mt. Bethel United Methodist Church recognized a need for Christian education among their young people. Adding a grade each year, the academy became a middle school and in the fall of 2015 the newly acquired upper school campus will add high school classes for the first time. Its serene and stimulating campus includes indoor and outdoor gymnasiums, soccer and baseball fields and a fully stocked pond for fishing.

Roger and Beverly were familiar with the church for it was only eight miles from the Life University campus. It was also the church where the Reverend Don Harp — assisted by the Reverend Randy Mickler, the Mt. Bethel pastor — married Chip and Christy. The Kaisers were already acquainted with Mickler who previously served at the First Methodist Church in Bowdon, eleven miles from Carrollton.

They also knew Darren DeVore, Chip's brother-in-law and an influential member at Mt. Bethel, the third largest Methodist church in the world and the largest east of the Mississippi River. It was DeVore who came to Roger in 2002 with an interesting proposition. Roger said no at first, but successful businessmen do not go away so easily. He came back again and this time Roger listened.

And that offer changed his life.

DAVID JONES HAD known Roger since he was a teenager at his summer camp in the hills of North Georgia. Jones played basketball in college at Mercer University before going to medical school and becoming a respected pediatric cardiologist. Through the years he had been there when the Kaiser family needed medical support and now he had a favor to ask of his old friend.

They met at a simple restaurant near the Atlanta airport. Jones told Roger how he had expanded his portfolio to a number of private businesses and that he believed one of his managers was stealing from him. Roger had just retired as athletic director at Life University and Jones assumed he was available, forgetting that he was the brand-new grandfather of triplets and that he had promised Beverly they would finally have time to travel. But Jones had been so helpful to his family and he was only asking Roger to run his company until they figured out where the problems were so he agreed to do what he could.

Roger was a basketball man, not a businessman, but he was honest, which was a valuable commodity to Jones. Accepting the temporary position, Roger commuted from Marietta to Fairburn every day. He was part detective and part manager and soon the coach and the physician figured out what had to be done.

Meanwhile, DeVore was not giving up. He was the founding chairman of the board at Mt. Bethel Christian Academy and he wanted Roger to be athletic director and head of the physical education department. DeVore was a graduate of the University of Georgia and a member of the board of trustees of the UGA Foundation. He overlooked Roger's Georgia Tech ties and believed he would bring stability and credibility to a burgeoning sports program.

"We did everything in excellence and we believed Roger represented excellence," he says. "We wanted him because of who he was. If we could get a man like Coach Kaiser it would bring prominence to the school and provide for our future."

Roger became intrigued at the prospect of working with adolescents. He earnestly believed he had something to offer them beyond basketball. What he did not imagine was how much those young people had to offer him. He finally told DeVore he would give them three years.

He had spent most of his adult life working on college campuses but from the beginning Roger felt at home at Mr. Bethel. As a young person, he never thought he was cut out for coaching. But at the age of sixty-four he could not imagine doing anything that did not involve coaching and teaching. He was as focused and intense dealing with boys not old enough to drive as he was with gifted college athletes. DeVore sensed that excitement right away. He is principal of The Carroll Organization, one of the nation's leading privately held real estate companies. He is fervent about business so it was easy for him to recognize Roger's passion.

He describes an eighth grade basketball game soon after Roger took over. "The refs were giving Coach Kaiser a hard time and he wouldn't quit riding them. He got a technical foul and the next thing I knew the referee came over and threw him out of the game. I followed him to the dressing room and he felt terrible. He said he had played since he was a kid, in high school, college and the pros and then spent forty years as a coach. And that was the first time he had ever been thrown out of a game."

Roger's three-year commitment stretched into more and his value to Mt. Bethel grows each year. In his first thirteen years on the bench, his boy's teams won 178 games and lost 52 times and between 2007 and 2012 brought home four division championships. The North Atlanta Metro League has honored the Eagle athletic program five different years for overall excellence in sports. But Callis looks beyond victories and trophies. "He's a coach. He's a basketball guy. But he loves all these kids, whether they can hit the broad side of a barn or not," the administrator says.

On campus he is a grandfatherly figure who loves to give hugs and get hugs and an engaged faculty member who is teaching if he is talking. Students benefit from his wisdom and in return they keep him young. The school has an annual grandparents day but many students do not have grandparents living nearby. That was the case for Abigail Ethridge, the daughter of school nurse Jennifer Etheridge. "She was 9 years old and she walked over to the gym and asked Coach Kaiser if he would be her grandfather for a day. I'm not sure who was happier," Callis recalls.

His physical education classes include more than basketball skills. When he learned that many of his affluent students had never been fishing Roger asked Callis if they could fish in one of the ponds on campus. "Can I buy some poles and worms?" he asked. He had to show students how to bait a hook and to his amazement, the girls were more comfortable with the worms than the boys.

There are more than a hundred faculty members and Roger prefers to be just another teacher. But on a field day when faculty and students participated in drills to build trust, everyone was startled to see Coach Kaiser swirling down from the tower on a zip line. They were also impressed at his performance during a coed softball game, bearing in mind that he was in his mid-seventies and a two-time cancer survivor.

Guys had to switch around and hit from the other side, which in Roger's case meant he had to swing the bat from the left side. Oh, and if a male player hit the ball over the fence it was an automatic out.

Photographs of Roger at the plate show his typical intense expression as he waited on the pitch.

Hitting left-handed he slammed the ball over the fence. Twice.

ROGER KAISER RUNS the same practice drills and has the same expectations coaching middle school guys as he did when he was a college coach. Chip Kaiser agrees that his father coaches the same way, but he points out one major difference: "The language is different."

Boys at Mt. Bethel are not like he and Bob Reinhart were when they were growing up in Indiana. Basketball was what they played and basketball was what they dreamed about. Youngsters today enjoy the game but it is only one activity on a crowded daily agenda. So while a coach can teach traditional offenses and defenses he must come up with clever ways to motivate and encourage players that do not have the patience or desire to spend endless hours alone honing individual skills.

"We talk about pride," Roger says. "Some people consider pride a sin but it isn't to me. A person must have self-pride, team-pride, school-pride and family-pride —especially if you want to be a shooter. I've always heard that a good coach improves your game but a great coach improves your life."

Even with middle school players, that is still the way he coaches. In 2015, he was blessed with three talented players that had been with him for several seasons. Ryan Billig, Coleman Boyd and Ryan Greer enjoyed playing, enjoyed working and along the way they discovered they enjoyed winning. They are students of the game, but does their basketball knowledge include their coach?

"I Googled him," Billig says.

"He was considered a shooter," Greer says.

"He has a good basketball IQ," Billig says.

Greer repeats Roger's mantra about pride and adds his own point of view: "It's all about pride. He shares his experiences with us and they don't always have to do with basketball. He teaches us lessons he has learned about life."

The boys heard about their coach's shooting ability, especially at the free throw line. They have seen him hit 55 in a row. They have challenged him but they have yet to beat him. "That's okay," Greer adds. "I knew I could learn from him."

Roger has also learned from them. "I'm a better person because of my experiences at Mt. Bethel."

MT. BETHEL STUDENTS learn from him and in nearly seventy years around the game Roger has learned about basketball and life from scores of teachers and coaches — including the people who worked for him as assistant coaches.

"I had perfect coaches," he says, "good people who never raised their voices."

Like a coach scouting an opponent, Roger runs down what he learned from them going all the way back to Gervais Hollander, a strict disciplinarian who taught boys on the grade school team to take the game seriously. As protégés of Hurst Livengood, he and Bob Reinhart learned nuances of the game, starting with the pick-and-roll. But Roger's basketball education really started in high school taught by a trio of coaches in that cozy gym in Dale:

- Jerry Kemp —A mathematician, he defied the odds and brought two ninth grade boys — Roger and Bob — up to the varsity and put them in the lineup ahead of more experienced players. He saw in Roger a teen-ager blessed with unusual skills and an unparalleled work ethic. It would have been interesting to see what kind of teams Kemp would have turned out had he stayed at Dale High and what kind of individual player Roger would have become.

- Roy Yenowine — He only coached Roger one year, the season Bob was ineligible during the first semester. He was wise enough to recreate the offense and give Roger the basketball. The numbers Roger put up helped the Golden Aces win a lot of games and caused college recruiters to begin to notice a small-town high school junior.

• Billy Livengood — He pushed Roger to show people who he was and urged him to have no regrets when a game was over. He said he needed a shot he could depend on and helped him refine his jump shot. Even before high school, he taught him the change of pace, a valuable tool that helped Roger get his own shot. Things Livengood taught him instilled the confidence that made Roger want the ball in crucial situations.

Coaches bounced through his life at a rapid pace in high school but in college there were only two: Whack Hyder and Joe Pittard. Ultimately, they were the reasons Roger came to Georgia Tech.

Perhaps no other coach in the game could have developed Roger like Hyder did. The harshest thing he ever said to him was, "Roger, you're a better person than that." Hyder was nurturing, kind and encouraging and provided Roger the opportunities he needed to become the player, coach and person he is. The affection and friendship they shared never waned.

Coach Joe was also a special person who as a baseball coach developed good citizens as well as good players. He wanted his players to behave on the field and be in church on Sunday morning. If Roger was struggling, he would say, "You're not living right."

Though Roger never aspired to be a coach, it was apparent that he was born for the job though he got into the profession for the wrong reason. "I wanted summers off," he confesses.

His style of coaching has been an amalgamation of coaches he played under and those he observed, including the educational philosophy of John Wooden and the simplicity of Bobby Knight and Norm Sloan who always warned against over-coaching. It is no accident that each of them is identified with the state of Indiana.

HIRING ASSISTANT COACHES was a new adventure. Since he had never been a head coach, Roger wanted aides familiar with sides of the game that he knew little about as a player. As much as anything he looked for someone who had the loyalty of a teammate.

"I wanted my assistant coaches to work with me as a team as we worked with the basketball teams. I wanted them to be involved in what we were doing and wanted them to jump in with both feet. Often I thought they would do some things better than me and truthfully, other things that I did not enjoy doing. I tried to make it possible for everyone involved to enjoy the job. It was nice to see smiling faces," he says.

When Roger took the job at Decatur High, Bob Reinhart already had three years of coaching experience and Roger knew firsthand how much his lifelong friend loved the game. "I never thought it would come down to working together but from Bob I learned the art of coaching and gained the confidence to make the move into the college game."

Though Roger never lacked confidence as a player, he saw another brand of confidence in his self-assured friend. "Bob's a real competitor in everything but especially on the golf course where he spends so much of his time. When it comes down to making a putt, Bob always says, "Only two people in the world can make this putt. One of them is Raymond Floyd and the other one is me. He's not here, so let me putt."

Constantly chomping on an unlit cigar, Bob is a genuine character and so is Jerry Reynolds, the first assistant coach Roger hired at West Georgia College. Players Reynolds recruited built the foundation for the program and he made things fun.

"He's another Hoosier who would talk basketball for hours," Roger says. "He was a delight to have around with his humor and uncanny ability to recruit. We were a workable team and we surprised many basketball people with our 1974 national championship team, a team that worked tirelessly and respected one another. As much as anything, I enjoyed being in his company, and I still do."

Bob Lamphier was yet another Hoosier. He played at Valdosta State prior to Roger's stint at West Georgia and turned into a valuable recruiter and friend. He lives in New Mexico and Roger and Beverly have joined his family on several snow skiing trips.

David Fowlkes was the first of Roger's former players to join his coaching staff. Their relationship started at Decatur High where Roger taught him in physical education class. As a player at West Georgia, he was on the first team to beat Valdosta State in Valdosta. He was a basketball assistant for the Braves and was later head baseball coach.

After Fowlkes, a number of former players worked under Roger. That list includes Tim Criswell, Joey Godwin, Boyd Steele and, of course, Chip Kaiser. "Each of them had a pretty good idea how I coached and what I expected and accepted from the players. They also knew what irritated me — giving less than 100 percent effort."

When Roger became head coach at Life University, he needed assistants with a keen knowledge of basketball but he also needed coaches who knew what went into building a program from the ground up and were willing to put in the effort on unglamorous tasks.

John Barrett was an ideal choice. "What a wonderful addition to a new program. He showed up wanting to be a part of it but at that time there was not even a team. His love for the game and tireless efforts recruiting paid dividends and before long he became a fulltime member of the staff. We worked together for ten years through three national championships. We share many happy memories."

Barrett recommended Bill Firnbach and the former Georgia State University player became a valuable staff member. "Bill was the detail man that John and I needed. He is quiet and unassuming and no task was too big or too small for him. Bill helped us all by not getting too high or too low for the outcome of a game or a season."

His mother recommended Chip Kaiser, and Roger needed no more than that. He played for his father at West Georgia College so Chip understood his coaching philosophy at every level.

"He was our link to the players and he did whatever needed to be done. He was my answer man whenever players had suggestions or voiced individual concerns. Maybe it was his youth. Maybe it was because he had been a player under me. Or maybe he understood me better than anyone else. I just know it was a pleasure to have him with me all those years at Life. I saw him run his screen printing business while he was coaching and his work ethic made me very proud."

At West Georgia and Life, Roger was blessed with a steady stream of hardcore basketball people. That list includes: Jimmy Parker, Steve Sodell, Nikita Johnson, Julius Smith, Randy Dunn, Bill Gamble, Frank Sylvester, Tim Reeve and Dale Hatcher.

When he went to Mt. Bethel and started tutoring adolescents, Roger needed a deeper level of support. He found that in Dan Boswell.

He was the academy's Director of Recreation and one of the first people Roger met when he arrived. "He told me he would help me any way he could to get the athletic program going in a positive direction. I told him the first thing I needed was coaches. I said if he would coach the girl's basketball team, I would coach the boys and we would be each other's assistants. Dan and I spent many hours discussing our needs and our players. He was a tremendous asset to our program and a positive influence for the academy."

Pete Gonzalez started as a volunteer and has never left. "He's a tireless worker who loves the game and has the players best interest at heart. Pete is always giving me suggestions and if I don't do them, he gives them to me again. He calls me Old School. I like that because everything that is new is not necessarily the best. Like me, Pete is very competitive. We work together well and we've had some fine teams and great players."

Whether it was college, high school or middle school, Roger and his staff have worked together as if they were his teammates or members of his extended family. Even after the contracts expire, those feelings do not end. He was in charge, but has never ignored the contributions of those around him.

"All of them brought something to our teams. Chances are I wouldn't have hired them if I didn't have that feeling. My ego has never prevented me from wanting help, I want and need their help and have had no problem giving them the opportunity to coach. Without their input over the years, we would have not had the success we were able to achieve. I've no problem giving them opportunity and responsibility. Most assistants are looking for the opportunity to be a head coach. I just never wanted them to take my job."

27
Fishin' with Coach

"You don't stop laughing because you grow old—you grow old because you stop laughing."

Roger Kaiser has many layers. He is a small-town boy who has not forsaken the wholesome values he learned as a child. He is a husband who loves his energetic cheerleader. He is a father who is always there for his children and never stops missing the one he lost. He is a grandfather who acts as young as his grandchildren when they are together. He is a fiercely loyal friend and teammate. He is a teacher who enjoys sharing his wisdom. He is a cancer survivor who lives because of faith and a team of doctors he calls his angels. And, as always, he competes until the final buzzer on everything he does.

Basketball opened many doors for him. It started on that primitive court that his father built and its importance has never waned. It brought him to Atlanta before the Braves, Falcons or Hawks at a time that his name was splashed across the front page of the sports section in the morning and afternoon. It turned a humble young man into a star and a hero when those things meant something. It pushed him into coaching where the rewards continued to mount.

It has been more than fifty years since Roger played his last basketball game at Georgia Tech and more than a decade since he coached his final game at Life University. But people he has never met still walk up to him and want to replay a big bucket from long ago or talk about the days when he was one of the nation's top five college basketball players.

Stardom has given way to celebrity and Roger wears that cloak with the same dignity that he showed when he was the focus of Al

Ciraldo's colorful broadcasts. After Pete Maravich's death in 1988, Bob Dylan wrote a song about the legendary LSU great. His lyrics suggest that dignity is like the wind that it cannot be seen and cannot be captured on film. That is the kind of dignity that Roger possesses.

His carriage and sincerity are part of what former Georgia Tech Athletic Director Homer Rice calls the Total Person. That is based on his concept that a person's excellence is a result of a balanced life. He says Roger is an example of that philosophy and in 2012 Roger was presented the Dr. Homer Rice Total Person Outstanding Alumnus Award by the Georgia Tech Athletic Association.

Rice believes Roger is one of those athletes that people never forget because he is the person they think he is. "He has a special magic. He is a friend to everyone and when you are with him he makes you think he is your best friend. Roger has shown excellence in all areas of his life. He is one of those positive leaders that we need so badly today."

People frequently discover that the athletes and coaches they admire do not always live up to their clippings. Instead of heroes, they are disappointments, he says. "Roger is not one of those people. He is an all-around person, a family man with a positive attitude. He fits the mold of a Total Person in all of the important categories."

Though remembered as a prolific scorer and uncanny shooter, Roger is amazingly unselfish. Rice recalls a Tech alumni game when former player Bud Shaw was coaching one of the squads. Roger was being a facilitator instead of shooting the ball and Shaw called time out and quietly spoke to the former all-American.

"Roger, these people didn't come here to see you pass the ball. Shoot it."

BASKETBALL HAS BEEN the key but family is the foundation for everything Roger Kaiser has accomplished in life. When he was a boy his father Elmer was the rebounder when Roger practiced shooting, Louanna, his mother, participated in family free throw contests and cooked carrots for him if he was not hitting the baseball. His parents were there for just about every game he played in high school and years later, when he went into coaching, they were in the stands for many of his biggest games.

His sister Sharon was an athlete long before Title IX. Dale High did not have a girl's basketball team when she was in school but she was a cheerleader for the Golden Aces. She and Roger competed on the family court and bickered over card games. Sharon graduated from Indiana University and like her mother became a schoolteacher. She took summer classes one year in Colorado and liked that part of the country so much that she moved to the West Coast. She was sixty-two years old and a resident of California when she died of colon cancer in 1996.

Roger was in elementary school when his brothers were born. Like their big brother Van and Joe played basketball at Dale High, finding it difficult to live up to the standards he had set. They were in their teens by the time Roger found stardom at Georgia Tech.

Joe, the youngest, became an Indiana Hoosier fan and shared his siblings' dry wit. For years, he suffered from health problems that stemmed from a serious motorcycle accident. His windpipe was almost severed and he nearly choked to death. He never fully recovered and always had trouble breathing. Joe died of a heart attack in 2000 at the age of fifty-five, leaving behind his wife and four children.

Roger was six years old when Van came along and the younger Kaiser cherishes pictures of his brother tossing a baseball to him in the front yard when he was only two years old. Such moments were repeated throughout his life. "Roger is always there," Van says. "He had been there for most of the important moments in my life."

He also showed up for card games.

"He's competitive, all right," Van says. "He'll change the rules if you don't watch him."

Van admits that it was difficult for he and his brother to live up to Roger's exploits in sports. No matter how well Van played, someone brought up his brother's name and pointed out that he was not as good as Roger. Bob Reinhart told Van how to handle those situations. "When someone says you're not nearly as good as your brother just say, 'and you're aren't either.'"

Van still has a clipping from the *Louisville Courier-Journal* that includes an article about a grand slam home run he hit to win an important American Legion game. Roger was in the stands and after the game he came down to the field to offer his congratulations. The story in the paper the next day talked about Roger Kaiser's brother hitting the big home run.

"That never bothered me," he says. "I was proud of him too."

Van was still a high school kid when he followed Tech games in the newspaper and sometimes picked them up on the radio. The real treats came when Elmer and Louanna packed up the car and took the younger boys to Yellow Jacket games at Kentucky, Tennessee or Vanderbilt.

What Van saw at a game in Nashville made an impression on him and the memory still makes him feel proud. "I don't know who won the game or how many points Roger had. But after the game I watched him sit in the bleachers and sign autographs for more than 45 minutes. The fans stayed and he stayed. It was one of the proudest moments of my life."

Van went to the University of Evansville and was a member of the Purple Aces baseball team. He graduated at the height of the Vietnam War and he had a choice of enlisting in the military or being drafted. Van joined the United States Army and qualified for flight school. He became a test pilot and as he puts it, "I flew everything." He retired as a Lieutenant Colonel and lives on a cattle farm back home in Dale.

David and James Hevron might as well be Roger's brothers. They were in grade school when he started dating their older sister and long ago they began to treat him as a big brother.

David Hevron was nine-years-old when, as he puts it, "Roger began hanging around" their home in Lincoln City. From the beginning, his sister's high school boyfriend fit into their family and treated Beverly's little brothers the way they wanted to be treated. In high school or college, he never acted like he was a star. "He has always fit in like a glove fits a hand," David says.

When Roger was at Tech, David and James wanted to hear his games on radio. Elmer Kaiser learned that if he drove to the highest point in Spencer County he could pick up WSB Radio from Atlanta.

Sometimes he took the boys with him. "About game time we would start driving toward Patronville. We would pull off the road along the way and gets parts of the game. We had to keep moving," David says.

James saw Roger play several times in high school and college, usually hitching a ride with his Dad. He saw him play both games in the Indiana-Kentucky all-star series and later saw him play against Ohio State in the NCAA Tournament in Louisville. "Roger was just somebody you wanted to be around," James says. "I got to go with him to Atlanta one time and they were just finishing Interstate 75. We were pulling a U-Haul and around Chattanooga Roger hit somebody from the rear. It was scary for a kid. When we got to Atlanta I remember that everybody wanted to meet him."

Roger has never quit hanging around, and now that they are older, David and James have adopted him into their close-knit family. They have seen he and Beverly's partnership prosper through the years and David says they look to him as a family leader even though his name is not Hevron.

"He doesn't demand respect. He gets respect. He has an ability to fit into any situation and I don't think I've ever seen him get upset," David says. "He's real, and he always gets it done."

FORMER DELTA AIRLINES pilot Bill Buntin and southpaw Christy Fead Kaiser married into the clan, and each of them describes a warm reception from their new in-laws. Bill met Jenny in the airport in Frankfurt, Germany when she was a flight attendant and he learned who her father was in bits and pieces. A friend arranged a date for Christy and Chip and at first she heard more about Roger than his only son.

Not long after they met Roger and Beverly invited Bill to join them on a family trip to the Civil War battlefields at Gettysburg. In the years that followed, they went skiing, rafting and deep-sea fishing together. He discovered a couple that acts twenty or thirty years younger than the numbers on their Driver's Licenses.

"Roger is like a fun big brother," Bill says.

When Christy met Chip, she had no clue about who his father was. She figured out that Roger must be someone special when so many people talked about him in glowing terms. She finally asked her father who he was and he remembered him winning a championship at West Georgia College. "That's great, I thought. But I'm going to be dating his son," she says.

Christy's aunt worked at Life University where Roger was coaching and Chip was one of his assistants. She grew even more tired of hearing about Chip's father when her aunt also gushed over him.

"It's such a small world," Christy says. "My aunt saw Chip on campus and said she had heard he was dating her niece. When he finally called me he said, 'I hear I'm your boyfriend.'"

From the moment they met Roger teased Christy about being a lefthander and to date he has not stopped making comments. "If I burn the cookies it's because I'm left handed. Whatever I'm doing, he says, 'Come on, Lefty. You can do it.' When I told him I led the basketball team at Walton High School in free throw shooting, he didn't believe me. 'You're a lefty. You can't shoot free throws.'"

Christy and Bill agree that Roger and Beverly are world-class grandparents. They support their eight grandkids in whatever they do but they do not cater to them. They see them as individuals and treat them the way they want to be treated. "They want to be sure that each child gets his or her fair share," Bill says.

Sons-in-law are not ignored. When Beverly arrives at their home in Florida she takes over the kitchen and keeps the stove in action until she goes back home. She did this when Bill was flying and when Beverly was around he seldom left on an overseas assignment without one of her pound cakes tucked away in his bags.

On a layover in Germany he was jogging alongside the Main River in Frankfurt and his back went out. Making his way back to his hotel, Bill called Jenny and told her how much pain he was in. Her parents contacted Doctor Sid Williams and let him know what was happening. The Life University founder called a former student who operated a clinic in Hamburg, three or four hours away. The chiropractor came to Frankfurt and after he adjusted Bill's back he was pain free. "He wouldn't take money so I gave him one of Beverly's pound cakes," Bill says.

Roger does not bake pound cakes but if Chip is busy and cannot tend to the lawn, he goes over and cuts the grass for Christy. He also makes sure she has the latest edition of the Upper Room, one of her favorite daily devotionals.

"How can you not love Roger Kaiser?" she says.

BELIEVE IT OR not, if it feels like leather Roger still shoots it. At an age when his peers only watch, he continues to compete. He has a store-bought hip, one of his knees has been surgically repaired and twice he was diagnosed with cancer. Despite these medical reports, he refuses to be a relic in an easy chair.

Blame that on Paul Vickers. He was a senior football player at Georgia Tech when Roger was a freshman. Before that, he was on the 1953 state championship basketball team at North Fulton High School in Atlanta. After college, the long and lanky Vickers worked for IBM. He still played basketball and as he grew older he found great joy stealing the ball from a twenty-year-old or blocking a young guy's shot.

In the late 1990s, he recruited other aging fellows to play for the Atlanta Classics in the National Senior Games. They competed two times and never won a game, which did not set well with Vickers. "Floyd Williams, a friend of mine at church, knew about my failures. He's a big Tech man and he suggested I should get Roger Kaiser. I said go ahead and ask him, and never thought about it again. Floyd collects autographs and in 2004 he went to the Final Four in San Antonio — the year Tech lost to U-Conn in the finals. Floyd stopped Roger on the street and asked if he wanted to play ball with some old gym rats. Roger said for me to call him."

Roger can still score, Vickers found. The team started winning and Vickers remembers a game in the nationals against a group from Maryland that they won 36-35 with Roger scoring 33 points. "He shoots the ball very well and is a three-point threat if he has time to line it up. He can drive it to the basket too. He's strong and he can handle the ball. He either makes the bucket and gets fouled or gets two free throws. The thing about Roger is he is nice and friendly to everyone but he's also a fierce competitor."

Gordon Darrah, his old adversary from Georgia, is one of Roger's senior teammates. He marvels how Roger scores the basketball. "Scoring is one of the first things to go as you age but he has such strong hands and legs," Darrah says.

Competition is three-on-three. The only concession to age is that they play half-court with a running clock. Vickers says those factors are misleading, that you never stop running. If the other team makes a bucket, you take the ball out and fire it to the top of the key.

Roger cannot jump any more but he is not short on confidence, which bubbled over on a Caribbean cruise he and Beverly enjoyed one summer. Word went out of a basketball tournament on deck and Roger joined them. Sides were chosen and he was not selected.

"While the first group was playing I got together a team. We challenged the winners and beat them soundly," he says. They were from Boston and they were good. After his team embarrassed them, one of the fellows confronted Roger.

"You're a ringer. Who are you?"

"I'm the guy you didn't pick," he said.

At the 2013 National Senior Olympics in Cleveland the Georgians won their first three games. That earned them a good seed in the finals. "I'm confident if Roger hadn't hurt his knee we would have been runner-up and may have won the whole thing," Vickers says. "We managed to finish third in the nation."

The 2015 games were in Minneapolis-St. Paul where the Classics competed in the 75 and over division. They did not make it to the finals losing three games by a total of nine points, including one game where they fell to a free throw after the final buzzer. The team from Rhode Island that eliminated the Classics went on to win the bronze medal. "As a team, we didn't come through when we needed to, be it a big bucket, a key rebound or a great pass," Roger says.

The pace was grueling and though Roger was the team's leading scorer he could feel time catching up on him. "We played three games one day then had to come back and play the next morning at 8 a.m.," he said. "People don't treat animals that way. I wasn't nearly as good as I was two years ago, and I needed a lot more rest. My shoulder was hurting and I didn't have nearly as much range."

So why do they play?

"It's fun," says Vickers, the team's oldest player. "It keeps me in good physical condition. Unlike a lot of older guys, I'm still a legitimate six-foot-three with long arms. This is the way I exercise. I have three rules: Don't embarrass myself. Play good defense. And don't get hurt."

When the 2015 Senior Olympic Games were history, Roger told Vickers that he probably would not play the next time around, ending more than seventy years of competitive basketball.

"Keep your jersey," Vickers told Roger. "I'm gonna retire it."

HIS ACCOMPLISHMENTS ON the court are rivaled by only a few. So old friends cannot help but wonder why with so many victories and championships Roger Kaiser was never a head coach at a Division I school — especially at his alma mater.

Whack Hyder retired from Tech in 1973 with 292 victories. As the Engineers searched for his successor reporters zeroed in on Roger, who had been at West Georgia College for three seasons. Speculation swirled but Roger purposely stayed on the sideline. He had Foots Walker and he sensed good things were about to happen in Carrolton. Tech's cupboard was bare. Hyder went 6-20 and 7-18 in his last two seasons and privately he advised Roger not to entertain any offers. "You don't want this job," Hyder said. "This isn't the place for you now."

Dwane Morrison, head coach at Mercer University and a former Hyder aide, got the job. Morrison was 5-21 in 1974 — the year Roger guided West Georgia to a 29-4 mark and his first NAIA championship. Morrison had only three winning seasons and was fired after a 4-23 record in 1981. Tech turned to Appalachian State University's Bobby Cremins who became the most successful coach in Tech history with 354 victories in nineteen seasons.

Jerry Reynolds has been with the Sacramento Kings since 1988. Before the NBA he worked with Roger at West Georgia and in four years the team was 98-23. He believes Roger's talents were underappreciated and that he would have flourished as a Division I coach.

"Hey, coaching isn't nuclear physics for gosh sakes. Roger is smart and humble and he knows his own strengths and weaknesses. I have never understood why Georgia Tech or some other program didn't hire him. I know firsthand what he did at West Georgia. If you had put Pat Riley or Mike Krzyzewski there they couldn't have done any better than Roger. People look down at Division II basketball but all I know is that Gregg Popovich didn't fare well in small college coaching but he has done very well in the NBA."

Tear away the frills and the primary differences between major college and Division II are the salaries of the coaches, the size of the arenas, the length of the bus rides and the number of games they play on ESPN. Playbooks are the same but the skills of the athletes running those plays are different. The quality of the coaching can be better in small college basketball but coaches are often treated like second-class citizens when they are talked about for Division I openings.

That is shameful to Oregon Tech's Danny Miles, a close friend of Roger's and one of the NAIA's all-time greats. He is third on the current list of winning coaches with 1,017 victories, one behind Krzyzewiski, the only Division I men's coach who has ever broken a thousand. Miles has won three national titles and gone to the national tournament seventeen times. He also drives the van to away games, washes the sweat from uniforms and endures thirteen-hour bus rides up mountain passes.

"Coaches don't get the same respect and sometimes it is tougher to win in small college basketball than it is in Division I," says Miles, who has coached the Hustling Owls since 1971. "But the big time is where you're at."

Bob Hoffman has coached on both sides of the street. He spent decades in the NAIA and as head coach at Division I Mercer his mid-major Bears shocked Coach K and Duke in the first round of the 2014 NCAA Tournament. Hoffman's Oklahoma Baptist team and Life spent the 1990s battling for spots in the Top 10. They met in the 1997 NAIA finals, won by Roger's Eagles.

"Life had a great run. Roger had the ability to get his teams to play hard and to be unselfish, which was an amazing gift at that level. He had a knack of getting older guys and helping them as players and in life," Hoffman says.

Like others, Hoffman does not understand why Roger never had an opportunity to perform on a larger stage. "He would have been successful because he coached in the toughest venues and at Life he built a program from the ground up. Assistants are not always successful as head coaches because they can't work all the angles but as a small college coach you have to be all things to all people. Roger could communicate with anybody," he says.

Before hundreds of schools jumped to the NCAA, the brand of basketball played in the NAIA was often better than Division I. So was the coaching. "I saw guys better than me not get the chance to coach at a big school," Hoffman says. "That's why I think it is amazing that Roger never had an opportunity."

After Mercer's upset of third-seeded Duke, Hoffman received his twenty-four hours of fame. An article in *Time Magazine* reminded readers where basketball coaches like Hoffman and Roger have been:

> The Mercer win says even more about coaching. Mercer's Bob Hoffman coached the pants of Krzyzewski. Down the stretch, he made chess moves on defense that gave Duke shooters fits. Mike Krzyzewski is a Hall-of-Famer, winner of four national titles, two gold medals, and pulling in $7 million a year, at least. Hoffman is well, a guy named Bob Hoffman, not making nearly as much. The best basketball coaches are often the ones who make the least. They're scattered across the country, in high schools, junior colleges, Division III institutions. If Coach K has humility, and I think he does, he'd be the first to admit: Big-name" coaches, like himself, are most often ridiculously overrated, and overpaid.

How Miles and Roger met is interesting. Miles needed teams to come to Klamath Falls and play in the Cell Tech Classic. He asked his secretary to invite squads on the West Coast and she mailed an invitation to Life University, confusing it with a school of the same name in California. Roger accepted, thinking a trip to the northwest would be educational for his players. By the time Miles learned what was happening, it was too late to rescind.

After several visits, the two coaches learned how much alike they were in coaching and in how they treated people. On another visit to Oregon, Miles called Roger at two o'clock in the morning and said they had to get out of there right then. "If you don't, you'll be snowed in." Then he did something that a Division I coach would never do. "He drove one of the vans to Medford, had breakfast with us, and made sure we made our flight," Roger says.

When a banquet marking Miles' 1000th victory was held in 2014, Roger went all the way to Oregon to speak. "We're both competitors. We would go hard to win at dominoes but after the game is over, it's over. I call Danny, 'The Coach.' He's in a class all his own. He does things the right way and sends a message he cares. And the greatest thing a leader can do is show that he cares."

His success in thirty-five years of coaching was not totally unnoticed. Roger had feelers from several schools about openings and was approached about head coaching jobs at Georgia State University, East Tennessee State University, Evansville University and the Citadel. The right offer never came at the right time and Roger harbors no regrets.

Working for Doctor Sid at Life University, Roger enjoyed many of the extras of a Division I program. He had a full staff, a new car every year and his basketball budget was more than adequate. The team traveled well and Roger was rewarded for his victories and titles.

Roger was comfortable with who he was. He never thirsted for the pressures of a major college job, especially the constant fear of getting fired. Nor did his ego need to be fed with TV time and courtside visits with Dick Vitale. Travel never appealed to him and he valued his time at home with his family.

He is at peace with his past and where it has led him. When he is asked about not getting an opportunity to coach at a major college, he recalls an exchange about such jobs that he had with Sonny Clements, the retired head coach at Columbus State University.

"Are you happy, Roger?"

"Yes, I am."

"Do you have enough money?"
"You never have enough, but yes, we're okay."
"Have you seriously thought about going Division I?"
"Not really."
"Then don't do it," Clements said. "Don't sell your soul."

HE KNOWS HOW to be a friend and in return people covet their friendship with Roger Kaiser. Some began when he was a kid in Indiana. Some were made on a basketball court and some started in a small town in Georgia where Roger played softball with his neighbors and went to church on Sunday mornings. Some were made in doctor's offices. When his phone rings it could be a high school classmate or a former ball player in need of advice.

Few go back further than David Dougan, a childhood buddy from across the street in Dale. They were together when they learned to cuss and tried to smoke. But the simple punishments their parents wielded did nothing to diminish their friendship. Many years later, after doctors removed most of Roger's colon in a successful fight against cancer, Dougan called Beverly every day. He wanted to come to Carrollton but she said no, everything was all right. Then one day she opened the front door and there was their dear friend from back home.

Fate or coincidence brought him there on one of Roger's worst days. Beverly needed help and there was Dougan. The families remain close and every year the Dougans drive to Georgia to work as volunteers at Lexi's Game, the annual celebrity golf tournament that is the primary fundraiser for the Alexis Kaiser Foundation. At the tournament in 2015, Dougan noted Roger's hearing problems and bragged about his new hearing aides. That July, Roger's old friend passed away and on a visit with Dougan's wife he asked for a keepsake to help him remember their friendship. She paused and she had just the thing. In a moment she returned with those hearing aides. "Dave would want you to have these," she said.

The golf tournament brings together Roger's assortment of friends. Participants appreciate the worthwhile cause but they also enjoy each other. Former NFL center Bill Curry does not play in the tournament but he joins Roger, his Georgia Tech classmate, as a greeter at one of the holes. When Leo Mazzone approached the green he recognized Curry from a distance. Here was a guy who with the Atlanta Braves coached three Hall of Fame pitchers but he was totally enamored with Curry.

When Mazzone shook the former Baltimore Colts lineman's hand he had tears in his eyes and he would not turn loose of Curry's hand. "I'm shaking hands with the hand that hiked the ball to Johnny Unitas," he said.

Curry and Roger enjoy discussing life and it often begins with talk about their families. In one exchange, Curry said he was with his mother when she died. He held her hand and reminded her that he loved her. This touched a nerve with Roger who was on his way to his mother's bedside when she passed away.

"You had a chance to tell her you loved her," an emotional Roger said.

"Yes, I did, but you told your mother you loved her by the way you lived your life," said Curry, now retired after eighteen seasons as a college football coach.

Roger's life has included more than his share of time in doctor's offices and hospitals dealing with everything from cataracts to gall bladders. He is grateful for the support he has received from a list of caregivers that he refers to as his "earth angels." It begins with Doctor John Barrow of Dale, who removed his tonsils, and Doctor Fielding Williams of Huntingburg, his family physician as a child. It includes Doctor John Ware of Carrollton who discovered his colon cancer; Doctor Tom Reeve of Carrollton who removed his colon; Doctor Anthony Malizia of Atlanta who treated his prostate cancer; and Doctor Jimmy Pope of Carrollton who provides annual cancer checkups.

Doctor Francis Owings of Atlanta removed his gall bladder and Doctor John Cantwell of Atlanta, whom he first met as a basketball player at Duke, is his cardiologist. Doctor Ken Kress of Atlanta installed his new hip and Doctor Scott Swayzee of Marietta repaired his knee. Doctor Aaron King, the team dentist at Georgia Tech, has cared for his teeth for more than fifty years. Offering support and referrals is Doctor G.B. Espy of Marietta, a close friend who was his college math tutor, and Doctor David Jones, of Atlanta his former summer camp participant.

Doctor Lee Stringfellow of Carrollton is Roger's family physician and a close personal friend. Through the years he has been the ringmaster for Roger's growing list of physicians.

Roger is blessed by their care and he shares those blessings with others. He lives the way a small town boy was taught to live. He cares for his friends and they care for him when he is need. He was there for Whack Hyder, when the old coach was dying and was a shoulder for former teammate Josh Powell to lean on. Today he makes frequent trips to Indiana to check on former teammate Alan Nass.

On Mother's Day 2015, with their children and grandchildren away, Roger and Beverly went to see Teeter Umstead. The former Tech basketball captain befriended Roger when he came to Atlanta and they have always been close. He trusted Roger so deeply that he sent his son to play for him at West Georgia College. Umstead's health is failing so he was glad to see his old friend that Sunday afternoon. These things come natural to Roger and Beverly. It was the way they were reared.

Friendships bring responsibilities and one of them has been to speak at the funerals of people he loved. Roger presented eulogies for Hyder, Powell and Doctor Sid — three people who played important roles in his life. He loved them, and openly sharing that love was not easy. But none was more difficult than speaking at a memorial for Orin Whitman, a wise old soldier who became a hero as well as a friend.

His beautiful friendship with Mr. Whitman began at a hamburger joint in Carrollton and it ended at a graveside service in the spring of 2015. Roger is usually unflappable but talking about his friend brought a flood of memories and emotions that were hard to keep in check. He remembered when Chip was in kindergarten and how most days he took him by Mr. Whitman's glass shop on the way to school. The storeowner would give Chip a quarter, which the little boy called a big nickel. He also remembered the patience his friend showed when he took Jenny and Jill fishing at his lake when they were young. He remembered trips to the Beaches of Normandy and the dedication of the World War II Memorial in Washington, D.C.

Their first stop in Europe was Omaha Beach. "He was 82 years old and it was a long and tiring flight. He used a cane, but when we walked over the American Cemetery, his cane never touched the ground. During the trip to Washington the decorated Mason had the honor of attending the Masonic Lodge that was the home lodge of George Washington. Mr. Whitman was invited to his lodge, and on top of that he sat in Washington's chair. He was so proud of that evening."

Mr. Whitman was a faithful follower of the Alabama Crimson Tide and its football team. But when a former Auburn football player contracted a rare and debilitating spinal disease, he took care of him every day. Jimmy Bonner was the head track coach and an assistant football coach at Carrollton High when he was crippled. The beloved coach's wife had a young son to care for so looking after her once robust husband was overwhelming.

"He was the man, who, for eight years went to Coach Bonner's house every morning before six o'clock and helped get him ready for his day. That meant bathing, dressing and cooking breakfast for him," Roger said in his eulogy.

Jimmy Bonner died in 1977.

Mr. Whitman was a homespun philosopher who did not bring his wisdom home from school. He loved his dogs. He loved bluegrass music. He loved Civil War history. He loved Bear Bryant. But as much as anything or anybody, he loved Roger and Beverly. To the Kaiser children and grandchildren, he was a surrogate grandpa who taught them common sense and how to appreciate people.

"I was always amazed at his wisdom," Roger said. "He could pretty well size up a person real quick. I have learned that almost anything that you want to learn about, you could listen and learn from Orin S. Whitman."

ROGER KAISER LIVES an all-American life. Athletics brought him honors and rewards and family and friends bring a flow of love and smiles. He is blessed in many ways and he never stops sharing those blessings. Though he never intended to coach, coaching has allowed him to teach and nurture young people in the same way his coaches did in high school and college.

As a student-athlete at Georgia Tech his childhood dreams came true. At West Georgia College and Life University, he accumulated the flashy rings of a champion. As a husband, father and grandfather he receives a warm love that disregards celebrity and recognition and touches him in ways a winning basket never could.

Though he has lived in Georgia for more than six decades he reserves a special spot in his heart for Indiana. He goes back to Dale regularly and every summer he joins Sam Alford and Chris May for the Indiana Basketball Hall of Fame golf tournament. At that event he exchanges barbs with old pals like Joe Todrank and Hugh Schaefer, the primary historian for basketball in Southern Indiana. He and Beverly also have been invited to serve as Grand Marshalls for the 2015 Fall Festival Parade in their hometown.

The world they knew in Dale has changed. You cannot buy a pair of shoes or slacks in Dale and the high school closed in 1972. His hometown does not have a Wal-Mart and the Interstates missed it years ago. Despite such changes, Roger and Beverly go home several times a year to see friends and family they left behind and he still has a tape of the radio play-by-play of the Golden Aces victory over Ferdinand in 1956.

Alexander Memorial Coliseum has become the McCamish Pavilion but Roger still has season tickets at Georgia Tech where he will always wear Number 21. West Georgia College grew into the University of West Georgia and Life University no longer wins championships. But Roger is still Roger. He collects Donald Ducks in all shapes and sizes and if you call him his cell phone plays a few bars of "Ramblin' Wreck."

Roger has not changed and neither has Beverly. They love each other. They stand by their children and they adore their eight grandchildren. They are seldom apart for she is his partner in whatever he does. They laugh about his amazing eye for the basket for on the road Roger is constantly lost. Before there was a GPS there was Beverly and she will always be her husband's navigator.

An unexpected reward is the time Roger spends as a teacher and coach at Mt. Bethel Christian Academy. When he retired from Life University in 2002 he assumed he and Beverly would take the trips they always talked about. They have been around the world several times, but he found true joy in Cobb County.

Working with students at Mt. Bethel Christian Academy has reinvigorated the old coach in ways he never imagined. Being around them has renewed his Christian faith and injected him with a new kind of energy. In return, the people at Mt. Bethel appreciate the wisdom that he shares in the classroom, the basketball court and even at a pond right there on campus.

His contributions to Mt. Bethel were cited in a column written for the *Eagle Eye* by Head of School Jim Callis. In a 2015 academy newsletter, Callis talked about those fishing trips behind the gym:

"Some might question why we would spend valuable physical education time teaching kids to bait a hook instead of games or exercises. But, I don't question it for a moment. For many of these students, it's the first time they've ever put a line in the water and I can't imagine a better person to do it with than Coach. There are a lot of things that make Mt. Bethel such an incredible place for children and near the top of that list is Coach Kaiser. They may not be catching catfish out there, but I guarantee you they are making memories. In forty years, these kids won't remember how many sit-ups they did in PE, but you can bet they'll remember fishin' with Coach. And that's a memory to treasure!"

And so is the all-American life of Roger Kaiser.

Epilogue

by Richard Hyatt

The birth of this book came on an unlikely Saturday afternoon in 2012 as old friends and lifelong readers filed into a Presbyterian church in Atlanta to mark the death of James Furman Bisher who for fifty-nine years told us everything we needed to know about sports.

Bisher was an institution before I knew how to spell the word. I was in grade school when I watched him climb the stairs to the press box at Ponce de Leon Ballpark. My parents read me his stories about Atlanta Cracker baseball games and I pushed myself to learn how to read them myself. When he switched from the morning Constitution to the afternoon Journal I whined until my folks followed him. Later on, I carried a Journal paper route and I read his column before I made my rounds.

For most of my adult life, I have tried to write as well as he did. We were colleagues and competitors and I considered him a friend but I was always the follower, as were most writers who for generations tried to emulate him. We were still chasing when he died at the age of ninety-three.

His eulogists had a tough assignment. First came Buck Riddle, who I remembered from a clinic at Poncey in which he offered tips on playing first base to a bunch of kids who thought we could play. Jim Minter, a crusty newspaperman who worked for Bisher and was behind so many opportunities in my career, followed Riddle. Then came the Reverend Tim Boggess, Bisher's pastor at Northwest Presbyterian Church. He had the unenviable job of summarizing in a few words the life of a master wordsmith.

Bisher, he said, came to that church originally because he lost to the pastor in a pickup basketball game. Now he was being memorialized during the NCAA Basketball Tournament, the pinnacle of the college season.

"He organized his life by the seasons around him … and he delighted in every one. He knew there was a time to pass and a time to punt … a time to bunt and a time to hit away … and a time to dribble and a time to dunk," the pastor said.

He said Bisher kept coming to that church because of the love he received and the love he gave. He also loved words, stories and games and Boggess said he was going to read an article he had clipped from the *Atlanta Journal-Constitution.* He had kept it tucked away for years knowing he would use it one day.

Bisher did not write it. Fact is the story did not have a byline. It told the story of Life University's comeback victory over Mobile College in the championship game of the 1999 NAIA Basketball Tournament, a game that the losing team dominated until the final four minutes. Victory came on a three-point bucket by Corey Evans at the buzzer.

"It is a story about a game that most of you don't remember," he said.

Roger Kaiser remembered. That was his team and it led to his third national title. He learned forward to the pew in front of him and tapped retired football coach Bill Curry on the shoulder.

"That's me, he's talking about," he told Curry.

Why would a minister who is not a huge basketball fan pick such a story to read at a funeral? He did not know that Bisher and Roger Kaiser were friends for more than fifty years. He was not acquainted with Roger and he did not know that the ex-coach and his wife were there that day.

It was all about the headline: "Life Wins."

To Boggess, those two words summarize the Christian faith. "It may seems like death wins but life wins. Even in the face of death and loss, life wins. If you remember nothing else from this service remember that life wins," he said.

Roger and Beverly stayed around long enough to introduce themselves to Boggess that afternoon. "I was blown away," the minister says. "Using that story was just a happy accident."

We all ended up in a reception at the church where I greeted Roger and Beverly for the first time in years. I told Beverly I was retired from active duty at the newspaper in Columbus but that I was busy writing books. I do not know who made the first connection but from that conversation came the idea that I should write a book about Roger Kaiser.

She had been trying to convince her husband that someone ought to do that for years. Beverly even tried to write it herself. The idea appealed to me for Roger Kaiser had been a hero of mine since I was a teenager and watched him play in the first college basketball game I ever saw in person.

From that brief conversation grew this book. This is the seventh biography I have written and each time I have uncovered a story worth telling and one worth preserving. It was my good fortune that Roger and Beverly are pack rats. They throw nothing away. I was able to go through scrapbooks that his mother began and Beverly continued. It was the same with photographs. They keep everything.

More than that they have opened their homes to me and have freely shared their memories. They talked about the happy times and did not sidestep the sadder moments. And Beverly usually sent me home with a bowl of macroni and cheese for my little girl. Family members also made themselves available. So did their endless army of friends. It has been a pleasure to get to know each of them.

That list includes the following:

Ryan Billig, Coleman Boyd, Bill Buntin, Jenny Kaiser Buntin, The Reverend Tim Boggess, Don Bryant, Jim R. Callis, Mitt Connerly, Tim Criswell, Bill Curry, Gordon Darrah, the late David Dougan, Bill Emmons, Derrick Engram, and Claude Felton.

Ryan Greer, Dan Grundhoefer, Stan Guth. Denson Hamby, Del Harris, The Reverend Don Harp, David Hevron, James Hevron, Bob Hoffman, John Hoffman, Bobby Howard, Doctor D.D. Humber, and Doctor David Jones.

Chip Kaiser, Christy Fead Kaiser, Van Kaiser, Jerry Kemp. John Logue, Daryl Lovell, Bruce Lyon, Steve McCutcheon, Dan Miles, Jim Minter, Alan Nass, Bob Reinhart, Jane Reinhart, Jerry Reynolds, and Homer Rice.

Mickey Sermersheim. Loren Smith, Mike Stamos, Doctor Lee Stringfellow, Brad Swann. Mike Tomasovich, Tom Turner, Teeter Umstead, Paul Vickers, Foots Walker, Herb White, and the late Orin S. Whitman.

To people who saw him play Roger Kaiser will always be Number 21. He was an all-American on the basketball court, a champion as a coach and through the writing of this book I conclude that his is an all-American life.

Like the preacher said: Life wins.

An Afterthought

by Roger Kaiser

This story would not have been told without the persistence and encouragement of Beverly Hevron Kaiser. It has been a labor of love for her and our entire family. Little did I know when I met that fifteen-year-old cheerleader from Lincoln City that she would become my biggest fan, my confidant, the love of my life and my very best friend. She has been at my side during most of the important chapters of my life.

Years ago, she encouraged me to write a book. She had me make a list of important events and on several long driving trips she had me tell old stories into a tape recorder. It was Beverly who cornered our old friend Richard Hyatt at Furman Bisher's funeral in 2012 and started a conversation that led to the writing of this book.

In the years since that unexpected meeting, Richard has proven to be a talented writer and a very patient man. He has spent countless hours wading through family scrapbooks and old newspaper clippings and talking to so many people from all walks and ages of our lives. He has counseled me and pushed me to discuss subjects that were painful. We appreciate his efforts and will always be grateful for his work.

To all of the people who gave their time and their cherished memories recalling moments of my life, thank you does not seem adequate. Because of their conversations, this book tells my story.

I am a fortunate man. I have a family I cherish and friends who show up at the very moment I need them. I have lived in Dale, Carrollton and Atlanta and each of these communities has blessed my soul. I dearly love the state of Georgia, but whenever I go back to Indiana I am living proof that you can go home again.

I have been honored in many ways. This book mentions most of them. But as I look back, I am persuaded that the true rewards are the wonderful people that have crossed my path in basketball and in life. Atop that list is that little cheerleader from Lincoln City.

Thank you, Beverly.

APPENDIX

ROGER AND BEVERLY KAISER'S FAMILY TREE

Roger Kaiser's Parents
Elmer Amos Kaiser 1904–1992
Louanna Frederica Niehaus Kaiser 1909–1985

Roger Kaiser's Siblings
Sharon Maxine Kaiser 1934–1996
Van Edward Kaiser (Diana Kruse) 1944
Joe Wayne Kaiser (Ann Boeglin) 1946–2000

Beverly Hevron Kaiser's Parents
Benjamin Romine Hevron 1911–1988
Helen Marie Woods Hevron 1913–1985

Beverly Kaiser's Siblings
James Roy Hevron (Barbara Michel) 1946–
David Allen Hevron (Margaret Nord) 1948–
Bonnie Karen Hevron Graman (Richard Graman) 1952–

Roger and Beverly's Children
Jennifer Kay Kaiser Buntin (William Russell Buntin) 1961–
William Kaiser (Billy) Buntin 2001–
Elizabeth Jill (Betsy) Buntin 2003–

Bill's children from previous marriage:
Courtney Alicia Buntin-Victor 1978–
Reese Eizabeth Victor 2015
Cameron Ashley Buntin 1985–

Susan Jill Kaiser Givens (Steve Givens) 1962–1997
Steven Robert (Bert) Givens Jr. 1993–
Susan Rachel Givens 1994–

Roger Allen (Chip) Kaiser Jr. (Christy Fead) 1967–
Kelli Jill Kaiser 2002–
Alexis Ensley (Lexi) Kaiser 2002–
Roger Allen (Trey) Kaiser III 2002–
Hallie Marie Kaiser 2005–

ROGER KAISER AS A PLAYER

Dale High School

	G	FG		PCT.	FG		PCT.	PTS.	
1954	13	32	61	52.4	27	44	61.4	91	7.0
1955	25	88	175	50.3	105	127	82.7	284	11.9
1956	24	198	401	49.4	230	276	83.3	626	26.1
1957	23	178	371	48.0	192	226	85.0	548	23.8
Career	85	496	1008	49.2	554	673	82.3	1549	18.2

Georgia Tech

	G	FG		PCT.	FT		PCT.	RB		PTS.	
1959	26	342	138	40.4	127	106	83.5	182	7.0	382	14.7
1960	28	503	237	47.1	190	164	86.4	154	5.5	638	22.8
1961	26	517	216	41.8	203	176	86.7	106	4.1	608	23.4
Career	80	1361	591	43.4	520	446	85.8	442	5.5	1628	20.4

American Basketball League

	G	FG		PCT	3P				FT	PCT	RB	AST		PTS			
1962	80	1258	528	42.0	238	72	30.3	481	428	89.0	261	3.3	232	2.9	1556	19.5	
1963	27	385	159	41.3	56	25	44.6	145	124	85.5	140	5.2	75	2.8	467	17.3	
Career	107	1643	687	41.8	294	97	33.0	626	552	88.2	401	3.7	307	2.9	2023	18.9	

ABL Postseason

1962	3	49	27	55.1	8	1	12.5	20	16	80.0	10	3.3	4	1.3	71	23.7

ROGER KAISER AS A COACH

Georgia Tech Freshman
1964–65 — 14–1

Decatur High School
1965–69 — 77–26

West Georgia College
1970–71 — 14–11
1971–72 — 28–6
1972–73 — 23–5
1973–74 — 29–4
1974–75 — 18–8
1975–76 — 17–10
1976–77 — 18–10
1977–78 — 20–8
1978–79 — 13–13
1979–80 — 24–6
1980–81 — 23–5
1981–82 — 15–11
1982–83 — 22–7
1983–84 — 26–4
1984–85 — 15–13
1985–86 — 21–8
1986–87 — 26–5
1987–88 — 4–22
1988–89 — 11–17
TOTALS — 381–186

Life University
1991–92 — 29–6

1992–93 — 30–5

1993–94 — 29–10

1994–95 — 31–3

1995–96 — 31–6

1996–97 — 37–1

1997–98 — 32–4

1998–99 — 29–10

1999–00 — 34–2

TOTALS — 282–47

LIFETIME COACHING RECORD

Georgia Tech Freshmen	—	14–1	.933
Decatur High School	—	77–26	.746
West Georgia College	—	381–186	.660
Life University	—	282–47	.857
TOTALS	—	**754–280**	**.743**

NAIA Championships

District 25 Champions — 1971–72, 1973–74, 1994–95, 1995–96, 1997–98,
National Tournament — 1971–72, 1973–74, 1993–94, 1996–97, 1998–99, 1999–2000.
National Champions — 1973–74, 1996–97, 1998–99, 1999–2000.

Conference Championships

South Atlantic Regular Season — 1973–74, 1974–75, 1979–80
South Atlantic Conference Tournament — 1974, 1978, 1980, 1981
Gulf South Conference Regular Season — 1985–86, 1986–87
Gulf South Conference Tournament — 1987
Georgia Intercollegiate Athletic Conference Regular Season — 1991–92, 1992–93

NCAA Tournament

Regionals — 1975, 1980, 1981, 1983, 1984, 1986, 1987.

Nationally Ranked Teams

1971–72 — 18th UPI, 13th NAIA; 1972–73 — 11th UPI; 1973–74 — 1st NAIA, 2nd AP; 1974–75 — 10th AP; 1977–78 — 12th NCAA; 1979–80 — 9th NCAA; 1980–81 — 7th NCAA; 1982–83 — 12th NCAA, 1st South Region; 1983–84 — 9th NCAA; 1985–86 — 12th NCAA; 1986–87 — 16th NCAA.

First Team All-Americans

Clarence "Foots" Walker (West Georgia) 1974; Billy Lewis (Life) 1994 and 1996; Jerry Jones (Life) 1995; Curtis Currington (Life) 1997; John Brown (Life) 1998; Jimmie Hunter (Life) 2000.

NBA Draft Choices

West Georgia College — Stanley Brewer, Dave Edmunds, Jerry Faulkner, Jarvis Reynolds, Tom Turner, Clarence "Foots" Walker.

LETTERMEN

West Georgia College

Earl Addison 1981–82; Barry Allen 1971–73; Greg Allen 1971–73; Ken Allen 1983–85; Willie Almon 1977–79; Glenn Andrew 1970–72; Emanuel Arnold 1990.

John Babbs 1979–81; Dennis Ballew 1981–82; Anthony Barge 1985–87; Donald Battles 1985–86; Warren Beaulah 1982–83; Aaron Bellamy 1990; Travis Benton 1986–87; Calvin Booker 1979–81; Nate Boyd 1990; Stanley Brewer 1979–81; Bobby Brill 1975–76; Fred Brooks 1985–86; Elton Brown 1986–87; Rick Brown 1973–74; Pat Bryant 1981–83; Ed Bryant 1983–84; Ben Bunt 1977–79.

Chip Chandler 1977–78; Sam Christian 1974–77; Derrick Clark 1980–85; Billy Cook 1970–71; Derrick Cooley 1990; Tim Cox 1984–86; Skeet Crigler 1969–72; Tim Criswell 1983–86.

Anton Daniels 1984–86; Mike DeBoer 1982–83; Rick DeLong 1984–85; Wilson Dugger 1981–82; Anthony Dunbar 1990.

Dave Edmonds 1973–75; Rusty Eliss 1982–84; Travis Ellison 1978–80.

Gregg Farmer 1969–71; Jerry Faulkner 1972–74; Terry Faulkner 1973–75; Jesse Fields 1974–75; David Fowlkes 1980–81; Lamar Frady 1977–81.

Tyrone Gates 1975–77; Melvin Gibson 1981–83; Jeff Glushakow 1978–79; Joey Godwin 1970–71; John Godwin 1978–80; Rusty Greiner 1979–81.

Mike Hamer 1976–77; Charlie Hamilton 1970–72; Kenny Hardy 1972–76; Tony Hardy 1987–90; Paul Harvey 1980–82; Bill Harvey 1979–81; Jeff Haynes 1981–83; Stanley Horton 1970–72; Tom Houghtaling 1973–76; Kevin Humphrey 1975–77.

Danny Jones 1978–81; Derek Jones 1982–84; Lonnie Jones 1982–84.

Chip Kaiser 1987–90; Jody Koonce 1990.

Jeff LaCava 1974–76; Terry Lawrence 1975–77; Scott Langford 1975–76; Kenny Lee 1981–83; Allen Lewis 1981–82; Willie Joe Lewis 1971–73.

Mike Maddox 1976–78; Pat Magley 1972–74; Whitt Matthews 1971–73; Mike Mayweather 1976–77; C.J. Mazzola 1985–88; Reggie Milbry 1986–87, 1988–89; Alexander Mitchell 1974–75; David Mitchler 1987–89; Milt Moss 1970–72; Jeff Myers 1987–90.

Danny O'Brien 1975–78.

Max Pfiefer 1971–74; Dave Pfister 1978–80; Floyd Phoenix 1973–75; Mike Pietrowski 1981–82; Bobby Pippens 1986–88; Clarence Porch 1977–79; Kevin Price 1975–76; Eric Pryor 1981–84.

Greg Rabideaux 1980–84; Jarvis Reynolds 1977–78; Tim Reynolds 1974–76; Daron Richardson 1979–81; Rodney Roberts 1983–88; Mike Robinson 1984–85; Ken Ross 1989–82; Randy Rountree 1972–74; Sherman Rowe 1984–86.

Warren Sellers 1984–87; Tommy Slocumb 1978–80; Darrell Smith 1983–86; Freddie Snyder 1990; Robert Speight 1976–77; Robert Stanley 1977–79; Boyd Steele 1969–71; Harley Stewart 1970–72; Martin Stokes 1985–86; Tony Stroud 1974–75; Mike Summers 1986–87.

Chris Thomas 1985–86; Scott Thomas 1977–79; Tom Turner 1972–74; Reggie Tyler 1975–76.

Corky Umstead 1976–80; Willie Upshaw 1978–80.

Clarence "Foots" Walker 1972–74; Mickey Williams 1988–90; Mike Wilson 1976–77; Ken Wilson 1975–77; Brister Wimbs 1976–77; John Wortham 1986–88; Stacy Worthy 1989–90; Tim Wyatt 1986–88.

Bobby York 1970–72; Ron Young 1984–85.

Life University

Herb Absher 1991–92, 92–93; Joseph Alexander 1995–96.

Rick Berry 1995–96; Daniel Brown 1993–94, 1994–95; John Brown 1997–98.

Brent Carraway 1991–92, 1992–93; Curtis Carrington 1996–97; Marvin Childs 1995–96; Mark Christian 1997–98; Isaac Cook 1998–99.

Richard Dodson 1991–92, 1992–93; Noble Duke 1993–94, 1994–95.

Ben Elliott 2000–01; Derrick Engram 1991–92, 1992–93; Kendrick Eskridge 1992–93; David Eubanks 1994–95, 1995–96; Corey Evans 1997–98, 1998–99, 1999–2000.

Derrick Folston 1996–97, 1997–98, 1998–99, 1999–2000.

Tyrone Gainer 1993–94, 1994–95, 1996–97; Ron Glover 1995–96, 1996–97, 1997–98, 1998–99.

Kevin Hagood 1993–94, 1994–95; Antwon Hall 1997–98; James Harris 1995–96, 1996–97; Lamar Harris 1991–92, 1992–93, 1993–94, 1994–95; Viren Harris 1997–98, 1998–99, 1999–00; Shawn Hill 1998–99, 1999–2000; Jamaal Horton 1998–99; Jimmie Hunter 1999–2000; Cy Hutcherson 1992–93.

Travis Ingram 1999–00.

Chummy Johnson 1996–97; 1997–98, 1998–99, 1999–2000; Larry Johnson 1997–98; Carlos Jones 1999–00; Ed Jones 1991–92, 1992–93; Jerry Jones 1992–93, 1993–94, 1094–95.

Kevin Ledoux 1991–92; Billy Lewis 1992–93, 1993–94, 1994–95, 1995–96; Patrick Lewis 1996–97; Keith Lundy 1994–95, 1995–96.

Dan Magett 1994–95; Wayne Mann 1995–96, 1996–97, 1997–98; Melvin Martin 1992–93, 1993–94; Anthony Maxwell 1996–97, 1997–98; Mike Maxwell 1996–97, 1997–98; Tyree McGhee 1991–92, 1992–93; Roger Montgomery 1992–93, 1993–94.

Pinchas Noyman 1991–92.

Wayne O'Neal 1991–92, 1992–93, 1993–94; Vernon Orr 1993–94, 1994–95.

Demetrius Palmer 1996–97, 1997–98; Keiffer Parker 1993–94, 1994–95; Tony Phillips 1997–98, 1998–99; Tyrone Prather 1991–92, 1992–93; Robert Richburg 1991–92, 1992–93.

Charles Sabourin 1991–92; Sahrad Sallette 1994–95, 1995–96; Tony Sanders 1995–96, 1996–97; Derrick Shaw 1998–99, 1999–2000; Richard Simpson 1994–95; Don Smiley 1996–97; Derrick Smith 1991–92, 1993–94; Jody Smith 1993–94, 1994–95; Allen Strozier 1998–99, 1999–2000; Jerome Sweeting 1993–94, 1994–95; Jason Sylvia 1999–2000.

Bruce White 1991–92, 1992–93; Jeff Wright 1995–96, 1996–97, 1997–98.

Tajai Young 1999–2000.

HONORS AND ACHIEVEMENTS

Lettered in basketball, baseball, track, and football at Dale High School, 1953–57; won Allen Brooner Award, 1956; named to all-State basketball team, 1957; cocaptain of basketball and baseball teams, 1956 and 1957; and named to Indiana-Kentucky All-Star Basketball Team, 1957.

Three-year letterman in basketball and baseball at Georgia Tech; unanimous selection all-SEC basketball, 1960 and 1961; SEC basketball player of the year, 1960 and 1961; captain of Georgia Tech basketball and baseball teams; consensus all-American, 1960 and 1961; participated in Olympic trials, 1960; all-SEC baseball, 1959; outstanding outfielder NCAA South Regional, 1959; played with Washington, New York, and Philadelphia Tapers of the American Basketball League, 1961–63.

First college basketball coach in Georgia to win a national title (1974); national coach of the year four times; NAIA Southeast Region coach of the year eleven times; conference coach of the year eight times; State of Georgia coach of the year eleven times; Georgia Sports Hall of Fame coach of the year three times; *Basketball Times Magazine* coach of the year; retired from college coaching in 2000 with 754 victories and four national titles, trailing only John Wooden of UCLA and Arad McCutcheon of Evansville College.

Indiana Basketball Hall of Fame Silver Anniversary Team, 1982; National Association of Basketball Coaches Silver Anniversary Team, 1986; named to NAIA's Top 75 in celebration of the NAIA's 75th anniversary in 2012.

Georgia Tech Sports Hall of Fame (inducted 1966); State of Georgia Sports Hall of Fame (inducted 1984); Indiana Basketball Hall of Fame (inducted 1996); National Alliance of Basketball Leagues Hall of Fame; State University of West Georgia Hall of Fame (inducted 1998); NAIA Hall of Fame (inducted 1999); Atlanta Sports Hall of Fame (inducted 2009).

Atlanta Tip-Off Club Steve Schmidt's Outstanding Contributions to Basketball Award, 1998; named to Top 100 Georgia Athletes for 20th Century by Atlanta Constitution; named to Top 100 Basketball Players in NCAA History; ACC Legend, 2001; presented Dr. Homer Rice Total Person Outstanding Alumnus Award by Georgia Tech Athletic Association in 2012.

Member of Seniors Basketball Team that won the Georgia Golden Olympics five times; member of Seniors Basketball Team that finished third and sixth in National Senior Olympics; started athletic program at Mt. Bethel Christian Academy, 2003.

Roger and Beverly spent many happy days walking the halls of their beloved Dale High School.

As a child in Indiana, Roger's dream was to wear the uniform of the Golden Aces.

In high school, Beverly led the cheers for her favorite basketball player.

Beverly and the Golden Aces cheerleaders had front row seats in the crowded gym at Dale High School.

Teammates watch as Roger and Dan Grundhoefer cut down the nets after a victory over Rockport in the 1956 season.

Roger was a high school junior when this team photo was taken. Left to right on the front row is Beverly Hevron, Theresa Knott, Jerry Stroud, Ruth O'Daniel and Priscilla Brown. On the middle row are Jerry Barnett, Mark Weller, Harold Huffman and Keith Roos. Standing is Assistant Coach Dave Robinson, Chuck Neighbors, Larry Walters, Roger Kaiser, Larry Knott, Bill Bockstahler, Dan Grundhoefer, David Knott, Head Coach Roy Yenowine and Dale High Principal Ralph Kifer.

Roger played two years of high school football.

Roger had a flat top most
of high school.

Tickets to the Sectionals in
Tell City were a hot item.

Beverly Hevron was a serious student.

Sharon Kaiser was a Dale cheerleader when her brother
Roger started playing organized basketball.

Sharon and Roger were the oldest children in the Kaiser family.

The Kaisers pose for an early family photo. Roger is in front, joined by Sharon and their parents Louanna and Elmer. Dad is holding little brother Van.

Beverly Hevron strikes a childhood pose.

Louanna and Elmer Kaiser got dressed up to celebrate their 50th wedding anniversary.

Before every basketball game in high school Roger and his father enjoyed a game of cribbage. And Elmer always won.

As a sophomore, Roger's big bat led Georgia Tech to post-season play for the first time in school history.

Broadcaster Al Ciraldo, right, met Whack Hyder when the future Georgia Tech basketball coach was playing for a New York Yankees farm club in Akron, Ohio.

Roger takes the ball to the basket in a Gator Bowl meeting with Navy.

After his final home game against Florida, Roger nervously awaits the ceremony marking his amazing career at Georgia Tech.

This photo of Roger and Beverly in their Atlanta apartment accompanied a Sunday magazine article published during his senior year of college.

This publicity photo of Roger was probably published more than any other picture.

When the minister lost his place during the wedding ceremony, Beverly fed him his lines.

No coach at Georgia Tech was more loved than Joe Pittard.

Boarding the plane on their way to the 1960 NCAA Tournament were, top to bottom, Josh Powell, John Hoffman, Roger Kaiser, Bobby Dews, John Gher and Wayne Richards.

Louanna Kaiser hugs her son
before a game at Georgia Tech.

Delmer Harris, right, organized a special day for
Roger back home in Dale. Joining the local barber were
Yellow Jacket Coach Whack Hyder and Bob Reinhart.

Beverly shows off her beautiful wedding gown to her grandmother, Mary Woods, and her mother, Helen Hevron.

Beverly was a junior at Dale High School.

Jenny and Jill were babies when Roger played in the ABL.

When Roger's West Georgia Braves won the 1974 NAIA Tournament they were the first college team from the state to win a national basketball championship.

Though he never intended to be a coach, Roger collected many awards at West Georgia College and Life University.

Mild mannered Roger Kaiser took on a different persona when he was on the bench. Just ask the officials that worked his games.

Teammates carried the legendary Foots Walker off
the court after he led the Braves to the 1974 NAIA title.

Roger was among the highest scorers in the
short-lived American Basketball League.

Looking dapper in their white shoes, Roger and loquacious assistant Jerry Reynolds accepted the hardware after the NAIA title game.

This band of basketball troubadours played all over the state of Georgia. Posing for a team picture are Roger Couch, Roger Kaiser, Tommy Norwood, J.G. Rowe, Jesse Weathers, Don Keiser and Billy Carter. Kneeling in front is their sponsor, Don Bryant.

Louanna and Elmer Kaiser joined their son when he
was inducted into the Georgia Sports Hall of Fame.

Jill and Jenny were basketball players and cheerleaders growing up in Carrollton.

More than sisters, Jenny and Jill were always best friends.

Big sisters Jenny and Jill always looked after their younger brother Chip.

Jenny and Jill were born before their father got into coaching.

As a basketball player in high school and college
Chip Kaiser always wore his father's Number 21.

Roger says every coach deserves to have a boss like Dr. Sid. Right after picture was taken, Life took the floor for its inaugural basketball game.

Before he was an Atlanta Brave, Rick Camp was a West Georgia Brave and a fishing buddy of Roger's.

To the Kaiser family, Orin Whitman was a hero and a dear friend.
Roger gave the eulogy at the World War II veteran's funeral in 2015.

He wanted his pal Bob Reinhart to get the job but instead Roger
spent four years as head coach at Decatur High in suburban Atlanta.

He was head basketball coach but Roger was also
the athletic director at West Georgia College and Life University.

Charlie Hamilton, left, and Bobby York were leaders
on the first team Roger took to the NAIA Tournament.

When he wasn't on the bench at West Georgia, Roger could be found on softball fields all over Carrollton.

Basketball coaches in the old South Atlantic Conference were a close-knit group. Flanking Roger is Marvin Vanover (Augusta), George Bianci (Armstrong), Sonny Clements (Columbus), Commissioner J.B. Scearce and James Dominey (Valdosta).

Roger guided the Running Eagles of
Life University to the 1999 national championship.

Roger and his Life players congratulate
Corey Evans, the hero of the 1999 championship game.

Roger joins basketball legends John McLendon and Marquis Haynes.

Wearing a 'I Beat Bisher' T-shirt, Roger displays one that did not get away.

Not many people know that Roger is an avid collector of Donald Duck memorabilia.

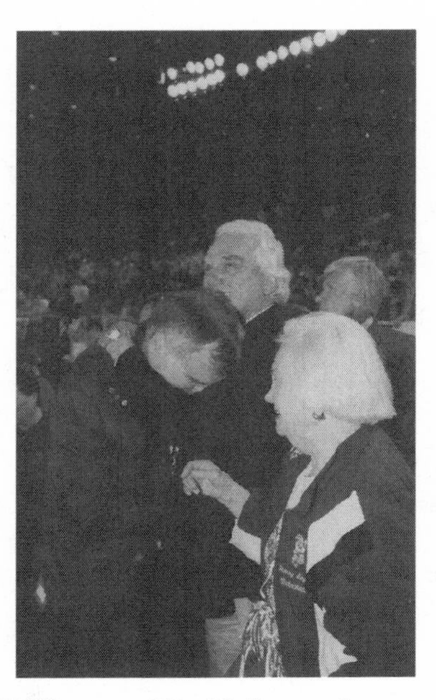

Dr. Sid Williams and Dr. Nell console an emotional Roger after Life's first NAIA championship.

Look closely at the center of this boisterous crowd
and you will find Jenny Kaiser waving her pom-pom.

His family joined Roger when he was inducted into the NAIA Hall of Fame. At his side, left to right, are daughter Jenny Buntin, daughter-in-law Christy Fead Kaiser, son Chip and the love of his life, Beverly.

Three All-American guards compare notes about backcourt play. Roger played at Georgia Tech then coached Billy Lewis at Life University and Foots Walker at West Georgia College.

Furman Bisher wrote about Roger as a player
and a coach and along the way became a close friend.

When he became head coach at West Georgia, the 1971-1972
team helped Roger revive a stagnant program. On the back row
are graduate assistant Boyd Steele, Harley Stewart, Bobby York,
Stanley Horton, Max Pfeifer, Glen Andrews, Charles Hamilton, Alan Gustavel,
assistant coach Jerry Reynolds and Roger. Kneeling is Greg Allen, Joey Godwin,
Barry Allen, Willie Joe Lewis, Skeet Crigler and Milt Moss.

NAIA Tournament MVP James Harris gives Roger a celebratory shower.

West Georgia basketball games became an event
that excited students and people from town.

Like his grandfather, Bert Givens is a college baseball player.

Cameron Buntin Crane and Courtney Buntin-Victor
are Bill Buntin's older daughters.

Hallie Marie is the youngest daughter of Chip and Christy Kaiser.

Alexis Ensley Kaiser is the daughter of Chip and Christy Kaiser.

William Kaiser Buntin has an IQ for basketball and baseball.

Chip and Christy Kaiser, joined by children Kelli, Hallie, Trey and Lexi.

Steve and Jill Givens join children Susan Rachel and Steven Robert Jr.

Bert and Rachel grew closer after the death of their mother.

The Kaiser cousins: Betsy, Billy, Lexi, Kelli, Trey and Hallie.

Jenny, Chip and their families help their parents celebrate their 50th wedding anniversary.

Roger and Beverly were joined by their three children at home in Carrollton.

The Kaiser family celebrates a big day at Georgia Tech.

Roger and Beverly were married in Dale on June 19, 1960.

The Elmer and Louanna Kaiser family in 1979.

Rachel Givens was a long distance runner in
high school and earned a scholarship to Auburn University.

Bill and Jenny Buntin are joined by children Billy and Betsy.

Reece Elizabeth Buntin-Victor is Roger and Beverly's only great-grandchild.

A proud Betsy Buntin competed in her first 5K run.

Kelli Kaiser enjoyed a week at Mt. Bethel's basketball camp.

Coach Kaiser welcomes grandchildren Betsy Buntin, Billy Buntin, Kelli Kaiser, Trey Kaiser and Lexi Kaiser to his annual camp.

Henry Rowling was Lexi's Challenger League helper and he became her friend.

Trey Kaiser pitched a shutout in Cooperstown in 2015.

When Del Harris and Roger Kaiser met as children they never dreamed they would spend their lives coaching basketball.

Roger helped the Reverend Don Harp celebrate his induction into the Young Harris College Sports Hall of Fame.

Students at Mt. Bethel Christian Academy huddle around Coach Kaiser.

The Class of 1957 celebrates its 57th class reunion.

Roger has broken in his favorite fishing hat.

These Hoosiers coached together at West Georgia College many years ago and Roger Kaiser and Jerry Reynolds are still in basketball.

Roger models a stylish hat that he bought to escape the sun on an African Safari.

Roger teaches his students at Mt. Bethel to fish as well as shoot free throws.

Before they were teammates and roommates at Georgia Tech, John Hoffman and Roger were high school competitors.

It was a historic moment at Georgia Tech when this group of players whose numbers have been retired gathered on the court. Left to right, John Salley, Matt Harpring, Roger, Tom Hammond and Rich Yunkus

Tech fans offer one more cheer for Roger and the school's first NCAA basketball team.

Roger takes a ride on a donkey in Greece.

Even on a cruise ship, Roger and Beverly raised money for cancer research.

Roger and Beverly enjoyed the scenery at a lodge in Tanzania.

Bobby Dews and Roger talk about the old days at
Georgia Tech. Dews was a longtime coach for the Atlanta Braves.

Roger met one of his heroes when Arnold Palmer graciously
donated items for an auction that benefited The Alexis Kaiser Foundation.

Old friends and teammates reunite at Lincoln State Park. Meeting in Indiana were Roger and Beverly Kaiser, Josh and Karen Powell, along with Alan and Connie Nass

The former Georgia Tech Athletic Director presented Roger the Homer Rice Total Person Award.

His middle school players at Mt. Bethel
Christian Academy have taught Roger many lessons.

True Classics: Gordon Darrah, Dave Hinderliter, Roger Kaiser and Paul Vickers.

About the Author

Photo by Gary Claborn

Richard Hyatt has been an award-winning reporter and columnist for newspapers in Georgia for nearly 50 years.

Most of his writing career has been spent with the *Ledger-Enquirer* in Columbus where he still provides readers a look at the fascinating stories behind the news. He previously worked for the *Atlanta Times* and the *Atlanta Constitution.*

Hyatt is the author of sixteen non-fiction books. He has also earned scores of state, regional and national awards in journalism, including the prestigious Green Eyeshade Award. *Georgia Trend* named him one of the state's most influential journalists.

He lives in Columbus with his wife Kaye and daughter Kamryn.

Books by Richard Hyatt

The Carters of Plains

Those Trees Are Mine

Lewis, Jack & Me

Buick Southern Open: The First 25 Years

Nothin' But Fine: The Music and the Gospel According to Jake Hess

Zell: The Governor Who Brought HOPE to Georgia

Mr. Speaker: A Biography of Tom Murphy

Charles Jones: A Biography

Home of the Infantry: A History of Fort Benning

Reflections on a Legacy: A History of the Country Club of Columbus

From These Hills: A History of Green Island Country Club

Richard Hyatt's Columbus: Remembering 40 Years of Daily Journalism

Ozzie's Boys: The Sylvan High School Story

Mr. Haskins of Hoylake

If It Feels Like Leather, Shoot It: The All-American Life of Roger Kaiser

Available at www.amazon.com